PRAISE FOR TIM FLANNERY
AND *THE EXPLORERS*

'Takes a part of Australian history that has meant
numbing boredom to generations of schoolchildren
and pummels it into robust and tragicomic shape.'
Bulletin

'Excellent.'
Herald Sun

'Tim Flannery is in the league of the all-time
great explorers like Dr David Livingstone.'
Sir David Attenborough

'In chronological order from Dutch shipwrecks to
Robyn Davidson's camel ride, this anthology of
Australian explorers' writings charts the range of
human emotions in a strange new land.'
Age

'Fascinating and often moving…If the insights
it gives stimulate fresh research and a reassessment
of the era of exploration, Flannery will have achieved
his purpose. Our explorers, as well as their
Aboriginal partners, deserve it.'
Canberra Times

T0363033

Born in Melbourne in 1956, Tim Flannery is a writer, scientist and explorer. He has published over a dozen books, including the award-winning bestsellers *The Future Eaters*, *Throwim Way Leg* and *We Are the Weather Makers*. He has also edited Watkin Tench's *1788* and John Nicol's *Life and Adventures 1776–1801*.

A leading thinker in environmental science, Tim is a member of the Wentworth Group of Concerned Scientists. He lives in a sustainable house on the Hawkesbury River with his wife and a lot of wildlife.

In January 2007 Tim Flannery was named Australian of the Year.

WHERE IS HERE?

350 YEARS OF EXPLORING
AUSTRALIA

EDITED AND INTRODUCED BY
Tim Flannery

TEXT PUBLISHING MELBOURNE AUSTRALIA

The Text Publishing Company
Swann House
22 William Street
Melbourne Victoria 3000
Australia
www.textpublishing.com.au

This edition, based on Tim Flannery's *The Explorers* anthology, first published 2007

Design by Chong
Map by Tony Fankhauser
Typeset by J & M Typesetting
Printed and bound by Griffin Press

National Library of Australia
Cataloguing-in-Publication data:

Where is here? 350 years of exploring Australia.

Bibliography.
For secondary school students.
ISBN 9781921145810 (pbk.).

1. Explorers - Australia. 2. Australia - Discovery and exploration. I. Flannery, Tim, 1956- .

919.404

To Anna —
may all your explorations
be happy ones

This unknown country is the fifth part of the terrestial globe, and extendeth itself to such length that in probability it is twice greater in kingdoms and seignories than all that which at this day doth acknowledge subjection and obedience unto your Majesty...to all the titles which you already do possess you may adjoin this which I represent, and that the name TERRA AUSTRALIS INCOGNITA may be blazoned and spread over the face of the whole world.

Pedro De Quiros,
Report to King Phillip III of Spain, 1610

CONTENTS

INTRODUCTION

This Extraordinary Continent
BY TIM FLANNERY

Wherever you live in Australia, it's possible that at some time an explorer passed through your area. That's because just 350 years ago almost all of inland Australia was unknown to everyone except its Aboriginal owners. Can you imagine what it was like to be an explorer? They had to travel in very different ways from what you are used to: on foot in hobnail boots, or in a bullock dray, on camel or horse. It was a slow and uncertain way to go into the great unknown, where they might meet death at any time from thirst, a wild river, or a spear.

Today we can jump in a car and go fifty times as far as those explorers could go in one day. And we can find a bed to sleep in, while they had to make camp, and find water and feed for their animals. It was a hard life, but they were seeing things that no outsider had ever seen before. Wondrous things, like the world's largest rock, the wierdest animals, and previously unknown creatures.

Now that we are trying to imagine a sustainable

future for our planet, these explorers tell us what the land was like and how the environment was treated by the Aborigines before white people arrived.

Some people think that history is boring. But as you read these passages you'll discover that the explorers' accounts include some of the most awesome, terrifying and amazing experiences ever had by a human being. I hope that you'll also see your country of Australia differently through their eyes. Perhaps you'll even be inspired to follow in their footsteps one day, and to see the wild country they saw.

Drunken camels were the curse of the Burke and Wills expedition. They drank gallons of the explorers' rum, which would have been better used to drown the doomed men's sorrows. The only female member of Ernest Favenc's expedition to Queensland's Gulf country in 1882–83 never got to publish her remarkable story of endurance in the face of sickness, death and privation. Her journal lies all but forgotten in the archive of Sydney's Mitchell Library, the list of baby clothes at the back suggesting she was pregnant for at least part of the journey. In February 1869 G. W. Goyder, surveyor-general of South Australia and petty tyrant, set out to found the settlement of Darwin. He was watched by the Larrakia people who, when they decided it was safe to contact the strangers, held a corroboree. They gave word perfect renditions of 'John Brown's Body', 'The Glory, Hallelujah', and 'The Old Virginia Shore'. This 'white-fella corroboree' had been traded from the Woolna people, who memorised the tunes while lying in the wet grass at night, spying on surveyors who were working near the Adelaide River. Who, in this instance, were the explorers?

In assembling these accounts I wanted to offer the reader the experience of being a fly on the wall at important moments in Australia's history. To be there, looking over Governor Phillip's shoulder as he chooses the location for the infant settlement of Sydney; to accompany John McDouall Stuart in his moment of triumph at reaching the centre of the continent; and to join the young William Wills as he lies alone, dying of starvation on a full stomach, at Cooper Creek. You will find humanity at its extreme; acts of unimaginable cruelty are juxtaposed with those of compassion and self-sacrifice. George Evans played games with frightened Aboriginal children to cheer them up. Other explorers were murderers.

Why were the explorers there? What made them do it? The answers are as varied as the explorers themselves. Some were simply obeying orders. Others had set out in search of new grazing land, illusory cities or imaginary seas. Some were careful calculators of risk, while others played a terrifying sport of brinkmanship with their own lives. Some were looking for lost comrades, while a few were made explorers by fate, having set out to do something completely different.

Mark Twain, the author of *Huckleberry Finn*, said that Australian history was like so many beautiful lies, but it all actually happened. And our written history is so short. It's hard to imagine that a few centuries ago almost nothing was known of Australia. Parts of its coastline had been charted, but all that was known of the land itself had been learned through the lens of a modest telescope and a handful of fleeting visits.

Back then, some visiting Europeans imagined that Australia was a land peopled by giants, others a green countryside with a vast inland ocean at its heart. It has taken the next 200 years to dispel most of the myths surrounding this country of ours, and the toughest job of all fell to the men and women who trudged into the unknown during the golden century of exploration: 1830–1930. Before that time exploration had been almost entirely restricted to the coasts, and at the end of that period even the driest deserts had been traversed and broadly mapped.

I sometimes try to put myself into the boots of the great explorers like Sturt, Stuart and Bourke and Wills. When their exploring parties left the last settlements surrounding Adelaide and Melbourne, they were entirely alone. Just them, their animals and supplies. No way to even send a letter, and no idea what lay ahead. They trudged on, at the rate of thirty kilometres a day, into what must have seemed an endless wasteland. Quite a number—including Ludwig Leichhardt, Kennedy and Gibson, left their bones bleaching in the outback. Others, like Stuart, arrived back on stretchers, little more than blackened skeletons. When Sturt arrived home after his 1845 exploration, there was no letter or telegram to announce his arrival. He just knocked on the front door, and his wife nearly fainted, thinking that the weatherbeaten figure of her husband was a ghost!

Although the explorers believed that they were entering a wilderness, they were in fact just going visiting, for all of Australia was inhabited, and had been so for at least 40,000 years. This was Aboriginal land, and one of the most fascinating things about Australia's explorations is what happened when the explorers met the Aborigines.

There is a certain moment in Australian exploration which has always transfixed me. It is the instant when white looks on black, and black on white, for the first time. Neither knows it, but such meetings bridge an extraordinary gulf in time, for they unite people who became separated at least 50,000 years ago. That's 40,000 years longer than people have been in the Americas or Ireland, 20,000 years before the Neanderthals finally surrendered Europe to my ancestors, and 25,000 years before the worst of the last ice age turned most of Australia into a howling desert, a vast dunefield. No other cultures, meeting on the frontier, have been separated by such an unimagineable chasm of time.

The thing that fascinates me about such meetings is just how clearly both sides managed to make themselves understood. A smile, anger or fear are immediately comprehended—as if the separation of the millennia never existed. That understanding is a tribute to the great commonality of experience that shaped humanity on the African savannah for a million years before the diaspora of the late Pleistocene era brought people to Australia. It speaks to me of a common humanity that makes differences in colour, race and culture almost invisible in their triviality.

That magic second of reunion between black and white in Australian exploration has resolved itself in as many different ways as there are explorers. James Cook watched the Aborigines behave as if it never happened. They simply kept fishing or walking, not looking up, as the *Endeavour* passed by a few hundred yards offshore. Sometimes, a spear or a gun saw this remarkable reunion terminated in bloodshed and shame; yet, at its best, the moment was followed by a celebration, a gift or a song.

And then there were the eccentric, almost comic, responses. John McDouall Stuart records that one fine morning in 1858 near Lake Torrens he surprised an Aboriginal man who was hunting: 'What he imagined I was I do not know...in an instant, he threw down his waddies, and jumped up into a mulga bush...He kept waving us off with his hand...I expected every moment to see the bush break with his weight.' What, indeed, did he imagine this white spectre on a horse was? Did the hunter guess (correctly as it turns out) that horses could not climb?

If you read these accounts carefully, you will discover that often the real explorers were the Aborigines. It was they who scouted ahead, found the trail and food, and met the local Aborigines for the first time.

As you read these journals, I hope that you discover

or rediscover something of Australia yourself. Its history is varied beyond belief. Eora warriors, Polish patriots, French aristocrats, currency lads and lasses, fools and wise men, black and white, have all played their part in shaping what the dying William Wills called 'this extraordinary continent'. It's a continent we are just beginning to explore.

Although the explorers often refer to Aborigines in terms which today we find unacceptable—'gins', 'blacks', 'savages', 'niggers', not to mention the strange but surprisingly popular 'children of nature'—the use of such expressions is not always intended to diminish. I have left the judgment of these instances to the reader. Where necessary, I have modernised punctuation and spelling, silently corrected a handful of obvious errors, inserted the occasional explanatory date, and sometimes added a word or two of clarification in a footnote, marked by a dagger. The explorers' own footnotes are indicated by an asterisk (*). Otherwise, their writings are presented as they were first printed, with any omissions of text indicated by an ellipsis (…).

Jan Carstensz

Coal-Black and Stark Naked, 1623

 In 1623 Dutch mariner Jan Carstensz, sailing in the yacht Pera, entered the Gulf of Carpentaria. After passing the verdant Spice Islands and glimpsing the eternal snows of New Guinea's highest mountains, he was disappointed by the arid country of western Cape York. Worse, the 'coal-black and stark naked' inhabitants repulsed Carstensz's attempts to go 'landinward' to complete his explorations. The crew of the Pera kidnapped an Aboriginal man, whose fate, like that of so many others, is not recorded. The theme of kidnapping was to become a recurring tragedy of Australian exploration.

We join Carstensz on a deserted and forbidding part of the coast.

May—...I went ashore myself with ten musketeers, and we advanced a long way into the wood without seeing any human beings. The land here is low-lying and without hills as before, in latitude 15°20'. It is very dry and barren for, during all the time we have searched and examined this part of the coast to our best ability, we have not seen one fruit-bearing tree,

Jan Carstensz

nor anything that man could make use of: there are no mountains or even hills, so that it may be safely concluded that the land contains no metals, nor yields any precious woods, such as sandalwood, aloes or columba.

In our judgment this is the most arid and barren region that could be found anywhere on the earth. The inhabitants, too, are the most wretched and poorest creatures that I have ever seen in my age or time; as there are no large trees anywhere on this coast, they have no boats or canoes whether large or small...I went ashore myself in the pinnace which was duly armed.† The blacks here attacked us with their weapons, but afterwards took to flight, upon which we went landinward for some distance, and found divers of their weapons, such as assegais and callaways, leaning against the trees.‡ We took care not to damage these weapons, but tied pieces of iron and strings of beads to some of them, in order to attract the blacks who, however, seemed quite indifferent to these things, and repeatedly held up their shields with great boldness and threw them at the muskets. These men are, like all the others we have lately seen, of tall stature and very lean to look at, but malignant and evil-natured...

The skipper went ashore with the pinnace, with strict orders to treat the blacks kindly, and try to attract them with pieces of iron and strings of beads; if practicable, also to capture one or more. When at noon the men

† Pinnace: a light boat propelled by sails or oars.

‡ Assegais and calloways: spears.

returned they reported that on their landing more than 100 blacks had collected on the beach with their weapons, and had with the strong arm tried to prevent them from coming ashore. In order to frighten them, a musket was accordingly fired, upon which the blacks fled and retreated into the wood, from where they tried every means in their power to surprise and attack our men.

These natives resemble the others in shape and figure: they are quite black and stark naked, some of them having their faces painted red and others white, with feathers stuck through the lower part of the nose...

In the morning of the 8th, I went ashore myself with ten musketeers. We saw numerous footprints of men and dogs (running from south to north). We accordingly spent some time there, following the footprints aforesaid to a river where we gathered excellent vegetables or potherbs. When we had got into the pinnace again, the blacks emerged with their arms from the wood at two different points; by showing them bits of iron and strings of beads we kept them on the beach, until we had come near them, upon which one of them, who had lost his weapon, was by the skipper seized round the waist, while at the same time the quartermaster put a noose round his neck, by which he was dragged to the pinnace.

The other blacks, seeing this, tried to rescue their captured brother by furiously assailing us with their assagais. In defending ourselves we shot one of them, after which the others took to flight, upon which we returned on board without further delay. These natives resemble all the others in outward appearance: they are coal-black and stark naked with twisted nets round their heads...

We cannot, however, give any account of their customs and ceremonies, nor did we learn anything about the thickness of the population, since we had few or no opportunities for inquiring into these matters. Meanwhile I hope that with God's help Your Worships will in time get information touching these points from the black we have captured, to whose utterances I would beg leave to refer you.

Abel Tasman

Men of Extraordinary Stature, 1642

 In 1642 Abel Tasman, wanderer on the sea from Batavia, now modern Jakarta, sailed into a great blank on the world map. At latitude 42° S he sighted a mountainous island. Among the tall timbers, his men found a tree with notches cut at five-foot intervals. They heard the sounds of trumpets and small gongs, and saw the pawprints of an animal like a tiger. Tasman's island is rather like the magical place Shakespeare dreamed up in his play, *The Tempest*, 'full of noises, sounds and sweet airs', a land of preternatural imaginings and monstrous possibilities.

Tasman left the island destined to bear his name convinced it was inhabited by giants and, to judge by the gongs and tigers, somewhat similar to Java. He was not to know that he had crossed the most profound zoological barrier on the planet—Wallace's Line—the imaginary divide that separates the Australian region (with its eucalypts and kangaroos) from Asia (with its elephants and tigers). In Tasmania, men climbed trees by leaps and bounds, ascending from notch to notch with their toes and a stone hatchet. There, the currawong and bellbird called their melodious songs, and of course there were

tigers—Tasmanian Tigers. We join Tasman near Storm
Bay in the south-east of the island.

25 November—This land being the first land we
have met with in the South Sea, and not known
to any European nation, we have conferred on
it the name of Anthoony van Diemenslandt in honour of
the Hon. Governor-General, our illustrious master, who
sent us to make this discovery...

2 December—Early in the morning we sent our pilot-
major Francoys Jacobsz in command of our pinnace,
manned with four musketeers and six rowers, all of them
furnished with spikes and side-arms, together with the
cockboat of the *Zeehaen* with one of her second mates
and six musketeers in it, to a bay, situated north-west of
us at upwards of a mile's distance, in order to ascertain
what facilities (as regards fresh water, refreshments, timber
and the like) may be available there.

About three hours before nightfall the boats came
back, bringing various samples of vegetables which they
had seen growing there in great abundance, some of them
in appearance not unlike a certain plant growing at the
Cabo de Bona Esperance and fit to be used as pot-herbs,
and another species with long leaves and a brackish taste,
strongly resembling *persil de mer* or samphire. The pilot-
major and the second mate of the *Zeehaen* made the
following report, to wit:

That they had rowed the space of upwards of a mile

round the said point, where they had found high but level land, covered with vegetation (not cultivated but growing naturally by the will of God), abundance of excellent timber, and a gently sloping watercourse in a barren valley...

That they had heard certain human sounds and also sounds nearly resembling the music of a trump or a small gong not far from them, though they had seen no one.

That they had seen two trees about two or two and a half fathom in thickness, measuring from sixty to sixty-five feet from the ground to the lowermost branches, which trees bore notches made with flint implements, the bark having been removed for the purpose. These notches, forming a kind of steps to enable persons to get up the trees and rob the birds' nests in their tops, were fully five feet apart, so that our men concluded that the natives here must be of very tall stature, or must be in possession of some sort of artifice for getting up the said trees; in one of the trees these notched steps were so fresh and new that they seemed to have been cut less than four days ago.

That on the ground they had observed certain footprints of animals, not unlike those of tiger's claws; they also brought on board certain specimens of animal excrements voided by quadrupeds so far as they could surmise and observe, together with a small quantity of gum of a seemingly very fine quality, which had exuded from trees and bore some resemblance to gum-lac...[†]

That in the interior they had in several places observed numerous trees which had deep holes burnt into them at the upper end of the foot, while the earth had here and there been dug out with the fist so as to form a fireplace, the surrounding soil having become as hard as flint through the action of the fire.

A short time before we got sight of our boats returning to the ships, we now and then saw clouds of dense smoke rising up from the land, which was nearly west by north of us, and surmised this might be a signal given by our men because they were so long coming back; for we had ordered them to return speedily...

When our men had come on board again, we inquired of them whether they had been there and made a fire, to which they returned a negative answer, adding, however, that at various times and points in the wood they also had seen clouds of smoke ascending. So there can be no doubt there must be men here of extraordinary stature.

[†] quadruped: mammal

William Dampier

The Miserablest People in the World, 1688

 William Dampier was a privateer, a commander of a private ship that was also used in wartime, or for exploration, by the English government. He provided the first extended account in English of the Great South Land and its inhabitants when he landed on the northern Western Australian coast in January 1688. Both the land and the people clearly appalled him. His realistic description stands in contrast to the fantastical Dutch interpretations. Perhaps Dampier's bleak account helped create the great gap of seventy years in the exploration of Australia, from the late seventeenth century until Cook arrived on the eastern seaboard in 1770.

New Holland is a very large tract of land. It is not yet determined whether it is an island or a main continent; but I am certain that it joins neither to Asia, Africa nor America. This part of it that we saw is all low even land, with sandy banks against the sea. Only the points are rocky and so are some of the islands in this bay.[†]

[†] King Sound.

William Dampier

The land is of a dry sandy soil, destitute of water except you make wells, yet producing diverse sorts of trees; but the woods are not thick nor the trees very big...We saw no sort of animal, nor any track of beast, but once; and that seemed to be the tread of a beast as big as a great mastiff dog. Here are a few small land birds, but none bigger than a blackbird; and but few sea fowls. Neither is the sea very plentifully stored with fish unless you reckon the manatee and turtle as such.[†] Of these creatures there is plenty, but they are extraordinarily shy; though the inhabitants cannot trouble them much, having neither boats nor iron.

The inhabitants of this country are the miserablest people in the world. The Hodmadods of Monomatapa, though a nasty people, yet for wealth are gentlemen to these, who have no houses, and skin garments, sheep, poultry, and fruits of the earth, ostrich eggs, etc., as the Hodmadods have.[‡] And, setting aside their human shape, they differ but little from brutes. They are tall, straight-bodied and thin, with small long limbs. They have great heads, round foreheads and great brows. Their eyelids are always half closed to keep the flies out of their eyes; they being so troublesome here that no fanning will keep them from coming to one's face and, without the assistance of both hands to keep them off, they will creep into one's nostrils and mouth too, if the lips are not shut very close.

[†] Manatee: Dampier is referring to the dugong.
[‡] Hodmadods: the Hottentots of South Africa.

So that from their infancy being thus annoyed with these insects, they do never open their eyes as other people, and therefore they cannot see far unless they hold up their heads as if they were looking at something over them.

They have great bottle noses, pretty full lips and wide mouths. The two fore-teeth of their upper jaw are wanting in all of them, men and women, old and young; whether they draw them out, I know not. Neither have they any beards. They are long-visaged, and of a very unpleasing aspect, having no one graceful feature in their faces. Their hair is black, short and curled like that of the negroes, and not long and lank like the common Indians. The colour of their skins, both of their faces and the rest of their body, is coal-black, like that of the negroes of Guinea…

These people speak somewhat through the throat; but we could not understand one word that they said. We anchored, as I said before, on January the 5th, and seeing men walking on the shore, we presently sent a canoe to get some acquaintance with them, for we were in hopes to get some provision among them. But the inhabitants, seeing our boat coming, ran away and hid themselves…

At last we went over to the islands, and there we found a great many of the natives. I do believe there were forty on one island, men, women and children. The men at our first coming ashore threatened us with their lances and swords, but they were frighted by firing one gun which we fired purposely to scare them. The island was so small that they could not hide themselves, but they were much disordered at our landing, especially the women and children, for we went directly to their camp. The lustiest of the women, snatching up their infants, ran away howling, and the little children ran after squeaking and bawling; but the men stood still.

Willem De Vlamingh

A Land of Miracles, 1696–97

 At the time of de Vlamingh's visit, unicorns, mermaids and giants were still found in the pages of respectable books of natural history. Despite Dampier's pragmatic assessments, the possibilities raised by the Great South Land remained monstrous: fish with arms and legs—even hands—like men, footprints half a metre long, and water as red as blood.

Willem de Vlamingh, master of the *Geelvinck*, captained the last large-scale voyage of exploration made by the Dutch East India Company. He had been despatched to investigate the fate of an East Indiaman lost off the coast of Western Australia. The expedition gives us a glimpse of the land beyond the shore, for de Vlamingh's men were the first Europeans to penetrate any distance inland. They found the uncanny 'Land of Eendracht', with its elusive inhabitants and eerie environment, little to their liking. Here we join him as he sights Rottnest Island—his first taste of Australia.

Willem De Vlamingh

December 1696—...Here our people saw a miraculous fish about two feet long with a round head and arms and legs of a kind, nay even something like hands; likewise several branches of vegetation. And we came to anchor at fourteen to fifteen fathoms, about half a mile off the island, on the south coast, good bottom, the wind sw by s...

The 31st I rowed ashore again with our skipper, and having gone some distance into the interior of the island I found there a great variety of herbs of which a great many were not unknown to me and some of which were similar in smell to those at home; likewise also several trees and among these a kind whose wood had an aromatic fragrance, almost like *Lignum rhodii*.[†] The ground is covered with little or no soil, mostly white sand and rocky, in my opinion unsuitable for cultivation.

There are few if any birds to be seen and no animals except a kind of rat as large as a common cat, whose dung is to be found in abundance all over the island;[‡] also very few seals and fish other than a kind of sardine and grey rock bream...

While returning to the beach, the people found a piece of Dutch timber with nails still sticking in it, which it seems must be from a wrecked ship. On the mainland coast smoke was seen to rise up in several places, about three to four miles from us. The country appears

---

[†] A hardwood, thought previously to have great medicinal qualities.

[‡] These were quokkas.

much higher than it really is and looks like that of Holland...

I again in company of the skipper, made for the mainland coast, where having stepped ashore, we found ourselves to amount to eighty-six men (both soldiers and seamen and two of the abovementioned blacks whom we had brought from the Cape) all well provided with weapons. We marched eastward and encountered after about an hour's advance a small hut quite as bad as those of the Hottentots; somewhat further on a large basin with brackish water, which later was found to be a river on whose banks we saw several footprints, no larger than ours, as well as some holes in which there was fresh and somewhat brackish water.

But however thoroughly we explored everything, we found no people. Further on we found still more poor huts and footprints. Towards the evening it was resolved to remain ashore that night and so we camped in a wood in a place where we found a fire started by the inhabitants, whom, however, we did not see. It was kept going by throwing on wood while in the meantime four guards were posted every quarter of an hour...

The 7th all the people were ferried back to the ships in the boats, bringing along two young black swans...

The 12th two hours before sunrise I went ashore again with our upper-steersman, several seamen and the said two blacks, upon seeing several fires. We met...no people, wherefore recognising that nothing was to be achieved by us here, we returned to our ship, which we came to at noon.

Concerning the country, it is sandy and, in the area where we have been, wooded with many trees, among which some as much as three to four fathoms thick, but without fruit: in short, full of thistles and thorns. Several of these trees yielded a kind of resin, almost like lacquer, brownishred in colour. Everything was timid in our presence, both men and birds, swans, brent-geese, pelicans, cockatoos, parakeets, etc. The best part of it is that no vermin is found here, but by day the flies are a terrible torment...

The 25th early in the morning I went ashore...Having come to the beach, we found many oysters and started at once out on our march but sometimes had to rest through fatigue caused by the heat of the sun and the heavy going through thick scrub, until we came to the mountain range, where we camped. But if the march had been hard, the greatest grief struck us now, for finding no water, we thought we would perish from thirst. We could see our ships clearly from here and wished a thousand times to be back on board.

Meanwhile, the commander of the soldiers had descended with another two men and brought back a report, with a cheerful face when he returned, that he had found fresh water as well as a hut and footprints eighteen inches long, about an hour's march from our camp.

The 26th in the morning before sunrise we started marching again and arrived at the said hut after a while, around which we found a great many eggshells, but those eighteen-inch footprints changed into ordinary ones. We also passed this night on shore, camped again by the waterhole mentioned, without, although having split up, finding either humans or animals, there being nothing but scrub.

William Dampier

Crying Pooh, Pooh, Pooh, 1699

 Dampier seems to have matured as an explorer by the time of his second voyage to Australia in 1699, this time representing the British Admiralty. His careful descriptions of wildlife indicate that he had overcome his initial horror at the sterility of the country, and he was filled with regret at the first spilling of blood between Aborigines and the English, at Roebuck Bay near Broome, an event he recounts here. When homeward bound, his ship sprang a leak and had to be run ashore on Ascension Island. Dampier finally reached England in 1701. Fittingly, he later rescued Alexander Selkirk, better known as that most famous of castaways, Robinson Crusoe.

August—The 28th day we had between twenty and forty fathom.[†] We saw no land this day, but saw a great many snakes and some whales. We saw also some boobies and noddy-birds; and in the night caught one of these last. It was of another shape and colour than

---

[†] Fathom: unit of length in the Imperial system. 1 fathom = 1.8288 metres.

any I had seen before.[†] It had a small long bill, as all of them have; flat feet like ducks' feet; its tail forked like a swallow but longer and broader, and the fork deeper than that of the swallow, with very long wings.

The top or crown of the head of this noddy was coal-black, having also small black streaks round about and close to the eyes; and round these streaks, on each side, a pretty broad white circle. The breast, belly and underpart of the wings of this noddy were white; and the back and upper part of its wings of a faint black or smoke colour...

The 30th day, being in latitude 18° 21', we made the land again, and saw many great smokes near the shore; and having fair weather and moderate breezes I steered in towards it...This evening we saw an eclipse of the moon...

The 31st of August betimes in the morning I went ashore with ten or eleven men to search for water. We went armed with muskets and cutlasses for our defence, expecting to see people there; and carried also shovels and pickaxes to dig wells. When we came near the shore we saw three tall black naked men on the sandy bay ahead of us, but as we rowed in they went away.

When we were landed, I sent the boat with two men in her to lie a little from the shore at an anchor, to prevent being seized; while the rest of us went after the three black men, who were now got on the top of a small hill about a

---

[†] Boobies: seabirds.

quarter of a mile from us, with eight or nine men more in their company. They, seeing us coming, ran away.

When we came on the top of the hill where they first stood, we saw a plain savannah, about half a mile from us, farther in from the sea. There were several things like haycocks standing in the savannah, which at a distance we thought were houses, looking just like the Hottentot's houses at the Cape of Good Hope—but we found them to be so many rocks. We searched about these for water, but could find none, nor any houses, nor people, for they were all gone. Then we turned again to the place where we landed, and there we dug for water.

While we were at work there came nine or ten of the natives to a small hill a little way from us, and stood there menacing and threatening of us, and making a great noise. At last one of them came towards us, and the rest followed at a distance. I went out to meet him, and came within fifty yards of him, making to him all the signs of peace and friendship I could; but then he ran away, neither would they any of them stay for us to come nigh them, for we tried two or three times.

At last I took two men with me, and went in the afternoon along by the seaside, purposely to catch one of them, if I could, of whom I might learn where they got their fresh water. There were ten or twelve of the natives a little way off, who, seeing us three going away from the rest of our men, followed us at a distance. I thought they would follow us: but there being for a while a sandbank between us and them, that they could not then see us, we made a halt, and hid ourselves in a bending of the sandbank. They knew we must be thereabouts and, being three or four times our number, thought to seize us. So they dispersed themselves, some going to the seashore, and others beating about the sandhills.

We knew by what rencounter we had had with them in the morning that we could easily outrun them; so a nimble young man that was with me, seeing some of them near, ran towards them; and they for some time ran away before him. But, he soon overtaking them, they faced about and fought him. He had a cutlass, and they had wooden lances; with which, being many of them, they were too hard for him. When he first ran towards them I chased two more that were by the shore; but fearing how it might be with my young man I turned back quickly, and went up to the top of a sandhill, whence I saw him near me, closely engaged with them.

Upon their seeing me, one of them threw a lance at me that narrowly missed me. I discharged my gun to scare them, but avoided shooting any of them; till, finding the young man in great danger from them, and myself in some; and that, though the gun had a little frighted them at first, yet they had soon learnt to despise it, tossing up their hands, and crying *pooh, pooh, pooh*, and coming on afresh with a great noise.

I thought it high time to charge again, and shoot one of them, which I did. The rest, seeing him fall, made a stand again; and my young man took the opportunity to disengage himself, and come off to me; my other man also was with me, who had done nothing all this while, having come out unarmed; and I returned back with my men, designing to attempt the natives no farther, being very sorry for what had happened already.

They took up their wounded companion; and my young man, who had been struck through the cheek by one of their lances, was afraid it had been poisoned; but I did not think that likely. His wound was very painful to him, being made with a blunt weapon, but he soon recovered of it.

James Cook

James Cook is justly regarded as the greatest maritime explorer of his age, perhaps of all time. In 1770 he charted the east coast of Australia, touching land five times—first of all at what is now Botany Bay. Cook initially named it Stingray Bay, for the enormous stingrays caught there, and he correctly surmised that these creatures were never hunted by the Aborigines. After giving the botanists Banks and Solander time to collect a cornucopia of plant specimens, he changed the name in honour of their work, set sail, and coasted serenely past a safe anchorage he named Port Jackson—thus failing to discover Sydney's astonishing harbour.

6May—In the evening the yawl returned from fishing having caught two stingrays weighing near 600 pounds. The great quantity of new plants etc. Mr Banks and Dr Solander collected in this place occasioned my giving it the name of Botany Bay. It is situated in the latitude of 34° 0' south, longitude 208° 37' west. It is capacious, safe and commodious...

The entrance of the harbour lies about the middle of

this land; in coming from the southward it is discovered before you are abreast of it which you cannot do in coming from the northward; the entrance is little more than a mile broad and lies in WNW...

We anchored near the south shore about a mile within the entrance for the conveniency of sailing with a southerly wind and the getting of fresh water, but I afterwards found a very fine stream of fresh water on the north shore in the first sandy cove within the island, before which a ship might lay almost landlocked, and wood for fuel may be got everywhere.

Although wood is here in great plenty yet there is very little variety; the largest trees are as large or larger than our oaks in England and grow a good deal like them and yield a reddish gum; the wood itself is heavy, hard and black like lignum vitae; another sort that grows tall and straight something like pines, the wood of this is hard and ponderous and something of the nature of American live oaks; these two are all the timber trees I met with.

There are a few sorts of shrubs and palm trees and mangroves about the head of the harbour. The country is woody, low and flat as far inland as we could see and I believe the soil is generally sandy; in the wood are a variety of very beautiful birds such as cockatoos, lorikeets, parrots etc., and crows exactly like those we have in England. Waterfowl are no less plenty about the head of the harbour where there are large flats of sand and mud on which they seek their food: the most of these unknown to us, one sort especially which was black and white and as large as a goose but most like a pelican.

On the sand and mud banks are oysters, mussels, cockles etc., which I believe are the chief support of the inhabitants, who go into the shoaled water with their little canoes and pick them out of the sand and mud with their hands and sometimes roast and eat them in the canoe, having often a fire for that purpose as I suppose, for I know of no other use it can be for.

The natives do not appear to be numberous, neither do they seem to live in large bodies but dispersed in small parties along by the water side; those I saw were about as tall as Europeans, of a very dark brown colour but not black, nor had they woolly frizzled hair, but black and lank like ours. No sort of clothing or ornaments were ever seen by any of us upon any one of them, or in or about their huts, from which I conclude they never wear any. Some we saw that had their faces and bodies painted with a sort of white paint or pigment.

Although I said that shellfish is their chief support yet they catch other sorts of fish, some of which we found roasting on the fire the first time we landed; some of these they strike with gigs and others they catch with hook and line; we have seen them strike fish with gigs, and hooks and lines were found in their huts. Stingrays I believe they do not eat because I never saw the least remains of one near any of their huts or fireplaces. However, we could but know very little of their customs as we were never able to form any connections with them; they had not so much as touched the things we had left in their huts on purpose for them to take away.

During our stay in this harbour I caused the English colours to be displayed ashore every day and an inscription to be cut in one of the trees near the watering place setting forth the ship's name, date, etc. Having seen everything this place afforded we at daylight in the morning weighed with a light breeze at NW and put to sea...We steered alongshore NNE and at noon we were...about two or three miles from the land and abreast of a bay or harbour wherein there appeared to be safe anchorage which I called Port Jackson.

Joseph Banks

The Endeavour Holed, 1770

 Perhaps it's his well-known portrait as the corpulent, bewigged president of the Royal Society that makes us think of Sir Joseph Banks as stuffy. His *Endeavour* writings, however, reveal a lively, enquiring young man with a delightful sense of humour, fully worthy of the maidens bestowed upon him by Queen Purea of Tahiti.

The holing of the *Endeavour* on the Great Barrier Reef in June 1770 is one of the most dramatic events in Australian exploration history. Banks's account of the catastrophe is full of life, wonderment and terror. In it we meet a landlubber faced with the prospect of a watery death, and the marvelling of an outsider at the coolness of the ship's crew in a moment of crisis.

Banks was perhaps secretly jubilant at the enforced stay at the Endeavour River in north Queensland, where Cooktown now is. It must have been frustrating for the great botanist to watch the coastline slip by for weeks at a time, with a captain unwilling to land. It was at Endeavour River that a European first saw a kangaroo, and where a sailor from the *Endeavour* encountered what appeared to be the devil himself!

Joseph Banks

8 June 1770—Still sailing between the main and islands; the former, rocky and high, looked rather less barren than usual and by the number of fires seemed to be better peopled. In the morn we passed within a quarter of a mile of a small islet or rock on which we saw with our glasses about thirty men, women and children standing all together and looking attentively at us. The first people we have seen show any signs of curiosity at the sight of the ship...

10 June—At nightfall rocks and shoals were seen ahead, on which the ship was put upon a wind offshore. While we were at supper she went over a bank of seven or eight fathom water which she came upon very suddenly; this we concluded to be the tail of the shoals we had seen at sunset and therefore went to bed in perfect security, but scarce were we warm in our beds when we were called up with the alarming news of the ship being fast ashore upon a rock, which she in a few moments convinced us of by beating very violently against the rocks.

Our situation became now greatly alarming: we had stood offshore three hours and a half with a pleasant breeze so knew we could not be very near it: we were little less than certain that we were upon sunken coral rocks, the most dreadful of all others on account of their sharp points and grinding quality which cut through a ship's bottom almost immediately.

The officers, however, behaved with inimitable coolness void of all hurry and confusion; a boat was got out in

which the master went and after sounding round the ship
found that she had ran over a rock and consequently had
shoal water all round her. All this time she continued to
beat very much so that we could hardly keep our legs
upon the quarterdeck; by the light of the moon we could
see her sheathing-boards etc. floating thick round her;
about twelve her false keel came away.

11 June—In the meantime all kind of preparations were
making for carrying out anchors, but by reason of the
time it took to hoist out boats etc. the tide ebbed so much
that we found it impossible to attempt to get her off till
next high water, if she would hold together so long; and
we now found to add to our misfortune that we had got
ashore nearly at the top of high water and as night tides
generally rise higher than day ones we had little hopes of
getting off even then...

Orders were now given for lightening the ship which
was begun by starting our water and pumping it up; the
ballast was then got up and thrown overboard as well
as six of our guns (all that we had upon deck). All this
time the seamen worked with surprising cheerfulness
and alacrity; no grumbling or growling was to be heard
throughout the ship, no not even an oath (though the ship
in general was as well furnished with them as most in His
Majesty's service). At night the tide almost floated her but
she made water so fast that three pumps, hard worked,
could but just keep her clear and the fourth absolutely
refused to deliver a drop of water. Now in my own opinion

I entirely gave up the ship and packing up what I thought I might save prepared myself for the worst.

The most critical part of our distress now approached. The ship was almost afloat and everything ready to get her into deep water but she leaked so fast that with all our pumps we could just keep her free. If (as was probable) she should make more water when hauled off she must sink and we well knew that our boats were not capable of carrying us all ashore, so that some, probably the most of us, must be drowned: a better fate maybe than those would have who should get ashore without arms to defend themselves from the Indians[†] or provide themselves with food, on a country where we had not the least reason to hope for subsistence had they even every convenience to take it as nets etc., so barren had we always found it; and had they even met with good usage from the natives and food to support them, debarred from a hope of ever again seeing their native country or conversing with any but the most uncivilised savages perhaps in the world.

The dreadful time now approached and the anxiety in everybody's countenance was visible enough. The capstan and windlass were manned and they began to heave: fear of death now stared us in the face. Hopes we had none but of being able to keep the ship afloat till we could run her ashore on some part of the main where out of her materials we might build a vessel large enough to carry us to the East Indies.

[†] Indians: Aborigines.

At ten o'clock she floated and was in a few minutes hauled into deep water where to our great satisfaction she made no more water than she had done, which was indeed full as much as we could manage, though no one there was in the ship but who willingly exerted his utmost strength.

12 June—The people who had been twenty-four hours at exceeding hard work now began to flag; myself, unused to labour, was much fatigued and had laid down to take a little rest; was awaked about twelve with the alarming news of the ship's having gained so much upon the pumps that she had four feet water in her hold...

One of our midshipmen now proposed an expedient which no one else in the ship had seen practised, though all had heard of it by the name of fothering a ship, by the means of which he said he had come home from America in a ship which made more water than we did.

He was immediately set to work with four or five assistants to prepare his fother which he did thus. He took a lower studding sail and, having mixed together a large quantity of oakum chopped fine and wool, he sticked it down upon the sail as loosely as possible in small bundles each about as big as his fist: these were ranged in rows three or four inches from each other.[†] This was to be sunk under the ship and the theory of it was this: wherever the leak was must be a great suction which would probably catch hold of one or other of these lumps of oakum and

---

† Oakum: tarred fibre used in shipbuilding.

wool and, drawing it in either partly or entirely, stop up the hole...

In the afternoon the ship was got under way with a gentle breeze of wind and stood in for the land; soon after the fother was finished and applied by fastening ropes to each corner, then sinking the sail under the ship and with these ropes drawing it as far backwards as we could; in about half an hour to our great surprise the ship was pumped dry and upon letting the pumps stand she was found to make very little water, so much beyond our most sanguine expectations had this singular expedient succeeded...

During the whole time of this distress I must say for the credit of our people that I believe every man exerted his utmost for the preservation of the ship, contrary to what I have universally heard to be the behaviour of seamen who have commonly as soon as a ship is in a desperate situation began to plunder and refuse all command. This was no doubt owing entirely to the cool and steady conduct of the officers, who during the whole time never gave an order which did not show them to be perfectly composed and unmoved by the circumstances howsoever dreadful they might appear...

The captain and myself went ashore to view the harbour and found it indeed beyond our most sanguine wishes: it was the mouth of a river the entrance of which was, to be sure, narrow enough and shallow but, when once in, the ship might be moored afloat so near the shore that, by a stage from her to it, all her cargo might be got out and in again in a very short time; in this same place she might be hove down with all ease, but the beach gave signs of the tides rising in the springs six or seven feet which was more than enough to do our business without that trouble. The meeting with so many natural advantages in a harbour so near us at the very time of our misfortune appeared almost providential...

17 June—Weather a little less rough than it was. Weighed and brought the ship in but in doing it ran her twice ashore by the narrowness of the channel; the second time she remained till the tide lifted her off. In the meantime Dr Solander and myself began our plant gathering. In the evening the ship was moored within twenty feet of the shore afloat and before night much lumber was got out of her...

20 June—Weather cleared up so we began to gather and dry plants of which we had hopes of as many as we could muster during our stay...

22 June—In the morn I saw her leak which was very large: in the middle was a hole large enough to have sunk a ship with twice our pumps, but here providence had most visibly worked in our favour, for it was in great measure plugged up by a stone which was as big as a man's fist. Round the edges of this stone had all the water come in which had so near overcome us, and here we found the wool and oakum or fothering which had relieved us in so unexpected a manner. The effects of the coral rock upon her bottom is difficult to describe but more to believe; it had cut through her plank and deep into one of her timbers, smoothing the gashes still before it so that the whole might easily be imagined to be cut with an axe.

Myself employed all day in laying in plants. The people who were sent to the other side of the water in order to shoot pigeons saw an animal as large as a greyhound, of a mouse colour and very swift.[†] They also saw many Indian houses and a brook of fresh water.

24 June—Gathering plants and hearing descriptions of the animal which is now seen by everybody. A seaman who had been out in the woods brought home the description of an animal he had seen, composed in so seamanlike a style that I cannot help mentioning it: it was (says he) about as large and much like a one gallon cagg, as black as the devil and had two horns on its head; it went but slowly but I dared not touch it.[‡]

25 June—In gathering plants today I myself had the good fortune to see the beast so much talked of, though but imperfectly; he was not only like a greyhound in size and running but had a long tail, as long as any greyhound's; what to liken him to I could not tell, nothing certainly that I have seen at all resembles him…

29 June—One of our midshipmen, an American who was out a shooting today, saw a wolf, perfectly he said

---

[†] The first European sighting of a kangaroo. Previous explorers had seen only various kinds of wallabies.

[‡] This was probably the black flying fox.

like those he had seen in America; he shot at it but did not kill it.[†] The seine was hauled today for the first time and 150 pounds of fish caught in it...

1 July—Being Sunday all hands were ashore on liberty; many animals were seen by them. The Indians had a fire about a league off up the river...[‡] The ship was now finished and tomorrow being the highest spring tide it was intended to haul her off, so we began to think how we should get out of this place, where so lately to get only in was our utmost ambition...

6 July—Set out today with the second lieutenant resolved to go a good way up the river and see if the country inland differed from that near the shore. We went for about three leagues among mangroves, then we got into the country which differed very little from what we had seen. From hence we proceeded up the river which contracted itself much and lost most of its mangroves; the banks were steep and covered with trees of a beautiful verdure particularly what is called in the West Indies mohoe or bark tree (*Hibiscus tiliaceus*). The land within was generally low, covered thick with long grass, and seemed to promise great fertility were these people to plant and improve it.

In the course of the day Tupia saw a wolf, so at least I guess by his description, and we saw three of the animals

---

[†] The midshipman was James Maria Magra (Matra). He probably saw a dingo.

[‡] A league: no longer an official unit of length. The distance a person can walk in an hour (about 3 miles or 5 kilometres).

of the country but could not get one; also a kind of bats as large as a partridge but these also we were not lucky enough to get.[†]

At night we took up our lodgings close to the banks of the river and made a fire, but the mosquitoes, whose peaceful dominions it seems we had invaded, spared no pains to molest as much as was in their power: they followed us into the very smoke, nay almost into the fire, which hot as the climate was we could better bear the heat of than their intolerable stings.

Between the hardness of our beds, the heat of the fire and the stings of these indefatigable insects the night was not spent so agreeably but that day was earnestly wished for by all of us; at last it

7 *July*—came and with its first dawn we set out in search of game. We walked many miles over the flats and saw four of the animals, two of which my greyhound fairly chased, but they beat him owing to the length and thickness of the grass which prevented him from running while they at every bound leaped over the tops of it. We observed much to our surprise that instead of going upon all fours this animal went only upon two legs, making vast bounds just as the jerboa (*Mus jaculus*) does.

We returned about noon and pursued our course up the river, which soon contracted itself into a freshwater brook where, however, the tide rose pretty considerably; towards

---

[†] Tupia was a Tahitian who had joined the expedition. The animals they saw were probably a dingo and flying foxes.

evening it was so shallow, being almost low water, that we were obliged to get out of the boat and drag her, so finding a convenient place for sleeping in we resolved to go no farther.

Before our things were got up out of the boat we observed a smoke about a furlong from us; we did not doubt at all that the natives, who we had so long had a curiosity to see well, were there.[†] So three of us went immediately towards it, hoping that the smallness of our numbers would induce them not to be afraid of us. When we came to the place, however, they were gone, probably upon having discovered us before we saw them. The fire was in an old tree of touchwood; their houses were there, and branches of trees broken down, with which the children had been playing, not yet withered; their footsteps also upon the sand below the high-tide mark proved that they had very lately been there; near their oven, in which victuals had been dressed since morn, were shells of a kind of clam and roots of a wild yam which had been cooked in it.

Thus were we disappointed of the only good chance we have had of seeing the people since we came here by their unaccountable timidity, and night soon coming on we repaired to our quarters, which was upon a broad sandbank under the shade of a bush where we hoped the mosquitoes would not trouble us. Our beds of plantain

---

† Furlong: an Imperial measure of distance, equal to 600 feet or 201.168 metres.

leaves spread on the sand as soft as a mattress, our cloaks for bedclothes and grass pillows, but above all the entire absence of mosquitoes made me and, I believe, all of us sleep almost without intermission; had the Indians came they would certainly have caught us all napping but that was the least in our thoughts...

12 July—Indians came again today and ventured down to Tupia's tent, where they were so well pleased with their reception that three stayed while the fourth went with the canoe to fetch two new ones; they introduced their strangers (which they always made a point of doing) by name and had some fish given them. They received it with indifference, signed to our people to cook it for them, which was done, and they eat part and gave the rest to my bitch. They stayed the most part of the morning but never ventured to go above twenty yards from their canoe. The ribbands, by which we had tied medals round their necks the first day we saw them, were covered with smoke; I suppose they lay much in the smoke to keep off the mosquitoes.

They are a very small people or at least this tribe consisted of very small people, in general about five feet six in height and very slender; one we measured five feet two and another five feet nine, but he was far taller than any of his fellows...Their colour was nearest to that of chocolate, not that their skins were so dark but the smoke and dirt with which they were cased over, which I suppose served them instead of clothes, made them of that colour.

Their hair was straight in some and curled in others; they always wore it cropped close round their heads; it was of the same consistence with our hair, by no means woolly or curled like that of Negroes. Their eyes were in many lively and their teeth even and good; of them they had complete sets, by no means wanting two of their fore-teeth as Dampier's New Hollanders did.

They were all of them clean limned, active and nimble. Clothes they had none, not the least rag, those parts which nature willingly conceals being exposed to view completely uncovered; yet when they stood still they would often or almost always with their hand or something they held in it hide them in some measure at least, seemingly doing that as if by instinct. They painted themselves with white and red, the first in lines and bars on different parts of their bodies, the other in large patches. Their ornaments were few: necklaces prettily enough made of shells, bracelets wore around the upper part of their arms, consisting of strings lapped round with other strings as what we call gimp in England, a string no thicker than a pack thread tied round their bodies which was sometimes made of human hair, a piece of bark tied over their forehead, and the preposterous bone in their noses which I have before mentioned were all that we observed. One had indeed one of his ears bored, the hole being big enough to put a thumb through, but this was peculiar to that one man and him I never saw wear in it any ornament.

Their language was totally different from that of the

islanders; it sounded more like English in its degree of harshness though it could not be called harsh neither. They almost continually made use of the word *chircau*, which we conceived to be a term of admiration as they still used it whenever they saw anything new; also *cherr, tut tut tut tut tut*, which probably have the same signification.

Their canoe was not above ten feet long and very narrow built, with an outrigger fitted much like those at the islands only far inferior; they in shallow waters set her on with poles, in deep paddled her with paddles about four feet long; she just carried four people so that the six who visited us today were obliged to make two embarkations. Their lances were much like those we had seen in Botany Bay, only they were all of them single-pointed, and some pointed with the stings of stingrays and bearded with two or three beards of the same, which made them indeed a terrible weapon; the board or stick with which they flung them was also made in a neater manner.

After having stayed with us the greatest part of the morning they went away as they came. While they stayed two more and a young woman made their appearance upon the beach; she was to the utmost that we could see with our glasses as naked as the men...

14 July—Our second lieutenant who was a shooting today had the good fortune to kill the animal that had so long been the subject of our speculations. To compare it to any European animal would be impossible as it has not the least resemblance to any one I have seen. Its forelegs are extremely short and of no use to it in walking, its hind again as disproportionally long; with these it hops seven or eight feet at each hop in the same manner as the jerboa, to which animal it bears much resemblance except in size, this being in weight thirty-eight pounds and the jerboa no larger than a common rat.

15 July—The beast which was killed yesterday was today dressed for our dinners and proved excellent meat...

18 July—Indians were over with us today and seemed to have lost all fear of us and became quite familiar; one of them at our desire threw his lance which was about eight feet in length—it flew with a degree of swiftness and steadiness that really surprised me, never being above four feet from the ground and stuck deep in at the distance of fifty paces. After this they ventured on board the ship and soon became our very good friends, so the captain and me left them to the care of those who stayed on board and went to a high hill about six miles from the ship.

Here we overlooked a great deal of sea to leeward, which afforded a melancholy prospect of the difficulties we were to encounter when we came out of our present harbour. In whichever direction we turned our eyes shoals innumerable were to be seen and no such thing as any passage to sea but through the winding channels between them, dangerous to the last degree.

Arthur Phillip

One of the Finest Harbours in the World, 1788

 Soon after the arrival of the First Fleet, Governor Phillip realised that its original destination, Botany Bay, was an unsuitable site for settlement. He set out to explore Port Jackson which Cook had sailed past eighteen years earlier. One can imagine the idyllic cove which caught Phillip's attention: the small sandy beach, the brook running through Port Jackson figs, ferns and rock orchids, and the slopes behind with their massive pink-barked angophoras (related to the eucalyptus) growing straight from the stone.

Unfortunately Phillip named the cove for the incompetent and forgettable Lord Sydney. If he had simply asked the 'chief of the tribe' what the place was called, Australia's first city might today be known as Werrong.

Phillip's published account of the founding of the settlement at Port Jackson was probably compiled from various sources. We join the narrative at Phillip's first meeting with the Eora people, then at the discovery of Sydney Cove.

18 January—At the very first landing of Governor Phillip on the shore of Botany Bay, an interview with the natives took place. They were all armed, but on seeing the governor approach with signs of friendship, alone and unarmed, they readily returned his confidence by laying down their weapons. They were perfectly devoid of clothing, yet seemed fond of ornaments, putting the beads and red baize that were given them on their heads or necks, and appearing pleased to wear them. The presents offered by their new visitors were all readily accepted, nor did any kind of disagreement arise while the ships remained in Botany Bay. This very pleasing effect was produced in no small degree by the personal address, as well as by the great care and attention of the governor...

The next care after landing was the examination of the bay itself, from which it appeared that, though extensive, it did not afford a shelter from the easterly winds; and that, in consequence of its shallowness, ships even of a moderate draught would always be obliged to anchor with the entrance of the bay open, where they must be exposed to a heavy sea that rolls in whenever it blows hard from the eastward.

Several runs of fresh water were found in different parts of the bay, but there did not appear to be any situation to which there was not some very strong objection... Smaller numbers might indeed in several spots have found a comfortable residence, but no place was found in the whole circuit of Botany Bay which seemed at all calculated for the reception of so large a settlement.

While this examination was carried on, the whole fleet had arrived. The *Supply* had not so much outsailed the other ships as to give Governor Phillip the advantage he had expected in point of time. On the 19th of January, the *Alexander, Scarborough* and *Friendship* cast anchor in Botany Bay; and on the 20th the *Sirius*, with the remainder of the convoy. These ships had all continued very healthy; they had not, however, yet arrived at their final station.

The openness of this bay, and the dampness of the soil, by which the people would probably be rendered unhealthy, had already determined the governor to seek another situation. He resolved, therefore, to examine Port Jackson, a bay mentioned by Captain Cook as immediately to the north of this. There he hoped to find not only a better harbour, but a fitter place for the establishment of his new government...

On the 22nd of January they set out upon this expedition, and early in the afternoon arrived at Port Jackson, which is distant about three leagues. Here all regret arising from the former disappointments was at once obliterated; and Governor Phillip had the satisfaction to find one of the finest harbours in the world, in which a thousand sail of the line might ride in perfect security.

The different coves of this harbour were examined with all possible expedition, and the preference was given to one which had the finest spring of water, and in which ships can anchor so close to the shore that at a very small expense quays may be constructed at which the largest vessels may unload. This cove is about half a mile in length, and a quarter of a mile across at the entrance. In honour of Lord Sydney the governor distinguished it by the name of Sydney Cove.

On the arrival of the boats at Port Jackson, a second party of the natives made its appearance near the place of landing. These also were armed with lances, and at first were very vociferous; but the same gentle means used towards the others easily persuaded these also to discard their suspicions and to accept whatsoever was offered.

One man in particular, who appeared to be the chief of this tribe, showed very singular marks both of confidence in his new friends and of determined resolution. Under the guidance of Governor Phillip, to whom he voluntarily entrusted himself, he went to a part of the beach where the men belonging to the boats were then boiling their meat; when he approached the marines, who were drawn up near that place, and saw that by proceeding he should be separated from his companions, who remained with several of the officers at some distance, he stopped, and with great firmness seemed by words and gestures to threaten revenge if any advantage should be taken of his situation.

He then went on with perfect calmness to examine what was boiling in the pot and, by the manner in which he expressed his admiration, made it evident that he intended to profit by what he saw.

Arthur Phillip

Governor Phillip contrived to make him understand that large shells might conveniently be used for the same purpose, and it is probable that by these hints, added to his own observation, he will be enabled to introduce the art of boiling among his countrymen. Hitherto they appear to have known no other way of dressing food than broiling. Their methods of kindling fire are probably very imperfect and laborious, for it is observed that they usually keep it burning, and are very rarely seen without either a fire actually made, or a piece of lighted wood, which they carry with them from place to place, and even in their canoes.

The perpetual fires, which in some countries formed a part of the national religion, had perhaps no other origin than a similar inability to produce it at pleasure; and if we suppose the original flame to have been kindled by lightning, the fiction of its coming down from heaven will be found to deviate very little from the truth.

In passing near a point of land in this harbour, the boats were perceived by a number of the natives, twenty of whom waded into the water unarmed, received what was offered them, and examined the boat with a curiosity which impressed a higher idea of them than any former accounts of their manners had suggested. This confidence and manly behaviour induced Governor Phillip, who was highly pleased with it, to give the place the name of Manly Cove.

The same people afterwards joined the party at the place where they had landed to dine. They were then armed, two of them with shields and swords, the rest with lances only. The swords were made of wood, small in the grip, and apparently less formidable than a good stick. One of these men had a kind of white clay rubbed upon the upper part of his face, so as to have the appearance of a mask. This ornament, if it can be called such, is not common among them, and is probably assumed only on particular occasions or as a distinction to a few individuals.

One woman had been seen on the rocks as the boats passed, with her face, neck and breasts thus painted, and to our people appeared the most disgusting figure imaginable. Her own countrymen were perhaps delighted by the beauty of the effect.

During the preparation for dinner the curiosity of these visitors rendered them very troublesome, but an innocent contrivance altogether removed the inconvenience. Governor Phillip drew a circle round the place where the English were, and without much difficulty made the natives understand that they were not to pass that line; after which they sat down in perfect quietness. Another proof how tractable these people are, when no insult or injury is offered, and when proper means are to influence the simplicity of their minds.

On the 24th of January, Governor Phillip, having sufficiently explored Port Jackson and found it in all respects highly calculated to receive such a settlement as he was appointed to establish, returned to Botany Bay. On his arrival there, the reports made to him, both of the ground which the people were clearing, and of the upper parts of the bay, which in this interval had been more particularly examined, were in the greatest degree unfavourable. It was impossible after this to hesitate concerning the choice of a situation; and orders were accordingly issued for the removal of the whole fleet to Port Jackson.

Arthur Bowes Smyth

The Golden Age, 1788

 Of all the parts of Australia, just two tiny specks were truly virgin lands in 1788. Christmas Island in the Indian Ocean would remain unsettled until the last quarter of the nineteenth century, while people first stepped onto Lord Howe Island four months after the Europeans settled at Sydney Cove. Lord Howe Island was discovered by ships of the First Fleet, drawn there after hearing that the French mariner La Pérouse had seen great flocks of seabirds in the area.

The infant colony was desperately short of food, and Lord Howe proved to be an extraordinarily well-stocked larder. The birds were superabundant and entirely tame. Some species had lost the ability to fly. Smyth's account gives us a glimpse of how the animals of Australia might have behaved on the day the first humans, the ancestors of the Aborigines, set foot on the continent.

16th May 1788—This forenoon I went shore with Captain Sever and Mr Watts in the pinnace; we went through an opening in the reef over which the sea broke with a tremendous noise and swell.

Arthur Bowes Smyth

We landed in Hunter's Bay and saw great numbers of boobies, pigeons and many other birds...The sport we had in knocking down birds etc. was great indeed, though at the expense of tearing most of the clothes off our backs. We made a fire under the trees and supped upon part of our game broiled, which was very sweet and good—the pigeons were the largest I ever saw. We afterwards slept in thick greatcoats carried on shore for that purpose, covered over with the leaves of the cabbage tree, which are here innumerable and many of them so small and tender that you may cut them down with a pocket knife.

When I was in the woods amongst the birds I could... see the fowls or coots, some white, some blue and white, others all blue with large red bills and a patch of red on the top of their heads, and the boobies in thousands, together with a curious brown bird about the size of the landrail in England, walking totally fearless and unconcerned in all part around us, so that we had nothing more to do than to stand still a minute or two and knock down as many as we pleased with a short stick—if you throwed at them and missed them, or even hit them without killing them, they never made the least attempt to fly away and indeed they would only run a few yards from you and be as quiet and unconcerned as if nothing had happened.

The pigeons also were tame as those already described and would sit upon the branches of the trees till you might go and take them off with your hand, or if the branch was so high on which they sat, they would at all times sit till you might knock them down with a short stick—many hundreds of all the sorts mentioned above, together with many parrots and parakeets, magpies and other birds were caught and carried on board our ship and the *Charlotte*.

There has never been any quadruped or reptile seen on the island, which is five or six miles in length and one mile broad at the broadest part and in some parts not so much. The trees on it are chiefly mangroves, cabbage trees, bamboo canes, a species of large aloes plants...

I must take notice that our surprise was no less in the morning upon going into the pinnace to fish with hooks and lines in the bay within side the reef. The water in many parts not more than four or five feet deep with a fine white sandy bottom with coral, brainstones and many other marine plants growing at the bottom, with the sun shining bright upon them, and the innumerable quantities and varieties of fish swimming amongst this coral grove (if I may be allowed the expression) exhibited such a novel and beautiful a scene as but few places in the world I believe will afford. The fish bit so very fast that in about two or three hours we had caught some hundredweight—and the pinnace was half loaded...[†] The fish we caught in the space of three hours served the whole ship's company three days.

[†] Hundredweight: in Imperial measurement 8 stone, or 50 kg.

Watkin Tench

Gonin-Patta!, 1791

 In 1791 almost everything west of Rose Hill (Parramatta) was unknown territory. The First Fleeters mounted several expeditions to fill in the blanks on the map. Here we accompany Captain Watkin Tench, his friend Lieutenant Dawes, Governor Phillip and others into the wilds lying north and west of Sydney Cove, a region which today is rapidly disappearing under the city's vast sprawl. They wanted to discover if the Nepean and Hawkesbury rivers formed one stream.

Tench was a great wit, always ready to enjoy a joke at his own expense. His account of the expedition quickly turns into a comedy. He describes how the Aboriginal 'guides' Colbee and Boladeree would relive every fall and mishap the Europeans have experienced. Tench's most remote landmark is 'that pile of desolation' the governor was pleased to name Tench's Prospect Mount.

Tench's explorations revealed little in the way of new territory, but they have left us some extraordinary insights into the language and life of the Aborigines of the Sydney area. They also remind us of the good relations which existed between black and white at the very beginning of European settlement.

Monday, April 11th, 1791—At twenty minutes before seven o'clock we started from the governor's house at Rose Hill and steered for a short time nearly in a north-east direction, after which we turned to north 34° west, and steadily pursued that course until a quarter before four o'clock, when we halted for the night.

The country for the first two miles, while we walked to the north-east, was good, full of grass and without rock or underwood. Afterwards it grew very bad, being full of steep, barren rocks, over which we were compelled to clamber for seven miles, when it changed to a plain country apparently very sterile, and with very little grass in it, which rendered walking easy.

Our fatigue in the morning had, however, been so oppressive that one of the party knocked up. And had not a soldier, as strong as a pack-horse, undertaken to carry his knapsack in addition to his own, we must either have sent him back, or have stopped at a place for the night which did not afford water.

Our two natives carried each his pack, but its weight was inconsiderable, most of their provisions being in the knapsacks of the soldiers and gamekeepers. We expected to have derived from them much information relating to the country, as no one doubted that they were acquainted with every part of it between the sea coast and the river Hawkesbury. We hoped also to have witnessed their manner of living in the woods, and the resources they rely upon in their journeys.

Nothing, however, of this sort had yet occurred, except their examining some trees to see if they could discover on the bark any marks of the claws of squirrels and opossums, which they said would show whether any of those animals were hidden among the leaves and branches.† They walked stoutly, appeared but little fatigued, and maintained their spirits admirably, laughing to excess when any of us either tripped or stumbled, misfortunes which much seldomer fell to their lot than to ours.

At a very short distance from Rose Hill, we found that they were in a country unknown to them, so that the farther they went the more dependent on us they became, being absolute strangers inland. To convey to their understandings the intention of our journey was impossible. For, perhaps, no words could unfold to an Indian the motives of curiosity which induce men to encounter labour, fatigue and pain, when they might remain in repose at home, with a sufficiency of food. We asked Colbee the name of the people who live inland, and he called them Boòrooberongal; and said they were bad, whence we conjectured that they sometimes war with those on the sea coast, by whom they were undoubtedly driven up the country from the fishing ground, that it might not be overstocked; the weaker here, as in every other country, giving way to the stronger.

We asked how they lived. He said, on birds and

---

† Sugar-gliders.

animals, having no fish. Their laziness appeared strongly when we halted, for they refused to draw water or to cleave wood to make a fire; but as soon as it was kindled (having first well stuffed themselves), they lay down before it and fell asleep.

About an hour after sunset, as we were chatting by the fireside and preparing to go to rest, we heard voices at a little distance in the wood. Our natives catched the sound instantaneously and, bidding us be silent, listened attentively to the quarter whence it had proceeded. In a few minutes we heard the voices plainly; and, wishing exceedingly to open a communication with this tribe, we begged our natives to call to them, and bid them to come to us, to assure them of good treatment, and that they should have something given them to eat.

Colbee no longer hesitated, but gave them the signal of invitation, in a loud hollow cry. After some whooping and shouting on both sides, a man with a lighted stick in his hand advanced near enough to converse with us. The first words which we could distinctly understand were, 'I am Colbee, of the tribe of Càdigal.' The stranger replied, 'I am Bèreewan, of the tribe of Boòrooberongal.' Boladeree informed him also of his name and that we were white men and friends, who would give him something to eat. Still he seemed irresolute. Colbee therefore advanced to him, took him by the hand and led him to us. By the light of the moon, we were introduced to this gentleman, all our names being repeated in form by our two masters of the ceremonies, who said that we were Englishmen and *budyeree* (good), that we came from the sea coast, and that we were travelling inland.

Bèreewan seemed to be a man about thirty years old, differing in no respect from his countrymen with whom we were acquainted. He came to us unarmed, having left his spears at a little distance. After a long conversation with his countrymen, and having received some provisions, he departed highly satisfied.

Tuesday, April 12th, 1791. Started this morning at half past six o'clock, and in two hours reached the river. The whole of the country we passed was poor, and the soil within a mile of the river changed to a coarse deep sand, which I have invariably found to compose its banks in every part without exception that I ever saw. The stream at this place is about 350 feet wide; the water pure and excellent to the taste. The banks are about twenty feet high and covered with trees, many of which had been evidently bent by the force of the current in the direction which it runs, and some of them contained rubbish and driftwood in their branches at least forty-five feet above the level of the stream. We saw many ducks, and killed one, which Colbee swam for.

Our natives had evidently never seen this river before. They started at it with surprise, and talked to each other. Their total ignorance of the country, and of the direction in which they had walked, appeared when they asked which way Rose Hill lay; for they pointed almost oppositely to it. Of our compass they had taken early notice, and had talked much to each other about it. They comprehended its use, and called it *naa-mòro*, literally, 'to see the way': a more significant or expressive term cannot be found...

At four o'clock we halted for the night on the bank of the creek. Our natives continued to hold out stoutly. The hindrances to walking by the river side which plagued and entangled us so much seemed not to be heeded by them, and they wound through them with ease; but to us they were intolerably tiresome. Our perplexities afforded them an inexhaustible fund of merriment and derision. Did the sufferer, stung at once with nettles and ridicule, and shaken nigh to death by his fall, use any angry expression to them, they retorted in a moment by calling him by every opprobrious name[†] which their language affords.

Boladeree destroyed a native hut today very wantonly before we could prevent him. On being asked why he did so, he answered that the inhabitants inland were bad; though no longer since than last night, when Bèreewan had departed, they were loud in their praise. But now they had reverted to their first opinion; so fickle and transient are their motives of love and hatred.

Wednesday, April 13th, 1791. We did not set out this morning until past seven o'clock, when we continued to trace the creek. The country...was in general high and

---

[†] Their general favourite term of reproach is *gonin-patta*, which signifies, 'an eater of human excrement'. Our language has a concise and familiar translation.

universally rocky. 'Toiling our uncouth way', we mounted a hill, and surveyed the contiguous country…The view consisted of nothing but trees growing on precipices; not an acre of it could be cultivated. Saw a tree on fire here, and several other vestiges of the natives. To comprehend the reasons which induce an Indian to perform many of the offices of life is difficult; to pronounce that which could lead him to wander amidst these dreary wilds baffles penetration.

About two o'clock we reached the head of the creek, passed it and scrambled with infinite toil and difficulty to the top of a neighbouring mountain, whence we saw the adjacent country in almost every direction, for many miles.

I record with regret that this extended view presented not a single gleam of change which could encourage hope or stimulate industry to attempt its culture. We had, however, the satisfaction to discover plainly the object of our pursuit, Richmond Hill, distant about eight miles, in a contrary direction from what we had been proceeding upon. It was readily known to those who had been up the Hawkesbury in the boats, by a remarkable cleft or notch which distinguishes it. It was now determined that we should go back to the head of the creek and pass the night there; and in the morning cut across the country to that part of the river which we had first hit upon yesterday, and thence to trace upward, or to the left.

But before I descend, I must not forget to relate that to

this pile of desolation on which, like the fallen angel on the top of Niphates, we stood contemplating our nether Eden, His Excellency was pleased to give the name of *Tench's Prospect Mount*.

Our fatigue today had been excessive; but our two sable companions seemed rather enlivened than exhausted by it.[†] We had not sooner halted and given them something to eat than they began to play ten thousand tricks and gambols. They imitated the leaping of the kangaroo; sang, danced, poised the spear and met in mock encounter. But their principal source of merriment was again derived from our misfortunes, in tumbling amidst nettles and sliding down precipices, which they mimicked with inimitable drollery. They had become, however, very urgent in their inquiries about the time of our return, and we pacified them as well as we could by saying it would be soon, but avoided naming how many days.

Their method of testifying dislike to any place is singular: they point to the spot they are upon, and all around it, crying *weèree, weèree* (bad), and immediately after mention the name of any other place to which they are attached (Rose Hill or Sydney, for instance), adding to it, *budyeree, budyeree* (good). Nor was their preference in the present case the result of caprice, for they assigned very substantial reasons for such predilection. 'At Rose Hill,' said they, 'are potatoes, cabbages, pumpkins, turnips, fish and wine; here are nothing but rocks and water.'

[†] Sable: black, the dark colour of sable fur.

These comparisons constantly ended with the question of 'Where's Rose Hill? Where?' on which they would throw up their hands and utter a sound to denote distance, which it is impossible to convey an idea of upon paper.

Thursday, April 14th, 1791. We started early and reached the river in about two hours and a half. The intermediate country, except for the last half mile, was a continued bed of stones, which were in some places so thick and close together that they looked like a pavement formed by art. When we got off the stones, we came upon the coarse river sand beforementioned.

Here we began to trace upward.[†] We had not proceeded far when we saw several canoes on the river. Our natives made us immediately lie down among the reeds, while they gave their countrymen the signal of approach. After much calling, finding that they did not come, we continued our progress until it was again interrupted by a creek, over which we threw a tree and passed upon it.

While this was doing, a native, from his canoe, entered into conversation with us, and immediately after paddled to us with a frankness and confidence which surprised everyone. He was a man of middle age, with an open cheerful countenance, marked with the smallpox, and distinguished by a nose of uncommon magnitude and dignity.[‡] He seemed to be neither astonished or terrified

---

[†] upward: upstream.

[‡] An epidemic, apparently of smallpox, had swept through the Aboriginal population in April 1789.

at our appearance and number. Two stone hatchets and two spears he took from his canoe, and presented to the governor, who in return for his courteous generosity, gave him two of our hatchets and some bread, which was new to him, for he knew not its use, but kept looking at it, until Colbee showed him what to do, when he ate it without hesitation.

We pursued our course and, to accommodate us, our new acquaintance pointed out a path and walked at the head of us. A canoe, also with a man and a boy in it, kept gently paddling up abreast of us. We halted for the night at our usual hour, on the bank of the river. Immediately that we had stopped, our friend (who had already told us his name) Gombeèree introduced the man and the boy from the canoe to us. The former was named Yèllomundee, the latter Dèeimba.

The ease with which these people behaved among strangers was as conspicuous as unexpected. They seated themselves at our fire, partook of our biscuit and pork, drank from our canteens, and heard our guns going off around them without betraying any symptom of fear, distrust or surprise. On the opposite bank of the river they had left their wives and several children, with whom they frequently discoursed; and we observed that these last manifested neither suspicion or uneasiness of our designs towards their friends.

Having refreshed ourselves, we found leisure to enter into conversation with them. It could not be expected that they should differ materially from the tribes with whom we were acquainted. The same manners and pursuits, the same amusements, the same levity and fickleness, undoubtedly characterised them.

What we were able to learn from them was that they depend but little on fish, as the river yields only mullets, and that their principal support is derived from small animals which they kill, and some roots (a species of wild yam chiefly) which they dig out of the earth. If we rightly understood them, each man possesses two wives. Whence can arise this superabundance of females?

Neither of the men had suffered the extraction of a front tooth. We were eager to know whether or not this custom obtained among them. But neither Colbee nor Boladeree would put the question for us; and, on the contrary, showed every desire to waive the subject. The uneasiness which they testified, whenever we renewed it, rather served to confirm a suspicion which we had long entertained, that this is a mark of subjection imposed by the tribe of Cameragal (who are certainly the most powerful community in the country) on the weaker tribes around them.[†]

Whether the women cut off a joint of one of the little fingers, like those on the sea coast, we had no opportunity of observing. These are petty remarks. But one variety

---

[†] Tooth evulsion is part of some Aboriginal initiation ceremonies, whose secret nature may have made Colbee and Boladeree reluctant to discuss the practice. It is also interesting to note that Governor Phillip was missing a foretooth. Did this predispose the Aborigines to accept him?

struck us more forcibly. Although our natives and the strangers conversed on a par and understood each other perfectly, yet they spoke different dialects of the same language; many of the most common and necessary words used in life bearing no similitude, and others being slightly different.

English	Name on the sea coast	Name on the Hawkesbury
Moon	Yèn-ee-da	Con-dò-en
Ear	Goo-reè	Bèn-na
Forehead	Nùl-lo	Nar-ràn
Belly	Bar-an`g	Bin`-dee
Navel	Mùn-ee-ro	Boom-bon`g
Buttocks	Boong	Bay-leè
Neck	Càl-ang	Gan-gà
Thigh	Tàr-a	Dàr-a
Hair	Deè-war-a	Kee-war-a

That these diversities arise from want of intercourse with the people on the coast can hardly be imagined, as the distance inland is but thirty-eight miles; and from Rose Hill not more than twenty, where the dialect of the sea coast is spoken. It deserves notice that all the different terms seemed to be familiar to both parties, though each in speaking preferred its own.[†]

[†] How easily people, unused to speak the same language, mistake each other, everyone knows. We had lived almost three years at Port Jackson (for more than half of which period natives had resided with us) before we knew that the word *bèeal* signified 'no', and not 'good', in which latter sense we had always used it without suspecting that we were wrong; and

Stretched out at ease before our fire, all sides continued to chat and entertain each other. Gombeèree showed us the mark of a wound which he had received in his side from a spear. It was large, appeared to have passed to a considerable depth, and must certainly have been attended with imminent danger. By whom it had been inflicted, and on what occasion, he explained to Colbee; and afterwards (as we understood) he entered into a detail of the wars and, as effects lead to causes, probably of the gallantries of the district, for the word which signifies a woman was often repeated. Colbee, in return for his communication, informed him who we were; of our numbers at Sydney and Rose Hill, of the stores we possessed and, above all, of the good things which were to be found among us, enumerating potatoes, cabbages, turnips, pumpkins and many other names which were perfectly unintelligible to

---

even without being corrected by those with whom we talked daily. The cause of our error was this. The epithet *weeree*, signifying 'bad', we knew; and as the use of this word and its opposite afford the most simple form of denoting consent or disapprobation to uninstructed Indians, in order to find out their word for 'good', when Arabanoo was first brought among us, we used jokingly to say that any thing which he liked was *weeree*, in order to provoke him to tell us that it was good. When we said *weeree*, he answered *bèeal*, which we translated and adopted for 'good'; whereas he meant no more than simply to deny our inference, and say, 'no—it is not bad'. After this, it cannot be thought extraordinary that the little vocabulary inserted in Mr Cook's account of this part of the world should appear defective—even were we not to take in the great probability of the dialects at Endeavour River and Van Diemen's Land differing from that spoken at Port Jackson. And it remains to be proved that the animal called here *Patagaram* is not there called *Kangaroo*.

the person who heard them, but which he nevertheless listened to with profound attention.

Perhaps the relation given by Gombeèree, of the cure of his wound, now gave rise to the following superstitious ceremony. While they were talking, Colbee turned suddenly round and asked for some water. I gave him a cupful, which he presented with great seriousness to Yèllomundee, as I supposed to drink. This last indeed took the cup and filled his mouth with water but, instead of swallowing it, threw his head into Colbee's bosom, spit the water upon him and, immediately after, began to suck strongly at his breast, just below the nipple. I concluded that the man was sick; and called to the governor to observe the strange place which he had chosen to exonerate his stomach. The silent attention observed by the other natives, however, soon convinced us that something more than merely the accommodation of Yèllomundee was intended.

The ceremony was again performed; and, after having sucked the part for a considerable time, the operator pretended to receive something in his mouth, which was drawn from the breast. With this he retired a few paces, put his hand to his lips and threw into the river a stone, which I had observed him to pick up slyly and secrete. When he returned to the fireside, Colbee assured us that he had received signal benefit from the operation; and that this second Machaon had extracted from his breast two splinters of a spear by which he had been formerly wounded.[†]

[†] Machaon: A doctor to the Greeks in the Trojan War.

We examined the part, but it was smooth and whole, so that to the force of imagination alone must be imputed both the wound and its cure. Colbee himself seemed nevertheless firmly persuaded that he had received relief, and assured us that Yèllomundee was a *cáradyee*, or 'doctor of renown'. And Boladeree added that not only he but all the rest of his tribe were *cáradyee* of especial note and skill. The doctors remained with us all night, sleeping before the fire in the fullness of good faith and security. The little boy slept in his father's arms, and we observed that, whenever the man was inclined to shift his position, he first put over the child, with great care, and then turned round to him.

Friday, April 15th, 1791. The return of light aroused us to the repetition of toil. Our friends breakfasted with us, and previous to starting Gombeeree gave a specimen of their manner of climbing trees in quest of animals. He asked for a hatchet and one of ours was offered to him, but he preferred one of their own making. With this tool he cut a small notch in the tree he intended to climb, about two feet and a half above the ground, in which he fixed the great toe of his left foot, and sprung upwards, at the same time embracing the tree with his left arm. In an instant he had cut a second notch for his right toe on the other side of the tree, into which he sprung, and thus, alternately cutting on each side, he mounted to the height of twenty feet in nearly as short a space as if he had ascended by a ladder, although the bark of the tree was quite smooth and slippery and the trunk four feet in diameter and perfectly straight.

To us it was a matter of astonishment, but to him it was sport; for while employed thus he kept talking to those below and laughing immoderately. He descended with as much ease and agility as he had raised himself. Even our natives allowed that he was a capital performer, against whom they dared not enter the lists; for as they subsist chiefly by fishing they are less expert at climbing on the coast than those who daily practise it.

Soon after they bade us adieu, in unabated friendship and good humour. Colbee and Boladeree parted from them with a slight nod of the head, the usual salutation of the country; and we shook them by the hand, which they returned lustily.

John Price

Whom-Batts and Cullawines, 1798

From the very beginning, the Irish convicts were the most troublesome, for many were freedom fighters who considered themselves political prisoners. They had no idea where Port Jackson was, so constantly broke out, hoping to walk to China or to find some fanciful European settlement which was rumoured to exist in Australia.

Governor Hunter suffered constant thefts and irritation from such breakouts. In an effort to stop them and, as he said, 'save worthless lives', Hunter sent a few of the more persistent questers on an expedition to illustrate the nature of the country beyond the bounds of settlement. They were led by John Wilson, known as the wild white man by the colonists, and called Bunboe by his Aboriginal friends. Wilson was a convict who, after serving his time, left European society and joined the Aborigines.

Records of the travels were kept by John Price, Hunter's servant. They are important because they contain the first recorded account of the lyre bird (shot on what was to become Australia Day), and mention of a mysterious animal, the cullawine, later identified as the koala. Here we join the party on its way to the Wollondilly River.

January 24th, 1798—Left Mount Hunter for about twelve miles, till we fell in with the Nepean River, where the rocks run so steep it was with great difficulty we crossed them; the rest of the ground run very scrubby. We saw nothing strange except a few rock kangaroos with long black brush tails, and two pheasants which we could not get a shot at. Distance, eighteen miles.

January 25th—The country runs very open; good black soil. We saw a great many kangaroos and emus, and we fell in with a party of natives which gave a very good account of the place we were in search of, that there was a great deal of corn and potatoes and that the people were very friendly. We hearkened to their advice; we altered our course according to their directions. One of them promised that he would take us to a party of natives which had been there; but he not coming according to his promise, we proceeded on our journey as he had directed us. In the course of this day we found a great deal of salt. Distance, six miles.

January 26th—The ground run very rocky and brushy, so that we could scarce pass. We crossed one small river, the banks of which were so rocky and steep that we could scarce pass it. We saw no signs of any natives about it, but we saw several sorts of dung of different animals, one of which Wilson called a whom-batt, which is an animal about twenty inches high, with short legs and a thick body forwards, with a large head, round ears and very small eyes; is very fat, and has much the appearance of a badger.

There is another animal which the natives call a cullawine, which much resembles the sloths in America. Here I shot a bird about the size of a pheasant, but the tail of it very much resembles a peacock, with two large long feathers, which are white, orange, and lead colour, and black at the ends; its body betwixt a brown and green; brown under his neck and black upon his head; black legs and very long claws. Distance, sixteen miles…

Matthew Flinders

The Great Circumnavigator, 1802–3

 Few explorers were as admirable, and as ill-starred, as Matthew Flinders. A man of immense humanity and literary ability, he sailed to Westernport Bay with George Bass in 1797–98; the pair then circumnavigated Tasmania in 1798–99, proving the existence of Bass Strait. Between 1801 and 1803 he completed the first circumnavigation of Australia, making many discoveries, and beating the Frenchman Nicolas Baudin to mapping much of the coast.

On his way back to England his leaking vessel was forced to sail to Mauritius for repairs. There Flinders was incarcerated by the French for six years, during which time the Baudin expedition results were published, falsely claiming for France many discoveries actually made by Flinders.

Physically broken by the hardships of his exploration and captivity, Flinders returned to England and his beloved wife in 1810, after an absence of thirteen years. He began preparing the book from which these passages are taken, and on 18 July 1814 the first copy was rushed to his tiny house in London. But it was too late. The volume was placed in the hands of the already unconscious explorer, who died the next day.

We join Flinders at the discovery of Kangaroo Island, a place which remained uninhabited after the Aborigines who once lived on the island died out 3,500 years ago. As Flinders observes, the kangaroos there are enormous, the largest recorded anywhere.

21 March 1802—Neither smokes nor other marks of inhabitants had as yet been perceived upon the southern land, although we had passed along seventy miles of its coast. It was too late to go on shore this evening; but every glass in the ship was pointed there to see what could be discovered. Several black lumps, like rocks, were pretended to have been seen in motion by some of the young gentlemen, which caused the force of their imaginations to be much admired.

Next morning, however, on going toward the shore, a number of dark-brown kangaroos were seen feeding upon a grass plat by the side of the wood; and our landing gave them no disturbance. I had with me a double-barrelled gun, fitted with a bayonet, and the gentlemen my companions had muskets. It would be difficult to guess how many kangaroos were seen; but I killed ten, and the rest of the party made up the number to thirty-one taken on board in the course of the day; the least of them weighing sixty-nine, and the largest 125 pounds. These kangaroos had much resemblance to the large species found in the forest lands of New South Wales, except that their colour was darker, and they were not wholly destitute of fat.

After this butchery, for the poor animals suffered themselves to be shot in the eyes with small shot, and in some cases to be knocked on the head with sticks, I scrambled with difficulty through the brush wood and over fallen trees to reach the higher land with the surveying instruments; but the thickness and height of the wood prevented anything else from being distinguished. There was little doubt, however, that this extensive piece of land was separated from the continent; for the extraordinary tameness of the kangaroos and the presence of seals upon the shore concurred with the absence of all traces of men to show that it was not inhabited.

The whole ship's company was employed this afternoon in skinning and cleaning the kangaroos; and a delightful regale they afforded after four months privation from almost any fresh provisions. Half a hundredweight of heads, forequarters and tails were stewed down into soup for dinner on this and the succeeding days; and as much steaks given, moreover, to both officers and men as they could consume by day and by night. In gratitude for so seasonable a supply, I named this southern land Kangaroo Island...

Francis Barrallier

Portions of a Monkey, 1802

In November 1802, Francis Barrallier, French-speaking ensign of the New South Wales Corps, came within a whisker of crossing the Blue Mountains. Although Barrallier turned back too soon, he brought with him the first evidence of the koala, an animal which the colonists knew about only by rumour. The creature's feet, pickled in rum, at first confused and then amazed Europe's scientists. Was it a monkey—or a tree wombat?

7 November—After having walked for a little while, I perceived two natives seated under a bush, one of whom seemed as if he were anxious to run away, while the other one remained seated and appeared to be trying to persuade the former to stay. Gogy, the native I had in my service, started running, and went and sat with them, where he remained until we arrived. He came and told me that one of these natives was a mountaineer called Bungin, and the other knew the white men and was called Wooglemai.[†]

[†] Wooglemai, in the natives' language, signifies 'one-eyed'. This native knew Gogy, as he used to go from time to time to Parramatta and Prospect Hill.

I went to the mountaineer to examine a mantle with which he was covered. This mantle was made of skins of various animals sewn together. It was a very great curiosity and, as I was desirous of obtaining it, I proposed to him to exchange it for a new axe, but he would not part with it, and told me that the nights were very cold and his mantle was his only covering.

I was compelled to abandon my proposal, and in order to attach to me this mountaineer, who would be very useful to me in the country I was in, I had the head of the kangaroo given to him to appease his hunger, after which he came and proposed, as a token of friendship, to exchange his old axe for the new one I had offered him for his mantle. I filled him with joy by complying with his request.

I resumed my journey at half past five o'clock, and arrived with my party and baggage on the border of a small creek...The place where I decided to spend the night was on the territory of the mountaineer Bungin. He gave a proof of his friendship and gratefulness for my good treatment by building a hut for me, and I was very thankful for his kind attention...

On the 8th November I crossed the creek, the banks of which are nearly perpendicular; but the bullocks succeeded

---

The mountaineer called Bungin was an inhabitant of the south and had left the Canambaigle tribe because they wanted to kill him. He was the brother of a famous chief who had accidentally killed himself in falling from a tree. That chief was called Goonboole. He inhabited the mountains near Jervis Bay and was the terror of the neighbourhood.

in making a wide passage, quite practicable for men on foot, but too steep for a carriage to pass, and I was obliged to have the waggon carried by hand to the other side.

I walked until noon, when I stopped near another creek in order to rest ourselves until four o'clock. A soup made of boiled rice, with pickled pork, composed our repast, and I saw that the two natives had their share; but whilst one of the newly arrived mountaineers would not partake of this food the other ate it with avidity. The former, having caught a lizard, roasted it and devoured it. I tasted some of it and preferred it to the opossum…

After having travelled over a plain, I perceived fires in several places, and Bungin told me that it was a chief called Canambaigle with his tribe, who were hunting and had on that very day set the country on fire. He showed me the imprints of various feet, both of males and females, scattered here and there…

On the 9th November, at six in the morning when I was preparing to start, Bungin, one of the mountaineer natives, told me that he heard the voice of a native at some distance from us and, after having spoken to Gogy, they went together towards the spot whence the sound of the voice had appeared to come. I heard them repeat, several times, the word coo-ee, shouting with all their strength; and a quarter of an hour later after I had lost sight of them they came back, bringing two other mountaineers with them. One was called Bulgin and the other Wallarra. The latter had never seen a white man, but the former had seen several whilst kangaroo hunting.

Wallarra was seized with a great fright when I stepped forward to shake hands with him, and I was obliged to withdraw and leave him with the other natives, who tried to reassure him and give him confidence, telling him that I did not do them any harm, that I had come to gather some pebbles and plants and that I had the animals skinned to preserve their fur.[†]

The forenoon was already far advanced. I gave orders to yoke the bullocks to the waggon, and to place in it my utensils for my journey to Nattai, which I reached at 11 a.m., after having gone over a very difficult country, all covered with stones and bush, the soil of which is very arid...[‡] I told some of my people to cut some trees to make a hut large enough for the whole of my party, and to procure a good supply of water, as the nearest creek was almost one mile from us. Whilst my orders were being carried out, and the other portion of my people were preparing our dinner, I went to explore the neighbourhood and there gathered various plants. After dinner I took two men with me and went down the creek, which I followed until dusk, gathering flowers and fragments of a rather

---

[†] I had some boiled rice and sugar given to them. Bulgin ate it with greediness, but Wallarra ate only the sugar which I had to put on top. It would be difficult to describe his fright. He was standing with crossed arms and his eyes riveted on the ground. I had a second handful of sugar given to him which he ate; but when I again went near him his whole frame began to tremble.

[‡] Nattai: south-west of Camden.

peculiar sandstone. I returned to the depot at sunset, and about the same time Bulgin (one of the mountaineer newcomers), with Bungin, arrived with their wives and two children; but Wallarra, the other mountaineer, was not with them.

Gogy told me that they had brought portions of a monkey (in the native language *colo*) but they had cut it in pieces, and the head, which I should have liked to secure, had disappeared. I could only get two feet through an exchange which Gogy made for two spears and one tomahawk. I sent these two feet to the governor in a bottle of spirits.

Te Pahi

Trans-Tasman Explorer, 1805–6

 Te Pahi, leading chief of the Rangihoua on New Zealand's northern Bay of Islands, had long nurtured a desire to visit the strange new English colony. In late November 1805 the great chief got his chance, travelling by whaler first to Norfolk Island and then on to Sydney.

Te Pahi was feted in Sydney society, and must have cut a fine if rather terrifying figure, his deeply carved tattoos transforming his face into a largely immobile mask. His interactions with the Eora people give us an inkling of how different Maori and Aborigines were, and of how they regarded each other. Te Pahi formed emphatic views about the society he was exploring, and he certainly impressed Governor King who made these notes about him.

Tip-a-he is five feet eleven inches high, stout, and extremely well made. His age appears about forty-six or forty-eight. His face is completely tattooed with the spiral marks shown in *Hawkesworth's and Cook's Second Voyage*, which, with similar marks on his hips and other parts of his body, point him out as a considerable chief or *etangatida etikitia* of the first class. To say that he was nearly civilised falls far short of his character, as every action and observation shows an uncommon attention to the rules of decency and propriety in his every action, and has much of the airs and manners of a man conversant with the world he lives in. In conversation he is extremely facetious and jocose and, as he never reflected on any person, so Tip-a-he was alive to the least appearance of slight or inattention in others.

He never missed any opportunity of gaining the most particular information respecting the cause and use of everything that struck his notice, and but few things there were of real utility that did not entirely engross his most serious attention.

In communicating observations on his own country he was always very anxious to make himself understood, and spared no pains to convince us that the customs of his country were in several instances better than ours, many of which he looked upon with the greatest contempt, and some with the most violent and abusive disapprobation, of which the following is an instance:

Two soldiers and a convict were sent prisoners from Port Dalrymple to be tried by a criminal court for stealing some pork from the king's stores at that place. Tip-a-he attended their trial on the Friday, and one of them was ordered for execution on the following Monday. As is usual, they attended divine service on the Sunday. As everyone was much affected by their situation Tip-a-he was not wanting in commiseration; but the instant the service was ended he went to the criminals and embracing them accompanied them back to the jail, where it appeared they gave Tip-a-he a petition to present to me.

On returning to Government House he came into the room where I was writing, and in a very earnest manner, and I believe from the full force of conviction, he endeavoured to reason with me on the injustice of slaying men for stealing pork, and at the same time showing the severest sorrow and grief for their fate, which he concluded by taking the petition out of his pocket and giving it to me, at the same time shedding tears. He threw himself prostrate on the ground, sobbing most bitterly.

Observing that I did not give him any answer or hopes than by saying I should consider of it, he left the room and did not make his reappearance until the hour of dinner, having taken off the dress he had made here, and appeared very violent, exclaiming in most furious manner against the severity of our laws in sentencing a man to die for stealing pork, although he admitted that a man might very justly be put to death for stealing a piece of iron, as that was of a permanent use; but stealing a piece of pork which, to use his own expression, was eat and passed off, he considered as sanguine in the extreme. With much earnestness he urged his being allowed to take them to New Zealand, where taking provisions was not accounted a crime; and so earnest was he on this expedient that he went to the master of an American vessel, then lying here, to request he would take them to New Zealand, where his ship would be loaded with potatoes as a recompense for their passage.

During the three days that the fate of those criminals was pending Tip-a-he would take no nourishment whatever, and in several instances was inclined to be furious. However, on its being signified that two were forgiven and that neither of the others would be executed at Sydney, he came about by degrees, but would never be reconciled to the idea of men suffering death for taking wherewithal to eat—a natural reasoning for one who inhabits a country where everything of that kind is common, and where their other wants are but few.

A material object of Tip-a-he's visit here was to know if the ships that touched at the bay all belonged to King George, and whether the refreshments and assistance he and his people gave them were right and agreeable to me. On this subject I explained to him the difference between the English and American colours, and that both were equally entitled to his kindness. He complained that in one instance a New Zealander had been flogged by the captain of a whaler and hoped that I would give orders that no such act should be committed in future, and very liberally observed that he supposed the captain must have been a very bad man in his own country to commit such violence on a stranger who he had nothing to do with.

As all the whalers and other vessels which have visited Tip-a-he's residence have expressed the great convenience, hospitality and assistance they have uniformly received from this worthy chief and his people, I told him that I should impress on those who might visit him the necessity of their conducting themselves and people in a peaceable manner, and to give them articles in exchange for their potatoes and what stock he may in future have to spare—which the supplies of breeding swine and goats, with fowl etc., sent from Norfolk Island, will soon enable him to do.

To give him some proof of the estimation he was held in by me and the inhabitants of this place, I caused a medal to be made of silver with the following engraving: 'Presented by Governor King to Tip-a-he, a Chief of New Zealand, during his visit at Port Jackson, in January, 1806'; and on the reverse: 'In the reign of George the Third, by the Grace of God King of the United Kingdom of Great Britain and Ireland.' This medal was suspended by a strong silver chain round his neck.

With this and his other presents he was pleased and gratified—particularly with the numerous tools and other articles of iron given him from the public stores and by every class of individuals. As several New Zealanders of the lower class had come here by different vessels, it was a desirable and useful object to endeavour to get a number of people sent from that country to distribute about as shepherds. On communicating this wish to Tip-a-he he appeared to give very readily into the idea, but insisted on sending the middling order of people, who would be more expert at labour and tractable than the *emokis* or lower class, who were too idle and vicious to send here and from whom no good could be got...

On the subject of cannibalism we could get but little certain information, as Tip-a-he decidedly denied the existence of such a practice in his dominions, but said it was common in Mowpah's district. Ti-a-pe, a native of Moodee Whenua, also said it was a practice with Tip-a-he and his subjects. Where truth lies I am undecided; but I am of opinion, from everything I have heard and observed, that this practice most certainly prevails in New Zealand.

As our visitor was constant in his attendance at divine service, his ideas on the existence of a God and matters of religion were often conversed upon. The existence of a God who resides above they believe, and that his shadow frequently visits the earth; that it is in the power of the priests to invoke the appearance of this shadow (which is perceptible to them only) either for the purpose of succouring the sick or on any other exigency. The presence of the deity is made known by a gentle whistling. The rest of the cure or other benefit depends on the charms or incantations of the priests, in whose efficacy they have an implicit belief.

The dead are buried, and they believe that the spirit ascends; but if it enjoys a new state, or this 'death is an eternal sleep', we could not ascertain. But that there are future rewards and punishments they consider as certain; as well as the existence of an evil spirit as opposed to the deity, which they distinguish by the Otaheitian name of *Eatooa*; but they have no image to represent it, as have the Otaheitians.

Polygamy exists. Tip-a-he told us of several wives he has had, one of whom he killed for having a troublesome tongue; nor could he help testifying his surprise that many of the women here did not suffer the same fate. He has fifty-two children living, but he now attaches himself to only one young woman, by whom he has a son now eight years old, who accompanies him on his visit and of whom he is very fond.

Of the natives of this country he had the most contemptible opinion, which both he and Tookey did not fail to manifest by discovering the utmost abhorrence at their going naked, and their want of ingenuity or inclination to procure food and make themselves comfortable, on which subject Tip-a-he on every occasion reproached them very severely. Their battles he treated as the most trifling mode of warfare, and was astonished that when they had their adversary down they did not kill him, which it seems is a custom among the New Zealanders and is carried to the most unrelenting pitch; indeed, no race of men could be treated with a more marked contempt than the natives of this country were by our visitors, who, it must be confessed, were infinitely their superiors in every respect.

Of Tip-a-he's independent and high spirits a better proof cannot be given than the following circumstance that occurred a week previous to his departure. Every person, particularly the officers and their wives, had made him presents of some baubles, as well as the greater part being of great use to him, which was clothing and iron tools of most description. An officer's wife had given him, among other things, a pair of earrings, which he very inconsiderately bestowed on a young woman. The donation was soon after discovered, and the earrings taken from the girl, on which Tip-a-he was reproached for his want of respect for the original donor who, before this unlucky event, was very much respected by him.

However, the instant he found that the earrings had been taken away, he packed every article up which he had received from that person (and among which were some very useful things) and sent them by one of his sons; nor could he ever be persuaded to speak or see the lady who gave him the things, and constantly expressed his disgust at hearing of the presents he had received being in any way mentioned except by himself; and, to do him justice, he always took every opportunity of speaking of the donors with the most grateful respect.

A few weeks after he arrived Te Pahi witnessed a skirmish near the Brickfields between two groups of Aborigines, in which a young warrior named Blewit was encircled. On 22 December 1805 the *Sydney Gazette* published an account of Blewit's predicament.

The animosity of his assailants was uncommonly remarkable; their party was far the most powerful and, confident of their superiority, took every advantage of their numbers. The flights of spears were seldom less than six, and managed with a precision that seemed to promise certain fatality. After 170 had been thus thrown, ten of the most powerful stationed themselves so as nearly to encircle the culprit, and front and rear darted their weapons at the same instant. His activity and strong presence of mind increased with the danger, and five he dexterously caught with his feeble target. The others he miraculously managed to escape.

One of his friends, enraged at the proceeding, threw a spear and received ten in return. Blewit turned one of the assailants' spears upon themselves and passed it through the body of old Whitaker: the affray then became general, but terminated without further mischief.

Tip-a-he, who with several of his sons was present, regarded with contempt their warfare. He frequently discovered much impatience at the length of interval between the flights, and by signs exhorted them to dispatch. He considered the heel-a-man or shield an unnecessary appendage, as the hand was sufficient to put aside and alter the direction of any number of spears. He nevertheless praised highly the woomera or throwing stick, as from its elasticity he acknowledged the weapon to receive much additional velocity.

He was visibly chagrined when he saw the old man

wounded through the body and would certainly have executed vengeance upon its author had he not been restrained by the solicitations of the spectators.

The natives have formed some extravagant notions of this stranger: they dread to approach him and as much as possible avoid him…

One of his eldest sons, communing familiarly with a large group on the use of the spear, was very politely and generally acquiesced with. He requested the loan of one of their weapons, which was immediately presented; but as soon as he took it in his hand they all took to their heels, men, women and children, and could not by all his most friendly assurances be prevailed upon to return until he had lain it aside.

Gregory Blaxland

Blaxland, Wentworth and Lawson Breach the Barrier, 1813

 A modest man, Gregory Blaxland wrote his official account of the first crossing of the Blue Mountains in the third person, and referred to it in his title as 'a tour'. And the crossing itself, after so many frustrated attempts by others, seems to have been ridiculously easy. Aboriginal trails may have aided the explorers in finding their way through the maze of canyons, cliffs and isolated pinnacles that form the Blue Mountains, but the key was to stick to the ridges. Whatever the case, this defining moment in European Australian exploration seems like an anticlimax.

On Tuesday, May 11, 1813, Mr Gregory Blaxland, Mr William Wentworth and Lieutenant Lawson, attended by four servants, with five dogs, and four horses laden with provisions, ammunition and other necessaries, left Mr Blaxland's farm at the South Creek for the purpose of endeavouring to effect a passage over the Blue Mountains, between the Western River and the River Grose. They crossed the Nepean, or Hawkesbury River, at the ford, on to Emu Island, at four o'clock, p.m., and having proceeded, according to their calculation, two miles in a southwest direction, through forest land and good pasture, encamped at five o'clock at the foot of the first ridge. The distance travelled on this and on the subsequent days was computed by time; the rate being estimated at about two miles per hour...

On Monday the 17th, having laden the horses with as much grass as could be put on them, in addition to their other burdens, they moved forward along the path which they had cleared and marked, about six miles and a half...

The following day was spent in cutting a passage through the brushwood, for a mile and a half farther. They returned to their camp at five o'clock, very much tired and dispirited. The ridge, which was not more than fifteen or twenty yards over, with deep precipices on each side, was rendered almost impassable by a perpendicular mass of rock, nearly thirty feet high, extending across the whole breadth, with the exception of a small broken rugged track in the centre. By removing a few large stones, they were enabled to pass.

On Wednesday the 19th, the party moved forward along this path, bearing chiefly west and west-south-west...

At a little distance from the spot at which they began the ascent, they found a pyramidical heap of stones, the work, evidently, of some European, one side of which the natives had opened, probably in the expectation of finding some treasure deposited in it. This pile they concluded to be the one erected by Mr Bass to mark the end of his journey.[†] That gentleman attempted, some time ago, to pass the mountains, and to penetrate into the interior; but having got thus far, he gave up the undertaking as impracticable; reporting, on his return, that it was impossible to find a passage even for a person on foot. Here, therefore, the party had the satisfaction of believing that they had penetrated as far as any European had been before them...

On Saturday the 22nd instant, they proceeded in the track marked the preceding day rather more than three miles in a south-westerly direction, when they reached the summit of the third and highest ridge of the mountains southward of Mount Banks...On the top of this ridge, they found about two thousand acres of land clear of trees, covered with loose stones and short coarse grass, such as grows on some of the commons in England.

Over this heath they proceeded for about a mile and a half, in a south-westerly direction, and encamped by the side of a fine stream of water, with just wood enough on the banks to serve for firewood. From the summit, they had a fine view of all the settlements and country eastward, and of a great extent of country to the westward and south-west. But their progress in both the latter directions was stopped by an impassable barrier of rock, which appeared to divide the interior from the coast, as

---

[†] George Bass attempted to cross the mountains in 1796, equipped with scaling irons, hooks and long ropes.

with a stone wall rising perpendicularly out of the side of the mountain...

They now flattered themselves that they had surmounted half the difficulties of their undertaking, expecting to find a passage down the mountain more to the northward...

On the 28th, they proceeded about five miles and three-quarters. Not being able to find water, they did not halt till five o'clock when they took up their station on the edge of the precipice. To their great satisfaction, they discovered that what they had supposed to be sandy barren land below the mountain was forest land, covered with good grass and with timber of an inferior quality. In the evening, they contrived to get their horses down the mountain by cutting a small trench with a hoe, which kept them from slipping, where they again tasted fresh grass for the first time since they left the forest land on the other side of the mountain. They were getting into miserable condition...

On the 29th, having got up the horses, and laden them, they began to descend the mountain at seven o'clock, through a pass in the rock about thirty feet wide, which they had discovered the day before when the want of water put them on the alert. Part of the descent was so steep that the horses could but just keep their footing without a load, so that, for some way, the party were obliged to carry the packages themselves. A cart road might, however, easily be made by cutting a slanting trench along the side of the mountain, which is here covered with earth...

They encamped on the bank of a fine stream of water. The natives, as observed by the smoke of their fires, moved before them as yesterday. The dogs killed a kangaroo, which was very accceptable, as the party had lived on salt meat since they caught the last. The timber seen this day appeared rotten and unfit for building...

On the Monday...the party encamped by the side of a fine stream of water, at a short distance from a high hill in the shape of a sugar loaf. In the afternoon they ascended its summit, from whence they descried all around forest or grass land, sufficient in extent, in their opinion, to support the stock of the colony for the next thirty years.

This was the extreme point of their journey...They now conceived that they had sufficiently accomplished the design of their undertaking, having surmounted all the difficulties which had hitherto prevented the interior of the country from being explored, and the colony from being extended. They had partly cleared, or at least marked out, a road by which the passage of the mountain might easily be effected. Their provisions were nearly expended, their clothes and shoes were in very bad condition, and the whole party were ill with bowel complaints.

These considerations determined them, therefore, to return home by the track they came...On Sunday the 6th of June, they crossed the river after breakfast, and reached their homes, all in good health. The winter had not set in on this side of the mountain, nor had there been any frost.

George Evans

They Began to Laugh, 1814

 George William Evans arrived in Australia in 1804 and managed the government grain store at Parramatta. He went on to become acting surveyor-general, a farmer, an artist and a resolute explorer. In November 1813, in the wake of Blaxland, Wentworth and Lawson, he became the first European to roam the lush plains to the west of the Blue Mountains. For this work he was awarded the sum of £100 and a thousand acres of land in Tasmania. He was to join other expeditions in both New South Wales and Tasmania.

In his later years, Evans opened a bookshop in Sydney. I wonder how many people dropped in just to chat with the old explorer. He loved children, for he had at least twelve of them himself, and seems to have delighted in their company, regardless of whether they were black or white. We join him in April 1814 near Bathurst.

Fine weather very warm; halted at the commencement of Bathurst Plains early, as I was desirous to examine this part. I ascended Mount Pleasant: the west end led me on a ridge of beautiful hills, along which

I travelled about three miles; a small stream of water forming ponds run at their foot...

I cannot speak too much of the country. The increase of stock for some 100 years cannot overrun it, the grass is so good and intermixed with variety of herbs. Emus and geese are numerous, but cannot get any.[†] We counted forty-one emus this day: our dogs will not follow them.

Returning we saw smoke on the north side of the river. At sunset as we were fishing I saw some natives coming down the plain. They did not see us until we surprised them: there were only two women and four children. The poor creatures trembled and fell down with fright; I think they were coming for water. I gave them what fish we had; some fish hooks, twine and a tomahawk they appeared glad to get from us. Two boys ran away; the other small children cried much at first. A little while after I played with them they began to be good-humoured and laugh. Both of the women were blind of their right eye.

[†] The geese were probably magpie geese.

John Oxley

An Oval Grave, 1817

 An Englishman who initially pursued a career in the navy, John Oxley was the first of the great overland explorers. His expeditions into the country west and north of the Blue Mountains, with George Evans and others, can be said to mark the beginning of the classic phase of Australian exploration. Explorers are naturally curious. But here, on the banks of the Lachlan River in 1817, did Oxley go too far?

July 29—The stream where we stopped was about four feet from the banks, running with much rapidity; and I think the flood in it has rather increased than abated.

Almost directly under the hill near our halting-place, we saw a tumulus which was apparently of recent construction (within a year at most). It would seem that some person of consideration among the natives had been buried in it, from the exterior marks of a form which had certainly been observed in the construction of the tomb and surrounding seats. The form of the whole was semi-circular. Three rows of seats occupied one half, the grave and an outer row of seats the other; the seats formed segments of circles of fifty, forty-five and forty feet each, and were formed by the soil being trenched up from between them. The centre part of the grave was about five feet high, and about nine long, forming an oblong pointed cone.

I hope I shall not be considered as either wantonly disturbing the remains of the dead, or needlessly violating the religious rites of an harmless people, in having caused the tomb to be opened that we might examine its interior construction. The whole outward form and appearance of the place was so totally different from that of any custom or ceremony in use by the natives on the eastern coast, where the body is merely covered with a piece of bark and buried in a grave about four feet deep, that we were induced to think that the manner of interring the body might also be different.

On removing the soil from one end of the tumulus, and about two feet beneath the solid surface of the ground, we came to three or four layers of wood, lying across the grave, serving as an arch to bear the weight of the earthy cone or tomb above. On removing one end of those layers, sheet after sheet of dry bark was taken out, then dry grass and leaves in a perfect state of preservation, the wet or damp having apparently never penetrated even to the first covering of wood. We were obliged to suspend our operation for the night, as the corpse became extremely offensive to the smell, resolving to remove on the morrow all the earth from the top of the grave, and expose it for some time to the external air before we searched farther…

July 30—The rain continued throughout the day without intermission…This morning we removed all the earth from the tomb and grave, and found the body deposited about four feet deep in an oval grave, four feet long and from eighteen inches to two feet wide. The feet were bent quite up to the head, the arms having been placed between the thighs. The face was downwards, the body being placed east and west, the head to the east.

It had been very carefully wrapped in a great number of opossum skins, the head bound round with the net usually worn by the natives, and also the girdle. It appeared, after being enclosed in those skins, to have been placed in a larger net, and then deposited in the manner before mentioned. The bones and head showed that they were the remains of a powerful tall man. The hair on the head was perfect, being long and black; the under part of the body was not totally decayed, giving us reason to think that he could not have been interred above six to eight months. Judging from his hair and teeth, he might have been between thirty and forty years of age.[†]

To the west and north of the grave were two cypress trees distant between fifty and sixty feet. The sides towards the tomb were barked, and curious characters deeply cut

---

[†] Allan Cunningham, who was on this expedition, mentions in his diary that Oxley intended to remove the skull for studies in craniometry.

upon them, in a manner which, considering the tools they possess, must have been a work of great labour and time. Having satisfied our curiosity, the whole was carefully re-interred, and restored as near as possible to the station in which it was found. The river fell in the course of the day near two feet.

Hamilton Hume

They Quarrelled about the Frying-Pan, 1824

The names Hume and Hovell have been inextricably linked in the minds of countless Australian schoolchildren. In my case, it was some time before I could comprehend precisely what this 'human hovel' was or had achieved; and how their exploration was linked to the Hume Highway which our family travelled each Christmas holidays on visits to country relatives.

Hume and Hovell started just south of Sydney at Hume's farm on 17 October 1824 and ten weeks later looked out on the waters of Corio Bay. It appears from this passage—taken from the third edition of Hume's account, published posthumously fifty years after their journey—that the explorer would turn in his grave if he knew that posterity had linked his name so closely with that of William Hovell. We join the pair on 22 October 1824 as they attempt to cross the Murrumbidgee River.

Returning to the camp, I immediately set to work, took the wheels off my cart, covered the body of it with my tarpaulin and made of it a very excellent and serviceable punt. This expedient I had seen adopted by Mr Surveyor Meehan, in the year 1817, when crossing Bong-Bong River while flooded. Thomas Boyd, who is an excellent swimmer, and myself,swam across the river with a line in our teeth, and thus established a communication between either bank; when, with much trouble and not a little danger, the whole party, with the cattle and stores, were safely landed on the other side...

Thomas Boyd states his recollection of our crossing the Murrumbidgee as follows:

'When we came to the Murrumbidgee we found it very high. Captain Hovell was discouraged at this and wished to turn back. I heard him say to Mr Hume, "We shall never get on with our expedition, we cannot cross those rivers."

'Mr Hume replied, "If you think you can't you may go back, for I mean to go on."

'Mr Hovell then asked, "How do you mean to get across this river?"

'Mr Hume answered, "That's best known to myself; I'll soon get over. Boyd, you get a tomahawk."

'I then went with Mr Hume and we cut a canoe, but it would not answer: the bark cracked. When we returned to the camp Mr Hovell was doing nothing. Mr Hume then took his cart to pieces, made a punt of it with the tarpaulin, with which we crossed the men and the supplies. Our method was this. Mr Hume and I had stout fishing lines made fast to us, which were attached to the punt, and we swam and dragged the punt to and fro. Mr Hovell could swim, but gave us little or no assistance in getting across...'

James Fitzpatrick says, 'We crossed the Murrumbidgee, near Yass, by making Mr Hume's cart into a punt, taking it off the wheels, and covering the body of it with his tarpaulin. Mr Hovell had no hand in this, neither doing nor suggesting it. It was Mr Hume did it. Mr Hovell's cart was taken across the Murrumbidgee in Mr Hume's.'

From these statements it will be evident that my associate, had he been dependent on his own resources and left to his own shifts, would not, under the circumstances, have crossed the Murrumbidgee, though he might have proceeded to trace it downwards, and by so doing, he would have acted, so far, according to the instructions furnished for our guidance.

After crossing the river and advancing a day's journey or more, we found ourselves hemmed in by the mountains, and camped for two nights on the Narrengullen Meadows. In order to find an outlet Mr Hovell took one direction and I took another. I was fortunate enough to hit upon an outlet, and through it we were able to extricate ourselves, though with no small difficulty and toil.

On this occasion Mr Hovell lost himself for part of two days and, when I found him, he was actually, but unsuspectingly, travelling back in the direction of Yass or Bowning...He lost himself and his road. I did not.

Thomas Boyd relates: 'While camped at Narrengullen, Mr Hume went in one direction and Mr Hovell in another to seek for an outlet. I accompanied Mr Hovell; we two got lost, and were out all night, away from the camp and the rest of the party. About seven or eight o'clock next morning I heard Mr Hume firing guns for us, on which I remarked to Mr Hovell that we were out of our latitude altogether. He asked me, how? I replied that I judged from the direction from which the guns sounded. We made in that direction and shortly met Mr Hume looking for us. We returned with him to the camp.

'I remarked to Captain Hovell in the night, when we were out, that I would not be out another night with him—no more was I. In fact he never put himself forward in any single thing afterwards. This was his first and last expedition by himself. He never slept all night.'

'I recollect,' says Angel, 'of Mr Hovell and some of his men losing themselves, and Mr Hume being out looking for them and firing guns until he met in with them. I know well, from our own talk among ourselves, that none of the men had any confidence in Captain Hovell. We had no dependence on his taking us through. In fact, he was the worst man in the party, excepting Claude.'

On Tuesday, the 26th, we were engaged in sending the carts and supplies across the Cooradigby River, and finding ourselves in a difficulty country we were compelled to leave the carts, harness, and part of our supplies. I took my tarpaulin with me. Mr Hovell left his. We had then to use the pack saddles and, owing to the cattle not being accustomed to them, they gave us great trouble, as well as occasioning great delay.

It may be asked why such a seemingly trivial matter as the leaving of Mr Hovell's tarpaulin, and the taking of mine forward, should be so pointedly mentioned. The reason is very obvious when its use at the crossing of the Murrumbidgee is remembered. I calculated ('accidentally' or not) that we would encounter other rivers as formidable as the Murrumbidgee and that the tarpaulin being at hand would serve us a good turn again. My readers will judge whether my fellow traveller displayed the smallest foresight when he left his tarpaulin after he had both witnessed and experienced the usefulness of such an article so shortly before. Had I not taken mine, as will be seen, the expedition must have returned. One cause of our success, simple as it may appear, was my sticking to my tarpaulin, and lugging it along through all our weary journey.

A few days afterwards we crossed the Tumut River. As we advanced I found we were getting into too high a country, for the Snowy Mountains (the Australian Alps) were observed crossing our course. I proposed that we should take a direction more westerly, in order to avoid the formidable barrier which threatened to intercept our way—but Mr Hovell dissented from my proposal. After some wrangling and disputing, each being positive of the correctness of his own opinion, we resolved to part company and follow each his own course. Accordingly we did separate. Mr Hovell held his course south; I steered mine west. However, when my party turned into camp and lighted the fire for the night, great, indeed, was my surprise to hear one of my men call out, 'Here comes Mr Hovell.'

And, sure enough, there he was with his man Boyd running down our tracks. If my fellow traveller had had any confidence in himself, would he, after a lapse of a few hours, have deserted his determination to go south, returned upon my footsteps, and adopted for the future my westerly course?

Angel says: 'I recollect Mr Hume and Mr Hovell having a dispute about which course we were to travel after we came in sight of the Snowy Mountains. After some wrangling they separated, each going his own course. Before they parted they had a row about who was to have the tent; they were going to cut it in two, but Mr Hume let Mr Hovell have it. Then they quarrelled about the frying-pan[†] and broke it in pulling at it. It was not long, however, before Mr Hovell came after us, a few hours or half a day...'

After the rupture we again joined forces in the manner described, and travelled together to the Hume River, which we reached early on the 16th of November. I named it the Hume in compliment to my father. We crossed it above its junction with the Mitta Mitta. On the 20th, and after travelling four or five miles, we came upon the latter river.

[†] Mr Hovell left his pan at Cooradigby.

On my getting ready to cross the Mitta Mitta, to my surprise Mr Hovell objected, and volunteered an address to the men, in which he pointed out, as well as he could, the hazards existing in the rear, suggesting the probability of others ahead, and appealed to their sense of personal safety, in conclusion asking whether it would not be the most prudent step to turn back, recross the Hume, and trace down its nearest bank, according to part of our instructions.

Mr Hovell appealed to Claude Bossawa, a man of mine, and asked his opinion; of course he agreed with Mr Hovell. On this I got angry and told Mr Hovell that I would prefer being rid of him altogether rather than have one in his position setting such a bad example. I gave him to understand very plainly that for me, or all I cared, he might just remain on the side of the river he was standing on, but I was determined to pursue the journey as originally intended.

I also threatened to put Claude in the river if he did not cross it with me, at the same time seizing him by the throat, as if to make good my threat; in fact, I frightened the fellow into crossing along with me.

I then rigged out my tarpaulin boat[†] and crossed with

[†] The boat was made out of wattles, in this manner: the bottom was formed of three pieces of stout saplings, bound across the end and middle by similar transverse pieces; through these we laced wattles, which we bent up to form the sides, binding them across from the opposite heads to keep them from springing outwards. This formed a square body, like a cart body, on the outside of which we stretched the tarpaulin.

my men and my cattle. Mr Hovell, with his men, remained on the near side of the river, with the asserted purpose of recrossing the Hume and following down its northern bank.

After I had crossed the Mitta Mitta, taken my wattle-boat to pieces, and made a start onwards, Mr Hovell called after me, pressing me to stop and assist him over, and that he would accompany me. I did so. To his horror, on the very same afternoon, we made the Kiewa River (Little River), bank high; but were saved the trouble of using the boat, as a fallen tree assisted our crossing. We then passed over the present Ovens goldfields…

Had I, at this time, become in any way discouraged, or had I yielded in the least to the reluctance of Mr Hovell at crossing the Hume, and his refusal to cross the Mitta Mitta with me, our expedition must have ended on the north bank of the Hume. I can here safely affirm that, only for my own fixed determination to go on at this point, Bass's Straits would never have been reached by any of our party.

Charles Sturt

On the Importance of a Good Introduction, 1830

 Charles Sturt was as gifted with the pen as he was with the compass. We join him here in a boat on the Murray in January 1830, between the Murrumbidgee and the Darling. In contrast with most other explorers, he encountered vast numbers of Aborigines in this heavily populated region. Clearly, tribal boundaries were fiercely defended, and the use of messengers to provide an introduction for travelling groups was essential if conflict was to be avoided. All goes well for Sturt—until his boat outsails his Aboriginal heralds.

Of all expeditionary turning points, I like this one best. Sturt's progress is stopped by a vast fishing net strung across the Darling. Out of consideration for the Aborigines who depend upon it for survival, Sturt decides not to breach the net. Instead he raises the Union Jack, gives three cheers and turns around.

We had not seen any natives since falling in with the last tribe on the Murrumbidgee…It appeared singular that we should not have fallen in with any for several successive days, more especially at the junction of the two rivers, as in similar situations they generally have an establishment... Macnamee, who had wandered a little from the tents, declared that he had seen about a dozen natives round a fire, from whom (if he really did see them) he very precipitately fled, but I was inclined to discredit his story, because in our journey on the following day we did not see even a casual wanderer...[†]

On the night of the 16th, we had a strong wind from the NW, but it moderated with daylight, and shifted to the ENE, and the day was favourable and cool...

About 4 p.m. some natives were observed running by the river side behind us, but on our turning the boat's head towards the shore they ran away. It was evident that they had no idea what we were and, from their timidity, feeling assured that it would be impossible to bring them to a parley, we continued onwards till our usual hour of stopping, when we pitched our tents on the left bank for the night, it being the one opposite to that on which the natives had appeared.

We conjectured that their curiosity would lead them to follow us, which they very shortly did; for we had scarcely made ourselves comfortable when we heard their wild notes through the woods as they advanced towards the river; and their breaking into view with their spears and shields, and painted and prepared as they were for battle, was extremely fine. They stood threatening us and making

---

[†] Macnamee was a convict travelling with Sturt.

a great noise for a considerable time but, finding that we took no notice of them, they, at length, became quiet.

I then walked to some little distance from the party and, taking a branch in my hand as a sign of peace, beckoned them to swim to our side of the river, which, after some time, two or three of them did. But they approached me with great caution, hesitating at every step. They soon, however, gained confidence, and were ultimately joined by all the males of their tribe.

I gave the first who swam the river a tomahawk (making this a rule in order to encourage them) with which he was highly delighted. I shortly afterwards placed them all in a row and fired a gun before them: they were quite unprepared for such an explosion, and after standing stupified and motionless for a moment or two they simultaneously took to their heels, to our great amusement. I succeeded, however, in calling them back, and they regained their confidence so much that sixteen of them remained with us all night, but the greater number retired at sunset.

On the following morning, they accompanied us down the river, where we fell in with their tribe who were stationed on an elevated bank a short distance below—to the number of eighty-three men, women and children. Their appearance was extremely picturesque and singular. They wanted us to land, but time was too precious for such delays. Some of the boldest of the natives swam round and round the boat so as to impede the use of the oars, and the women on the bank evinced their astonishment by mingled yells and cries...

On the 19th, as we were about to conclude our journey for the day, we saw a large body of natives before us. On approaching them, they showed every disposition for combat, and ran along the bank with spears in rests, as if only waiting for an opportunity to throw them at us. They were upon the right, and as the river was broad enough to enable me to steer wide of them I did not care much for their threats; but upon another party appearing upon the left bank, I thought it high time to disperse one or the other of them, as the channel was not wide enough to enable me to keep clear of danger, if assailed by both, as I might be while keeping amid the channel.

I found, however, that they did not know how to use the advantage they possessed, as the two divisions formed a junction; those on the left swimming over to the stronger body upon the right bank. This, fortunately, prevented the necessity of any hostile measure on my part, and we were suffered to proceed unmolested for the present. The whole then followed us without any symptom of fear, but making a dreadful shouting, and beating their spears and shields together, by way of intimidation. It is but justice to my men to say that in this critical situation they evinced the greatest coolness, though it was impossible for anyone to witness such a scene with indifference.

As I did not intend to fatigue the men by continuing to pull farther than we were in the habit of doing, we landed at our usual time on the left bank, and while the people were pitching the tents I walked down the bank with M'Leay to treat with these desperadoes in the best way we could, across the water, a measure to which my men showed great reluctance, declaring that if during our absence the natives approached them they would undoubtedly fire upon them. I assured them it was not my intention to go out of their sight. We took our guns with us, but determined not to use them until the last extremity, both from a reluctance to shed blood and with a view to our future security.

I held a long pantomimical dialogue with them, across the water, and held out the olive branch in token of amity. They at length laid aside their spears, and a long consultation took place among them, which ended in two or three wading into the river, contrary, as it appeared, to the earnest remonstrances of the majority who, finding that their entreaties had no effect, wept aloud and followed them with a determination, I am sure, of sharing their fate, whatever it might have been.

As soon as they landed, M'Leay and I retired to a little distance from the bank, and sat down; that being the usual way among the natives of the interior to invite to an interview. When they saw us act thus, they approached, and sat down by us, but without looking up, from a kind of diffidence peculiar to them, and which exists even among the nearest relatives, as I have already had occasion to observe. As they gained confidence, however, they showed an excessive curiosity, and stared at us in the most earnest manner.

We now led them to the camp, and I gave, as was my custom, the first who had approached, a tomahawk; and to the others some pieces of iron hoop. Those who had crossed the river amounted to about thirty-five in number. At sunset, the majority of them left us; but three old men remained at the fireside all night.

I observed that few of them had either lost their front teeth or lacerated their bodies, as the more westerly tribes do. The most loathsome diseases prevailed among them. Several were disabled by leprosy, or some similar disorder, and two or three had entirely lost their sight. They are, undoubtedly, a brave and a confiding people, and are by no means wanting in natural affection. In person, they resemble the mountain tribes. They had the thick lip, the sunken eye, the extended nostril, and long beards, and both smooth and curly hair are common among them. Their lower extremities appear to bear no proportion to their bust in point of muscular strength; but the facility with which they ascend trees of the largest growth, and the activity with which they move upon all occasions, together with their singularly erect stature, argue that such appearance is entirely deceptive.

The old men slept very soundly by the fire, and were the last to get up in the morning. M'Leay's extreme good humour had made a most favourable impression upon them, and I can picture him, even now, joining in their wild song. Whether it was from his entering so readily into their mirth, or from anything peculiar that struck them, the impression upon the whole of us was that they took him to have been originally a black, in consequence of which they gave him the name of Rundi. Certain it is, they pressed him to show his side, and asked if he had not received a wound there—evidently as if the original Rundi had met with a violent death from a spear wound in that place.

The whole tribe, amounting in number to upwards of 150, assembled to see us take our departure. Four of them accompanied us, among whom there was one remarkable for personal strength and stature. The 21st passed without our falling in with any new tribe, and the night of the 22nd saw us still wandering in that lonely desert together. There was something unusual in our going through such an extent of country without meeting another tribe, but our companions appeared to be perfectly aware of the absence of inhabitants, as they never left our side...

The four natives joined us in the camp, and assisted the men at their various occupations. The consequence was that they were treated with more than ordinary kindness; and Fraser, for his part, in order to gratify these favoured guests, made great havoc among the feathered race. He returned after a short ramble with a variety of game, among which were a crow, a kite and a laughing jackass (*Alcedo gigantea*), a species of king'sfisher, a singular bird, found in every part of Australia.[†] Its cry, which resembles

---

[†] Fraser shot a kookaburra.

a chorus of wild spirits, is apt to startle the traveller who may be in jeopardy, as if laughing and mocking at his misfortune. It is a harmless bird, and I seldom allowed them to be destroyed, as they were sure to rouse us with the earliest dawn. To this list of Fraser's spoils a duck and a tough old cockatoo must be added. The whole of these our friends threw on the fire without the delay of plucking, and snatched them from that consuming element ere they were well singed, and devoured them with uncommon relish...

The natives, in attempting to answer my interrogatories, only perplexed me more and more. They evidently wished to explain something, by placing a number of sticks across each other as a kind of diagram of the country. It was, however, impossible to arrive at their meaning. They undoubtedly pointed to the westward, or rather to the south of that point, as the future course of the river; but there was something more that they were anxious to explain, which I could not comprehend. The poor fellows seemed quite disappointed, and endeavoured to beat it into Fraser's head with as little success.

I then desired Macnamee to get up into a tree. From the upper branches of it he said he could see hills, but his account of their appearance was such that I doubted his story; nevertheless it might have been correct. He certainly called our attention to a large fire, as if the country to the NW was in flames, so that it appeared we were approaching the haunts of the natives at last.

It happened that Fraser and Harris were for guard, and they sat up laughing and talking with the natives long after we retired to rest. Fraser, to beguile the hours, proposed shaving his sable companions, and performed that operation with admirable dexterity upon their chief, to his great delight. I got up at an early hour, and found to my surprise that the whole of them had deserted us. Harris told me they had risen from the fire about an hour before, and had crossed the river. I was a little angry, but supposed they were aware that we were near some tribe, and had gone on ahead to prepare and collect them...

We had proceeded about nine miles, when we were surprised by the appearance of a long line of magnificent trees of green and dense foliage. As we sailed down the reach, we observed a vast concourse of natives under them and, on a nearer approach, we not only heard their war song, if it might be so called, but remarked that they were painted and armed, as they generally are prior to their engaging in deadly conflict...

We approached so near that they held their spears quivering in their grasp ready to hurl. They were painted in various ways. Some, who had marked their ribs and thighs and faces with white pigment, looked like skeletons, others were daubed over with red and yellow ochre, and their bodies shone with the grease with which they had besmeared themselves.

A dead silence prevailed among the front ranks, but those in the background, as well as the women, who carried supplies of darts and who appeared to have had a bucket of whitewash capsized over their heads, were extremely clamorous. As I did not wish a conflict with these people, I lowered my sail and, putting the helm to starboard, we passed quietly down the stream in mid-channel.

Disappointed in their anticipations, the natives ran along the bank of the river, endeavouring to secure an aim at us; but, unable to throw with certainty, in consequence of the onward motion of the boat, they flung themselves into the most extravagant attitudes, and worked themselves into a state of frenzy by loud and vehement shouting.

It was with considerable apprehension that I observed the river to be shoaling fast, more especially as a huge sandbank, a little below us and on the same side on which the natives had gathered, projected nearly a third-way across the channel. To this sandbank they ran with tumultuous uproar, and covered it over in a dense mass. Some of the chiefs advanced to the water to be nearer their victims, and turned from time to time to direct their followers. With every pacific disposition, and an extreme reluctance to take away life, I foresaw that it would be impossible any longer to avoid an engagement, yet with such fearful numbers against us I was doubtful of the result.

The spectacle we had witnessed had been one of the most appalling kind, and sufficient to shake the firmness of most men; but at that trying moment my little band preserved their temper coolness, and if anything could be gleaned from their countenances it was that they had determined on an obstinate resistance.

I now explained to them that their only chance of escape depended, or would depend, on their firmness. I desired that, after the first volley had been fired, M'Leay and three of the men would attend to the defence of the boat with bayonets only, while I, Hopkinson and Harris would keep up the fire as being more used to it. I ordered, however, that no shot was to be fired until after I had discharged both my barrels. I then delivered their arms to the men, which had as yet been kept in the place appropriated for them, and at the same time some rounds of loose cartridge. The men assured me they would follow my instructions, and thus prepared, having already lowered the sail, we drifted onwards with the current.

As we neared the sandbank, I stood up and made signs to the natives to desist, but without success. I took up my gun, therefore, and, cocking it, had already brought it down to a level. A few seconds more would have closed the life of the nearest of the savages. The distance was too trifling for me to doubt the fatal effects of the discharge; for I was determined to take deadly aim, in hopes that the fall of one man might save the lives of many. But at the very moment when my hand was on the trigger, and my eye was along the barrel, my purpose was checked by M'Leay, who called to me that another party of blacks had made their appearance upon the left bank of the river.

Turning round, I observed four men at the top of their speed. The foremost of them, as soon as he got ahead of the boat, threw himself from a considerable height into the water. He struggled across the channel to the sandbank, and in an incredibly short space of time stood in front of the savage against whom my aim had been directed. Seizing him by the throat, he pushed him backwards, and forcing all who were in the water upon the bank, he trod its margin with a vehemence and an agitation that were exceedingly striking. At one moment pointing to the boat, at another shaking his clenched hand in the faces of the most forward, and stamping with passion on the sand, his voice, that was at first distinct and clear, was lost in hoarse murmurs. Two of the four natives remained on the left bank of the river, but the third followed his leader (who proved to be the remarkable savage I have previously noticed) to the scene of action.

The reader will imagine our feelings on this occasion: it is impossible to describe them. We were so wholly lost in interest at the scene that was passing that the boat was allowed to drift at pleasure. For my own part I was overwhelmed with astonishment, and in truth stunned and confused; so singular, so unexpected and so strikingly providential had been our escape.

We were again roused to action by the boat suddenly striking upon a shoal, which reached from one side of the river to the other. To jump out and push her into deeper water was but the work of a moment with the men, and it was just as she floated again that our attention was withdrawn to a new and beautiful stream, coming apparently from the north.[†]

The great body of the natives having posted themselves on the narrow tongue of land formed by the two rivers, the bold savage who had so unhesitatingly interfered on our account was still in hot dispute with them, and I really feared his generous warmth would have brought down upon him the vengeance of the tribes. I hesitated, therefore, whether or not to go to his assistance. It appeared, however, both to M'Leay and myself, that the tone of the natives had moderated and, the old and young men having listened to the remonstrances of our friend, the middle-aged warriors were alone holding out against him.

A party of about seventy blacks were upon the right bank of the newly discovered river, and I thought that by landing among them we should make a diversion in favour of our late guest; and in this I succeeded. If even they had still meditated violence they would have to swim a good broad junction, and that, probably, would cool them, or we at least should have the advantage of position.

I therefore ran the boat ashore, and landed with M'Leay amidst the smaller party of natives, wholly unarmed, and having directed the men to keep at a little distance from the bank. Fortunately, what I anticipated was brought about by the stratagem to which I had had

---

[†] The new river was the Darling.

recourse. The blacks no sooner observed that we had landed than curiosity took place of anger. All wrangling ceased, and they came swimming over to us like a parcel of seals.

Thus, in less than a quarter of an hour from the moment when it appeared that all human intervention was at an end, and we were on the point of commencing a bloody fray which, independently of its own disastrous consequences, would have blasted the success of the expedition, we were peacefully surrounded by the hundreds who had so lately threatened us with destruction; nor was it until after we had returned to the boat, and had surveyed the multitude upon the sloping bank above us, that we became fully aware of the extent of our danger, and of the almost miraculous intervention of providence in our favour. There could not have been less than six hundred natives upon that blackened sward...

It was my first care to call for our friend, and to express to him, as well as I could, how much we stood indebted to him, at the same time that I made him a suitable present; but to the chiefs of the tribes I positively refused all gifts, notwithstanding their earnest solicitations.

We next prepared to examine the new river, and turning the boat's head towards it endeavoured to pull up the stream. Our larboard oars touched the right bank, and the current was too strong for us to conquer it with a pair only; we were, therefore, obliged to put a second upon her, a movement that excited the astonishment and admiration of the natives. One old woman seemed in absolute ecstasy, to whom M'Leay threw an old tin kettle, in recompense for the amusement she afforded us.

The river preserved a breadth of one hundred yards and a depth of rather more than twelve feet. Its banks were sloping and grassy, and were overhung by trees of magnificent size. Indeed, its appearance was so different from the water-worn banks of the sister stream that the men exclaimed, on entering it, that we had got into an English river. Its appearance certainly almost justified the expression; for the greenness of its banks was as new to us as the size of its timber. Its waters, though sweet, were turbid and had a taste of vegetable decay, as well as a slight tinge of green. Our progress was watched by the natives with evident anxiety. They kept abreast of us, and talked incessantly.

At length, however, our course was checked by a net that stretched right across the stream. I say checked, because it would have been unfair to have passed over it with the chance of disappointing the numbers who apparently depended on it for subsistence that day. The moment was one of intense interest to me. As the men rested upon their oars, awaiting my further orders, a crowd of thoughts rushed upon me. The various conjectures I had formed of the course and importance of the Darling passed across my mind. Were they indeed realised? An irresistible conviction impressed me that we were now sailing on the bosom of that very stream from whose banks I had been twice forced to retire.

I directed the Union Jack to be hoisted, and giving way to our satisfaction we all stood up in the boat and gave three distinct cheers. It was an English feeling, an ebullition, an overflow, which I am ready to admit that our circumstances and situation will alone excuse. The eye of every native had been fixed upon that noble flag, at all times a beautiful object, and to them a novel one, as it waved over us in the heart of a desert. They had until that moment been particularly loquacious, but the sight of that flag and the sound of our voices hushed the tumult, and while they were still lost in astonishment the boat's head was speedily turned, the sail was sheeted home, both wind and current were in our favour, and we vanished from them with a rapidity that surprised even ourselves, and which precluded every hope of the most adventurous among them to keep up with us.

George Augustus Robinson

The Big River Tribe, 1831

 George Augustus Robinson was born the year Australia was settled. He emigrated to Tasmania in 1823, at a time when the war between settlers and Aborigines was escalating. A serious, religious man, Robinson believed that conciliation between black and white was possible. The opportunity to put his belief into practice came when he answered a government advertisement for a man of good character to 'effect an intercourse with natives'.

In September and October of 1830, Governor Arthur organised 2200 men into a massive line to sweep the Tasmanian bush free of Aborigines. The exercise was a dismal failure—just one man and one boy were captured.

We join Robinson here a year later in October 1831 as he tracks the Big River Tribe through central Tasmania. The tribe, a pathetic remnant of twenty-six individuals, had fought a brilliant guerilla war that had held white Tasmania to ransom. A leader of the tribe had lost an arm—after being shot by a settler's musket he had burnt the useless limb off in a fire.

By August 1834 the 'Aboriginal Problem', as the settlers called it , was ended. Robinson played a vital role in its resolution. It remains for the modern reader to decide whether his actions were for the best.

23 October   ...This morning crossed a deep gully whose sides consisted of rocks, and on ascending to the opposite hills observed a junction of gullies. The whole of these hills are covered with thick forest and scrub. These gullies communicate with Little Swanport River. At this place Mannalargenna procured himself a spear, as did another of the natives (Timmy). At meridian caught a boomer kangaroo which the natives roasted.[†] When the animal was opened the natives took the shavings of their spears and dipped them in the blood of the animal, probably with a view to act as a charm.

Whilst partaking of this repast the chief Mannalargenna said his spirit told him that the natives was on an adjacent hill looking at them. Though I felt convinced it was a delusion, yet in order to gratify his whim I sent two of the native men to see if there was any footmarks of natives. They shortly returned and had seen no signs of native footmarks or any indications whatever.

The strange native woman whom I had brought from the gaol and who belonged to the Big River tribe informed her husband Umurrah that she knew where there was plenty of guns and spears concealed. Tom and Umarrah informed me accordingly and it was agreed that the woman should conduct me to the place and that I should

---

[†] Meridian: noon

get them accordingly. This is another strong and striking proof of their confidence in me. These firearms had been taken by her countrymen in their attacks upon the whites and when she was present, and now she is desirous to make atonement by restoring them to the whites again.

One of the native women, Sall, found a bulbous plant called by the white people 'native bread', which they gave to me as a present.[†] At 4 p.m. came to the top of a hill and was informed by my natives that the white man's house was close by, and at the same time they showed me a tree which the white men had cut. I had not intended approaching so close to the whites lest my party should be discovered by stockkeepers, in which case I apprehended that some of my natives might get shot, as the practice of this class of individuals is to come upon them and to fire at them—a similar practice to the blacks in their attacks upon the whites—unless fear seizes the white and he seeks his safety by flight. I cautioned my natives and said if the whites saw them they would shoot them. They replied that they could see the whites first, and that they could not always shoot straight...

25 October—...Set off travelling in a south-east direction and with a view to procure the spears and guns which the native woman of the Big River tribe had disclosed and which had been concealed by her and the Oyster Bay tribe. She said there was two places where they had those various death instruments concealed.

---

† Native bread: a fungus.

In our way the natives showed me a dead tree where there was native bread growing. I saw no signs myself; they smelt the wood and said the plant was a long way in the ground. The natives showed me a bird's nest built in a hole in the ground, with three small white eggs. The bird resembled the honey bird, but smaller. Crossed the head of Prosser River and decamped in a small meadow on its banks, the natives having assured me that no grass would be met with after leaving this place.

Leaving the baggage and some of the people at this encampment I set off with five black men and the native woman of the Big River tribe to procure the muskets and spears which she had previously divulged to having been concealed. This woman led us over several stony hills covered with thick forest and across gullies. On arriving at a small grass plot enclosed by a green copse, the female guide pointed out the embers of a fire and where she said her and her tribe had enjoyed a little hilarity by dancing. This woman had previously said that those weapons would be found near to where they had had a fire and had danced. On beholding this spot again the woman evinced much feeling and all the circumstances connected therewith burst on her mind and with which she agreeably entertained her sable friends.

On leaving this place she proceeded to the distance of about forty yards further and on reaching a large fallen tree pointed out that as the place where the things were concealed. They were soon sought out by her and the rest of the natives, and was presented to me as a token of their confidence in me. They consisted of several bundles of spears tied round with pieces of blankets and check shirts, and amounted to forty-five spears, six waddies, one fowling piece and one tower musket, a bag containing bullets, slugs, buck and small shot, and a bag which had contained powder and a newspaper.[†] They were in tolerable condition; was placed under the tree.

On restoring those weapons of destruction they evinced much pleasure, and if any further proof was wanting of their confidence this alone would be sufficient. On our way from the place of encampment to this sequestered retreat the natives discovered a smoke, which they said was that of the natives. I loaded myself with the spears and one of the muskets and returned to the encampment with the native woman, who carried the fowling piece.

The men set off by a different route on an hunting excursion. Umarrah had selected from the spears one for himself, and two waddies. The rest would have followed his example but that I told them I purposed sending them to the governor, to which they agreed. I ascertained from this woman that these weapons had been placed there in concealment at the time of the Line and that some of the small spears belonged to the young lad that was taken at the time of the Line and the big ones to his father. She said that the embers of the fire I saw was where she and the other women, about eight in number, had *kar.ne.win.ne*,

---

[†] Waddies: clubs

i.e., danced, and that there was two men with them, that the rest of the men was dancing at another fire down in the bottom. Said that Memermannalargenna had speared a woman near the Blue Hills...

There is fine scope for reflection to consider that at this period last year the grand military operations was then in active service, that those spears had been manufactured by those very natives whom they was then in quest of and that when they took their departure they concealed those weapons, that the woman was then with them and now with me leading me in quest of her countrymen and telling me all the various schemes they adopted. The large spear that we found belonged to Montpelieratter and with which he had speared a white woman. The natives informed me that the white men about those parts had killed plenty of the natives, that they used to shoot them in their huts in the winter time.

This night the place to find the natives was a subject of deliberation. Tom said Mannalargenna would ask his devil. Accordingly, he went to work, Tom and his wife asking him occasionally where the natives rendezvoused. He said they was about the banks of the river. When he had finished he got up (it being dark) and said that a dead man's devil that had been put in a tree was walking about and would tell him about it. He set off in the woods; Tom and another native trembling followed him; the women lay as still as mice. They said I should know if he was there by his whistling. By and by heard a whistle and several whistles. They returned. I asked Tom if he had seen the devil; he said he had only heard him whistle. Said that when there was a small fire he would come and look at us at night.

I told them I would go and make a small fire in the woods and see if the devil would come, that if he made his appearance I would lay hold of his ears and pull him along and put him in the fire. I did not treat their superstition with that contempt I should do had I not been engaged in this anxious enterprise. Was therefore willing to indulge them in their whims, hoping thereby to succeed, as for their own credit they would find them out. Umarrah pointed out the way this afternoon he took when he left the Line.

John Batman

Batmania, 1835

John Batman, who sailed from Van Diemen's Land to explore the Port Phillip district, was not a modest man. He named Batman Creek 'after my good self', and I'm sure he would have been delighted if Melbourne had retained the name of its founder. Doubtless, the name of the city of Batman with its crowds of Batmanians would eventually have become commonplace—but the same colonial spirit that lumbered us with the name Sydney ensured that Melbourne would prevail.

What Batman thought he was doing by getting Bungett and Jagajaga to draw sacred designs on a tree, by way of concluding his purchase of 600,000 acres of tribal land in exchange for a barrow load of trinkets, God only knows.

Friday 29 May 1835—This morning as soon as daylight appeared, saw the heads of Port Phillip about eight miles off. With a fair wind we got between the heads about nine o'clock a.m., the tide running out, nearly low water. A very heavy surf running at the entrance. The wind was light, and with some difficulty we got in; width about one mile and a quarter, the depth five-and-a-half to seven fathoms of water. We got well into the port about ten o'clock, where the water is very smooth, and one of the finest basins of water I ever saw, and most extensive. I would not recommend anyone to come in until the tide was running in, when the surf is smooth at the mouth...

We anchored in a small bay about twelve miles up the port, and went on shore. Before we got into the boat we saw a dog on the sand. We put off and came up to the dog, which proved to be a native dog of New Holland, which had surely left the natives within a day or so, as he came quite close to my natives, and did not appear at all afraid, but would not allow them to take hold of him. Our dogs, after some time, took after him, and ran him into the water, where we shot him. He was a large dog, and much the same I have seen in New South Wales. We fell in with the tracks of the natives, which was only a day or two old; also huts on the bay where they had been eating mussels...

Saturday 30 May 1835—...I went on shore to look at the land, which appeared beautiful, with scarcely any timber on. On my landing I found the hills of a most superior description—beyond my most sanguine expectations. The land excellent and very rich—and light black soil, covered with kangaroo grass two feet high, and as thick as it could stand. Good hay could be made, and in any quantity. The trees were not more than six to the acre, and those small she-oak and wattle. I never saw anything equal to the land in my life. I walked over a considerable extent, and all of the same description.

This land forms an isthmus which is about twenty miles long by ten across it—upwards of 100,000 acres of good land or more. I could see five or six miles in every direction. Most of the high hills was covered with grass to the summit, and not a tree, although the land was as good as land could be. The whole appeared like land laid out in farms for some one hundred years back, and every tree transplanted. I was never so astonished in my life... We anchored in three fathoms water and, to my joy and delight, we saw at some distance the natives' fire. I intend to go off to them early in the morning and get, if possible, on a friendly footing with them in order to purchase land etc. from them...

Sunday 31 May 1835—...At daylight this morning we landed, to endeavour to meet the natives. We had not proceeded more than one and a half mile when we saw the smoke at seven large huts. My natives stripped off and went up to them quite naked. When they got to the huts, found that they had left this morning. Then, with the natives, went round, and found by their tracks the direction they went in. We followed on the tracks for ten miles or nearly, when Stomert, one of my natives, saw a black at the distance of a mile. We were at this time spread along. He made a sign to us, and all made in the same direction. He came up to the person (an old woman), quite cripple. She had no toes on one foot.

We then saw the remainder of the tribe about a mile further on. We made towards them, and got up to them about one o'clock p.m. They seemed quite pleased with my natives, who could partially understand them. They sang and danced for them. I found them to be only women and children: twenty of the former and twenty-four of the latter.

The women were all of a small size, and every woman had a child at her back except one, who was quite a young woman and very good-looking. We understood that the men went up the river. They had four native dogs, and every woman had a load of sixty pounds or seventy pounds on her back, of one thing or another.[†] Each had two or three baskets, net-bags, native tomahawks, bones etc. I found in one of the net-bags a part of a strake of a cart-wheel, which had two nail holes in. They had ground it down to a sharp edge, and put it in a stick to cut with as a tomahawk. They had also several pieces of iron hoop, ground sharp to cut with; several wooden buckets to carry water in. They had some water with them, which was very bad.

They came back with us to where I had some blankets, looking-glasses, beads, handkerchiefs, sugar, apples. I gave them eight pair blankets, thirty handkerchiefs, one tomahawk, eighteen necklaces of beads, six pounds sugar, twelve looking-glasses, a quantity of apples, which they

---

[†] The very large loads the women are carrying suggest a more sedentary lifestyle for these Aborigines.

seemed well pleased with. They then went off again. I promised to see them again tomorrow. The young woman, who I have spoke of before, gave me a very handsome basket of her own make. Other women gave me two others; also some spears. I got a native bucket, which I brought on board with me...

I never saw or could suppose there could be so extensive plains as I saw today. Five thousand sheep would be almost lost upon them. But the only thing I see at present is the want of water, but am sure it could be obtained by digging in almost any place.

The children were good-looking, and of an healthy appearance; they were dreadfully affrighted by the discharge of a gun, and all of them dropped down immediately. I think they never heard the report or saw a gun before. We saw a great number of wild turkeys today, but could not shoot one. We could not have walked less than thirty miles today.

Monday 1 June 1835—We left the vessel this morning at daybreak, and went round a bay to look at and examine some plains and clear hills at a distance, which looked very well...

We saw several places on going up which the natives had made with stones across the creek, to take fish, I suppose, in summer time. The walls were built of stones about four feet high, and well done and well planned out; two or three of these places following each other down the stream with gates to them, which they appear to stop with a bundle of bushes. We saw those in about ten or twelve different places up this stream.

On this stream we also met with the bones of an animal or beast of some kind which I had never met with before, and cannot accurately describe it. I counted twenty-four joints in the backbone, which is at least three inches each, therefore the animal must have been upwards of six feet in length. It must have been killed some time, and part of the bones were burnt. There may have been a greater number of bones in the back than I have seen. I have brought on board part of the head, thigh bones, and some joints of the back for the learned gents to study over on my return to Van Diemen's Land.[†]

Saturday 6 June 1835—The wind blew hard all night with some rain. We started this morning at eight and went to find the natives. We travelled over as good a country as I have yet met with and if possible richer land, thinly timbered. The grass was mostly three and four feet high and as thick as it could lie on the ground. The land quite black. We walked about eight miles when we fell in with the tracks of the natives, and shortly after came up with a family: one chief, his wife and three children. I gave him a pair of blankets, handkerchiefs, beads and three knives. He then went on with us and crossed a freshwater creek. The land on each side excellent. He took us on, saying he would take us to the tribe and mentioned the names of chiefs.

[†] The strange beast was probably a seal.

We walked about eight miles when, to our great surprise, we heard several voices calling after us. On looking back we saw eight men all armed with spears etc. etc. When we stopped they threw aside their weapons and came very friendly up to us. After shaking hands, and my giving them tomahawks, knives etc., they took us with them about a mile back, where we found huts, women and children.

After some time and full explanation, I found eight chiefs amongst them who possessed the whole of the territory near Port Phillip. Three brothers, all of the same name, were the principal chiefs, and two of them men of six feet high and very good-looking; the other not so tall, but stouter. The other five chiefs were fine men. After a full explanation of what my object was, I purchased two large tracts of land from them—about 600,000 acres, more or less, and delivered over to them blankets, knives, looking-glasses, tomahawks, beads, scissors, flour etc. etc., as payment for the land; and also agreed to give them a tribute or rent yearly. The parchment the eight chiefs signed this afternoon, delivering to me some of the soil, each of them, as giving me full possession of the tracts of land.

This took place alongside of a beautiful stream of water, and from whence my land commences, and where a tree is marked four ways to know the corner boundary. The country about here exceeds anything I ever saw, both for grass and richness of soil. The timber light, and consists of she-oak and small gum, with a few wattle. My natives gave the chiefs and their tribe a grand corroboree tonight. They seemed quite delighted with it. Each of the principal chiefs has two wives and several children each. In all, the tribe consists of forty-five—men, women and children.

Sunday 7 June 1835—Detained this morning some time drawing up triplicates of the deeds of the land I purchased, and delivering over to them more property on the banks of the river which I have named Batman Creek—after my good self. Just before leaving, the two principal chiefs came and brought their two cloaks, or royal mantles, and laid at my feet, wishing to accept the same. On my consenting to take them, they placed them round my neck and over my shoulders, and seemed quite pleased to see me walk about with them on. I asked them to accompany me to the vessels. They very properly pointed to the number of young children, and then at their feet, meaning that they could not walk but said they would come down in a few days.

I had no trouble to find out their sacred marks. One of my natives (Bungett) went to a tree, out of sight of the women, and made the Sydney natives' mark. After this was done, I took with me two or three of my natives to the principal chief and showed the marks on the tree. This he knew immediately, and pointed to the knocking out of the teeth. The mark is always made when the ceremony of knocking out the tooth in the front is done.

However, after this I desired, through my natives, for him to make his mark; which, after looking about some time, and hesitating some few minutes, he took the tomahawk and cut out in the bark of the tree his mark, which is attached to the deed, and is the signature of their country and tribe.

Sunday 7 June 1835—About 10 a.m. I took my departure from those interesting people. I think the principal chief stands six feet four inches high, and his brother six feet two inches, and as fine looking men as ever I saw...

Monday 8 June 1835—The wind foul this morning for Indented Head. We tried, but could not get out of the river. The boat went up the large river I have spoken of, which comes from the east, and I am glad to state, about six miles up found the river all good water and very deep. This will be the place for a village—the natives on shore.[†]

[†] Batman was on the Yarra River near where Queen Street now terminates.

Thomas Livingstone Mitchell

Australia Felix, 1836

 Sir Thomas Mitchell, surveyor-general, undertook four major expeditions in eastern Australia between 1831 and 1845. He was one of the very few explorers to discover rich pastoral land, and he called Victoria's Western District his 'Australia Felix', 'Lucky Australia'. Horses were still expensive in 1836, so Mitchell travelled by bullock dray.

Mitchell was a man of many skills. He patented the 'boomerang propellor for steamers' and later translated Camoens' sixteenth-century Portuguese epic, the *Lusiads*. On 30 June 1836 Mitchell climbed Pyramid Hill, not far from where the town of Warrnambool now stands, and beheld a 'scene...different from anything I had ever before witnessed...As I stood, the first European intruder on the sublime solitude of these verdant plains, as yet untouched by flocks or herds, I felt conscious of being the harbinger of mighty changes.' Two months later he had the unusual explorer's experience of discovering a European settlement: the Hentys had arrived from across Bass Strait and established a secret station. The mighty changes were already at hand.

August 29—...We crossed and then continuing through a thick wood we came out at length on the shore of Portland Bay, at about four miles beyond the little river...

On reaching the seashore at this beach, I turned to observe the face of Tommy Came-last, one of my followers, who being a native from the interior had never before seen the sea. I could not discover in the face of this young savage, even on his first view of the ocean, any expression of surprise; on the contrary, the placid and comprehensive gaze he cast over it seemed fully to embrace the grand expanse then for the first time opened to him.

I was much more astonished when he soon after came to tell me of the fresh tracks of cattle that he had found on the shore, and the shoe marks of a white man. He also brought me two portions of tobacco-pipes and a glass bottle without a neck. That whaling vessels occasionally touched there I was aware, as was indeed obvious from the carcases and bones of whales on the beach; but how cattle could have been brought there I did not understand.

Proceeding round the bay with the intention of examining the head of an inlet and continuing along shore as far as Cape Bridgewater, I was struck with the resemblances to houses that some supposed grey rocks under the grassy cliffs presented; and while I directed my glass towards them my servant Brown said he saw a brig at anchor, a fact of which I was soon convinced, and also that the grey rocks were in reality wooden houses.

The most northern part of the shore of this bay was comparatively low, but the western consisted of bold cliffs rising to the height of 180 feet.

We ascended these cliffs near the wooden houses, which proved to be some deserted sheds of the whalers. One shot was heard as we drew near them, and another on our ascending the rocks. I then became somewhat apprehensive that the parties might either be, or suppose us to be, bushrangers, and to prevent if possible some such awkward mistake I ordered a man to fire a gun and the bugle to be sounded; but on reaching the higher ground we discovered not only a beaten path, but the track of two carts, and while we were following the latter a man came towards us from the face of the cliffs. He informed me in answer to my questions that the vessel at anchor was the *Elizabeth of Launceston*; and that just round the point there was a considerable farming establishment belonging to Messrs Henty, who were then at the house.

It then occurred to me that I might there procure a small additional supply of provisions, especially of flour, as my men were on very reduced rations. I, therefore, approached the house and was kindly received and entertained by the Messrs Henty, who as I learnt had been established there during upwards of two years. It was very obvious indeed from the magnitude and extent of the buildings, and the substantial fencing erected, that both time and labour had been expended in their construction. A good garden stocked with abundance of vegetables already smiled on Portland Bay; the soil was very rich on the overhanging cliffs, and the potatoes and turnips produced there surpassed in magnitude and quality any I had ever seen elsewhere.

I learnt that the bay was much resorted to by vessels engaged in the whale fishery, and that upwards of 700 tons of oil had been shipped that season. I was likewise informed that only a few days before my arrival five vessels lay at anchor together in that bay, and that a communication was regularly kept up with Van Diemen's Land by means of vessels from Launceston. Messrs Henty were importing sheep and cattle as fast as vessels could be found to bring them over, and the numerous whalers touching at or fishing on the coast were found to be good customers for farm produce and whatever else could be spared from the establishment...

August 30—I was accommodated with a small supply of flour by Messrs Henty, who having been themselves on short allowance were awaiting the arrival of a vessel then due two weeks. They also supplied us with as many vegetables as the men could carry away on their horses. Just as I was about to leave the place, a whale was announced, and instantly three boats well manned were seen cutting through the water, a harpooneer standing up at the stern of each with oar in hand, and assisting the rowers by a forward movement at each stroke.

It was not the least interesting scene in these my Australian travels, thus to witness from a verandah on a beautiful afternoon at Portland Bay the humours of the whale fishery, and all those wondrous perils of harpooneers and whale boats, of which I had delighted to read as scenes of 'the stormy north'. The object of the present pursuit was a 'hunchback' and, being likely to occupy the boats for some time, I proceeded homewards. I understood it frequently happened that several parties of fishermen, left by different whaling vessels, would engage in the pursuit of the same whale, and that in the struggle for possession the whale would occasionally escape from them all and run ashore, in which case it is of little value to whalers, as the removal, etc, would be too tedious, and they in such cases carry away part of the head matter only.

The natives never approach these whalers, nor had they ever shown themselves to the white people of Portland Bay; but as they have taken to eat the castaway whales it is their custom to send up a column of smoke when a whale appears in the bay, and the fishers understand the signal. This affords an instance of the sagacity of the natives, for they must have reflected that, by thus giving timely notice, a greater number will become competitors for the whale, and that consequently there will be a better chance of the whale running ashore, in which case a share must fall finally to them.

John Graham

That Abject Captive Lady, 1836

The idea of a white woman living among the Aborigines provoked a powerful reaction in colonial Australia. She was a recurrent myth on the frontier, and searches for her were used more than once as an excuse for the massacre of Aborigines. There were, however, several actual instances of European women living with Aborigines. Perhaps the most famous is Eliza Fraser, whose story inspired Sidney Nolan to paint, and Patrick White to write *A Fringe of Leaves.* Shipwrecked with her husband on Swain Reef near present-day Rockhampton in May 1836, Fraser was lucky to survive. She was heavily pregnant and gave birth in a longboat to a baby who died.

Eventually she fell in with the Kabi people on Fraser Island. The Aborigines believed that she was Mamba, a woman who had died some time previously, and that she had lost both colour and language during her time in the grave. Her husband was speared to death, but she lived with her captors until rescued, three months later, in August 1836.

This breathless account is the verbal testimony of a convict, John Graham, who lived with the Aborigines for years before returning to Moreton Bay. He was known to them as Moilow, one of their clan who had returned from the dead. He was fluent in the Kabi language, and in his account of his expedition to rescue Eliza Fraser we gain a rare insight into what the Aborigines were thinking as they met the Europeans. Graham's account is addressed to Captain Foster Fyans, commandant at Moreton Bay.

Your Honour…I was determined to brave the worst of fates or finish a miserable existence to rescue that abject captive lady.

Though solicited by Mr Otter to accompany me with all the arms he had, it was of no avail, for had we been able to assail them she must have fallen a sacrifice to their spears or be carried by hundreds further through the mountains. I must act on other plans though doomed to face hundreds of savages, amongst whom were the very men but a few days before I fired at. I depended on a tribe whose former friendship I had experienced, several of whom acknowledged me their father, or spirit thereof.

There were several resolutions of detaining hostages and sending word, to see if they would give her up. This would have caused lives on both sides, and certainly would have proved fatal to her and also shown a coward in me, I alone knowing where she was. I think it a pleasure in giving your Honour an account of this transaction and every minute detail, showing I was determined, or die the worst of deaths, or fulfil my promise.

Lieutenant Otter wishing to accompany me to whom I refer, and spoke these words: 'Sir, I am but one, my life I do not care for, it being of little use to me. If I do not return in two days then take hostages and revenge for my blood.' The sentiments of his mind were seen by me in not being a co-partner; he must risk his life and follow me. He took me to his tent giving me a glass of rum and water. I here gave him directions of the route. He was to follow me on the following morning by the mark of the broad arrow which I was to leave for his instruction, and to sit where it was, stop till I should come next day if living.

I strove much to get two of those blacks to come with me. I brought them to the tents, showed two blankets, two tomahawks and two axes to induce them to come. They told me their hearts failed them, they would be killed. I recollect telling Mr Otter at the time what they said when, taking a roasted bream and a small piece of bread, I took my departure, my comrades saying they would revenge my fate, expecting no more to see me. I soon crossed the hills and was out of sight on Tuesday at eleven o'clock August the 16th.

Lest my bread should be took from me, expecting to meet several natives, I eat it. I had trousers on, and continued my route making the mark as I went along. Drawing near sundown I thought of my supper, having none, nor time to look for any. Your Honour can here read ideas of my mind, and think the arm of God alone strengthened and assisted me in this virtuous act of humanity. Proceeding on, I found a snake seven feet long which showed me providence was assisting and protecting me. On getting back I retired to a gully, made a fire and roasted my snake which I hung up for morning. Of all my life this was the most disturbed night I ever spent, too tedious to mention here. The dawn of day called me forth, after taking God for my guide, and my breakfast which his mercies sent me.

I descended from my gully twenty-five miles from the tents and continued my route, making the mark. On coming where I was to turn, I put a stop with those words, 'Stop. Here you will find fresh water at the rock.' This was thirty miles in all. I saw no blacks ascending the hills and crossing the forest ground. About four miles you descend into a boggy ground or swamp ankle-deep for a mile, after which a lake about thirty miles in circumference, four miles where I crossed it, knee-deep at low water, after which a freshwater river.

Being about to swim across, a black man and his wife appeared in their canoe. Being horror-struck at my appearance and thinking I had more confederates, they were making away saying they would bring plenty of men. I standing on the brink of the river telling them I was alone, and showing two fish hooks, the woman induced him to return. Their approach was timid, and asking me what he would get, I tore the leg of my trousers off and gave it to him. The hooks for her. After inquiring the different tribes that were there, and particularly after my own kindred, and what part of the field they were in, I made enquiry after my wife (the woman who said I was her husband's spirit and died in 1827), if she had strayed amongst them.

They told me there was a female spirit, but a man by the name of Mothervane claimed her as his wife's sister. As they had heard of the skirmages we had, which I left to the stupid spirits that were along with me, as I came to do no harm but take my wife down to the beach and there live on my ground as I had done before. Promising him my trousers, and her as many hooks as she could carry, if she would go and tell the men, especially my friends, not to be cross as I came to live amongst them and make axes and fish hooks at Thaying (my ground), and I would show Mothervane that spirit was Mamba, whose sons was there visiting. Murrow Dooling and Caravanty—two young men who always claimed me as their father's spirit, who had a great connection in several tribes.

The woman said they were there and dispatched to tell them, while the man and I hurried on, telling me he would assist me.

On coming in sight of the camp, I watched the woman going to the south side where I supposed my friends were. I made there. She was telling them I was making onward but, surrounded by numbers, I was forced to stand. Black and savage as they were, no horror struck me as the sight of that unhappy lady, who caught my eye as it wandered round their huts.

Could I then have armed myself with vengeance would I have been detained from giving the cannibal race any account of my demands? Courage flushed to me and I feared no fate. Hearing the sound of Mamba, which the woman had told she was, and my sons amongst the crowd, to whom I said: 'Is your eyes blind, don't you know your mother?' upon whose neck I fell, fancying to cry. My father-in-law jumped to his knife, saying, 'No crying, go and take her.' (This man's name is Mootemu.)

Upwards of 400 blacks had seized their spears when Mothervane came forward, to whom I said, 'Do you claim a spirit? And she my wife. She can't speak to tell having lost her speech, and I who have got sense do tell the truth and here are her two sons and father,' pointing to the people above-named.

A dead silence was here and all eyes were on me whilst I told them how she was along with me in a canoe after turtle, and being cast away she swam amongst the north men, who gave her nothing to eat. She being a stranger could not tell who were her friends, having lost her tongue, and if Mothervane would [be] cross I would call a challenge. Here throwing off my trousers, to make fresh friends, I impeached them with being stupid in not knowing her.

All the coast blacks here stood on my side, and said I always told the truth. Saying, 'Give her,' 'She is his,' being now satisfied that she was Mamba. As they wanted me to go along with them into the mountains as their friends had heard of that spirit and their hearts would be glad at seeing her.

I here said, 'You see she is near dead with hunger, let your friends wait till she is recovered and then I will go a season to the mountains.'

Mothervane said it was a pity to let that spirit go, but here Mootemu said, 'They are two ghosts and no men has any right to separate them. Moilow† has good sense and knows how to live as well as us, he must have his wife.'

The father of the child to whom I gave the skirt coming forward, telling him what I had done for his girl, and where I left her with a full belly, not as my wife was, starving among them. He said in an angry voice, 'You people hear that, he is coming with good fingers and why be cross?'

They began to retire to their respective huts, and a black man sitting opposite her hut, and again I seen the face of a Christian woman, and a black man sitting opposite her hut with a spear in his hand as a sentinel. On looking I recognised him to be a nephew of mine who has four wives, by name Dapen (left-handed man)—and coming to me said, 'Come uncle, I was watching my aunt, that the mountain blacks should not come near, whilst you were talking. I fear none. I'll give her to you.'

On approaching to the hut, could I believe—I lost my sense of surprise and joy, and a sense of gratitude to the most of those savages who stood my friend. With

† My native name.

a heartfelt sorrow for her then before me, I sunk to the ground. When roused by the voice of Dapen saying, 'The sun is going round uncle, you have far to go.'

Roused to a sense of my situation I rose, reached my hand, saying, 'Come with me. God has made me your deliverer.'

Fortitude was what I now called from heaven to assist me in seeing a woman survive in the most distressed state than can be painted, and one but a few months rolled in the affluence of plenty, doomed to subsist on the husks of the earth, and forced to bear the wood on them sunburnt shoulders where the tender skin hung in scales, ordered to hop on lacerated feet to fetch them water...What but heaven could have prolonged a life of such misery for a deliverance?

This lady rising and taking my hand, I proceeded through a camp of some hundreds of blacks. On the most judicious plan I asked four of those men to come with me to Nemberthan. Taking my leave of my friends, Mootemu wanted me to take some *bungwal* (a root), which I refused. Having come to the canoes, two were brought—three in each we crossed the lake. On her head was a south-wester, the smell of paint kept the blacks from taking it. Around her loins were part of the legs and waistband of a pair of trousers, which covered part of her thighs, wound round with vines twentyfold as well for delicacy as the preservation of her marriage and earrings which she concealed under the vines, and the only articles that were saved from those savage hands.

In ascending the forest ground I caused the blacks to follow my example which they did to the rocks, where arriving I saw that relief was come. Leaving the lady at the waterhole telling her to remain a few minutes, I took the blacks with me to the beach where was Lieutenant Otter, who came to meet me in such haste that almost frightened the blacks, enquiring where she was. I told him all was right, asking him for some clothes for her, at which he clasped his hands and thanked his God, going to his bag.

I seated the blacks along with corporals McGuire and Campbell of the 4th Regiment and Nathaniel Mitchell who came with Mr Otter, to whom I went and got a boat cloak and some other articles of dress and returned to prepare the lady for his reception, and for the first time them vines were pulled off which the hands of her dear and much lamented husband had put on...

Your Honour best can judge the situation of her mind, being about to enter into society, and the distress which attended this meeting when, assisting her forth, I gave her hand to that gentleman Mr Otter about one o'clock on Wednesday the 17th of August.

George Grey

A Horrid Dream, 1838

 Sir George Grey: now there was a man destined for greatness. One day he would be governor of South Australia, then of New Zealand, then of the Cape. But here we see a younger George Grey at the beginning of his career: an English officer of twenty-five who disliked military life, attempting to explore the Prince Regent River region in the Kimberley—some of the most difficult terrain in Australia.

The thing that I love most about Grey is that, despite incidents like the one related here, he had a gift for getting on with the Aborigines. He learned their language and understood them, and he never saw them as second-class. Later, he was to sum up the cause of their lack of progress in white society in one word: prejudice.

II February—On quitting the camp in the morning, I and my two companions traversed for some time portions of the elevated sandstone plains which I had passed on a former occasion; and after an hour's walking through the gloomy stringybark forest which covered them we reached a stream of water running

in a shallow valley; and as there was a bad route down
to this I halted to make a road which the ponies could
traverse. There was plenty of water and forage hereabouts,
and a fine level country for our proceedings, so that we
were all in high hopes and spirits and, as I then believed,
our principal difficulties were at an end.

Whilst at work at the road we all thought that we
heard a native call and that others answered him; having
listened for a repetition of these sounds, we again heard
them, but they were so indistinct in character that none of
us this time agreed as to what they were—I imagined that
it was the call of a bird, and when I again heard the same
sound very faintly in the distance, I felt convinced it was
not a human voice, and proceeded on my way perfectly
at ease...

It was the duty of the Cape man who accompanied me
to mark a tree every here and there by chipping the bark,
so that the party might the next day easily recognise the
route which they had to pursue; upon looking back I now
perceived that he had neglected a very remarkable tree
about twenty or thirty yards behind us...I desired him to
go back and chip it, and then to rejoin us; in the meantime
I stood musing as to the best means of avoiding the little
rocky ravine in our front. Finding that the man remained
absent longer than I had expected, I called loudly to him
but received no answer, and therefore passed round some
rocks which hid the tree from my view to look after him.
Suddenly I saw him close to me, breathless and speechless

with terror, and a native with his spear fixed in a throwing-stick, in full pursuit of him; immediately numbers of other natives burst upon my sight; each tree, each rock seemed to give forth its black denizen, as if by enchantment.

A moment before, the most solemn silence pervaded these woods, we deemed that not a human being moved within miles of us, and now they rang with savage and ferocious yells, and fierce armed men crowded round us on every side, bent on our destruction.

There was something very terrible in so complete and sudden a surprise. Certain death appeared to stare us in the face, and from the determined and resolute air of our opponents I immediately guessed that the man who had first seen them, instead of boldly standing his ground, and calling to Coles and myself for assistance, had at once, like a coward, run away; thus giving the natives confidence in themselves, and a contempt for us—and this conjecture I afterwards ascertained was perfectly true.

We were now fairly engaged for our lives; escape was impossible and surrender to such enemies out of the question.

As soon as I saw the natives around me, I fired one barrel of my gun over the head of him who was pursuing my dismayed attendant, hoping the report would have checked his further career. He proved to be the tall man seen at the camp, painted with white. My shot stopped him not; he still closed on us, and his spear whistled by my head but, whilst he was fixing another in his throwing stick, a ball from my second barrel struck him in the arm, and it fell powerless by his side. He now retired behind a rock, but the others still pressed on.

I now made the two men retire behind some neighbouring rocks which formed a kind of protecting parapet along our front and right flank, whilst I took post on the left. Both my barrels were now exhausted; and I desired the other two to fire separately whilst I was reloading; but to my horror Coles, who was armed with my rifle, reported hurriedly that the cloth case with which he had covered it for protection against rain had become entangled. His services were thus lost at a most critical moment, whilst trying to tear off the lock cover; and the other man was so paralysed with fear that he could do nothing but cry out, 'Oh, God! Sir, look at them; look at them!'

In the meantime, our opponents pressed more closely round; their spears kept whistling by us, and our fate seemed inevitable. The light-coloured man, spoken of at the camp, now appeared to direct their movements. He sprang forward to a rock not more than thirty yards from us and, posting himself behind it, threw a spear with such deadly force and aim that had I not drawn myself forward by a sudden jerk it must have gone through my body and, as it was, it touched my back in flying by. Another well-directed spear, from a different hand, would have pierced me in the breast but, in the motion I made to avoid it, it struck upon the stock of my gun, of which it carried away a portion by its force.

All this took place in a few seconds of time, and no shot had been fired but by me. I now recognised in the light-coloured man an old enemy who had led on the former attack against me on the 22nd of December. By his cries and gestures he now appeared to be urging the others to surround and press on us, which they were rapidly doing.

I saw now that but one thing could be done to save our lives, so I gave Coles my gun to complete the reloading, and took the rifle which he had not yet disengaged from the cover. I tore it off and, stepping out from behind our parapet, advanced to the rock which covered my light-coloured opponent. I had not made two steps in advance when three spears struck me nearly at the same moment, one of which was thrown by him. I felt severely wounded in the hip, but knew not exactly where the others had struck me. The force of all knocked me down, and made me very giddy and faint, but as I fell I heard the savage yells of the natives' delight and triumph; these recalled me to myself and, roused by momentary rage and indignation, I made a strong effort, rallied, and in a moment was on my legs; the spear was wrenched from my wound, and my haversack drawn closely over it, that neither my own party nor the natives might see it, and I advanced again steadily to the rock.

The man became alarmed, and threatened me with his club, yelling most furiously; but as I neared the rock, behind which all but his head and arm was covered, he fled towards an adjoining one, dodging dexterously according to the native manner of confusing an assailant and avoiding the cast of his spear; but he was scarcely uncovered in his flight when my rifle ball pierced him through the back, between the shoulders, and he fell heavily on his face with a deep groan.

The effect was electrical. The tumult of the combat had ceased: not another spear was thrown, not another yell was uttered. Native after native dropped away, and noiselessly disappeared. I stood alone with the wretched savage dying before me, and my two men close to me behind the rocks, in the attitude of deep attention; and as I looked round upon the dark rocks and forests, now suddenly silent and lifeless, but for the sight of the unhappy being who lay on the ground before me, I could have thought that the whole affair had been a horrid dream.

Warrup

Onwards, Onwards, 1839

Trust George Grey to give us what is probably the earliest first-hand Aboriginal account of exploration in Australia. In April 1839 Grey's expedition came to grief seeking an overland route south from Shark Bay. Grey split his party and struggled on to Perth with a handful of men. Here, Warrup, a Noongar man, memorably describes the journey of the relief expedition sent in search of the men who had been left behind, south of where Geraldton stands today.

I st day—At Dundalup we eat fish; then onwards, onwards, onwards, till we slept at Neerroba.

2nd day—Onwards, onwards, till we reached Nowergoop, where the horses drank water; then onwards, onwards, onwards, until Manbabee, where we eat flesh and bread. Onwards, onwards, onwards, until Yungee, where we shot ducks, and the horses drank water. Onwards, onwards, onwards, onwards, to Boongarrup, where we slept one sleep.

3rd day—Onwards through a forest, onwards through a forest, onwards through a forest. We slept at

Neergammy, a pleasant resting-place; the land was good, the herbage good; pleasant was our resting-place, and our hut was good.

4th day—Onwards, onwards, onwards, we entered a woody country. Onwards, through a forest, onwards through a forest; we now see the waters of Kajeelup; we eat flesh and bread. Onwards through the forest, onwards through the forest, onwards through the forest. We see the tracks of natives; we shout aloud, and then proceed conversing with natives; they sit down. Onwards go we, onwards, onwards, onwards; the horses drink water; by and by, we see tracks. Onwards, onwards, onwards; we see a large water; we shoot ducks. On the one side we see two waters, on the other side one water we see. Onwards, onwards, onwards, onwards, onwards; we see no other water. Onwards through the forest, onwards through the forest, onwards through the forest; we see a river. You had here eaten freshwater mussels: at this river we sleep. Barramba is the place's name.

5th day—Onwards through the forest, through the forest, through the forest, through the forest onwards; water we see not. Through the forest onwards; through the forest onwards; we see a water, but a worthless water. Yours and Kaiber's footsteps we see. Here there is no grass. You had here shot a bird—a cockatoo you shot. Maribara was this place's name.

Onwards through the forest, through the forest onwards, through the forest onwards; we see no other water; the herbage is worthless. We still go onwards, onwards through the forest. We see natives; a few natives we see: the men are two, the women one, the children two. We see the place called Nowergup.

We say, 'Where is there water? Here the water is bad.'

The natives say, 'Yonder the water is good—here it is bad. At Boranyup the water is good.'

We go onwards, onwards, onwards; at Boranyup we sleep—rain falls as we sleep at Boranyup.

6th day—Onwards through the forest, onwards through the forest, onwards through the forest; some of the others sit down; Auger sits down; Hunt sits down. Mr Roe, Mr Spofforth and I on horseback go onwards, onwards, onwards, onwards, through the forest onwards, through the forest onwards, through the forest onwards, through the forest onwards. We see the sea; then onwards, onwards, onwards; along the seashore onwards, along the seashore onwards, along the seashore onwards. We see the tracks of white men.

Then we turn back again, away we go back again, back again away; through the forest away, through the forest away, through the forest away; back again. We move, move, till we sit at Boranyup; we then eat kangaroo; Hunt and Auger had brought it in. At Boranyup we lie down; we sleep.

7th day—The next day away, away, away, away, returning, returning, on our tracks returning, on our tracks returning, on our tracks returning. At Barramba we sit down: we eat bread and meat; they eat freshwater mussels; the natives eat not freshwater mussels.

Away, away, away, away, away; we see the water of Djunjup; we shoot game. Away, away, away, through a forest away, through a forest away; we see no water. Through a forest away; along our tracks away, along our tracks away, along our tracks away, along our tracks away. We sleep at Ka-jil-up; rain falls; the water here is good: the horses feed—well did the horses feed.

8th day—Away, away; along our tracks away, along our tracks away; hills ascending: then pleasantly away, pleasantly away, away; through a forest away, through a forest away, through a forest away; we see a water—the water of Goonmarrarup. Along the river away, along the river away; a short distance along the river we go; then away, away, away, through a forest away; a short distance through a forest we go.

Then along another river away, away; we cross the river; away, a short distance away. At Neergammy we sleep, raising huts.

The others continue returning; we go away, away: in the forest we see no water; we see no footsteps; we see some papers—the papers put by Mr Mortimer we see: still we go onwards, along the sea away, along the sea away, along the sea away: through the bush away, through the bush away; then along the sea away, along the sea away. We see white men—three of them we see. They cry out, 'Where is water?' Water we give them—brandy and water we give them. We sleep near the sea.

Away, away go we (I, Mr Roe and Kinchela), along the shore away, along the shore away, along the shore away. We see no fresh water; along the shore away, along the shore away. We see a paper, the paper of Mortimer and Spofforth. Away we go, away, away, along the shore away, away, away, a long distance we go. I see Mr Smith's footsteps ascending a sandhill, onwards I go regarding his footsteps. I see Mr Smith dead. We commence digging the earth.

Two *sleeps* had he been dead; greatly did I weep, and much I grieved. In his blanket folding him, we scraped away the earth.

We scrape earth into the grave, we scrape the earth into the grave, a little wood we place in it. Much earth we heap upon it—much earth we throw up. No dogs can dig there, so much earth we throw up. The sun had just inclined to the westward as we laid him in the ground.

Edward John Eyre

Oh Massa, Oh Massa, Come Here, 1841

 Edward Eyre's crossing of southern Australia in 1840–41, in the company of Wylie (an Aborigine from the Albany area), is one of the most compelling stories in Australian exploration. Eyre's overseer, James Baxter, and two Aboriginal youths, Joey and Yarry, who accompanied the expedition, were destined not to complete the journey.

Eyre's brooding account illustrates the point that Aboriginal 'guides' were not always willing participants and reliable companions. When their interests conflicted with those of their white leaders, they had few means of being heard. Sometimes, frustration, fear and continual displays of white superiority would lead to an outburst—even to murder.

Eyre and Wylie trudged on to Albany where they had long been given up for dead. As they stood above the town in dismal weather Eyre wept, remembering the disasters of the journey. Wylie, on the other hand, was welcomed home by his people with wild joyous cries.

Edward John Eyre

Tonight the overseer asked me which of the watches I would keep, and as I was not sleepy, though tired, I chose the first. At a quarter before six, I went to take charge of the horses, having previously seen the overseer and the natives lay down to sleep, at their respective break-winds, ten or twelve yards apart from one another. The arms and provisions, as was our custom, were piled up under an oilskin between my break-wind and that of the overseer, with the exception of one gun, which I always kept at my own sleeping place...

Trifling as the arrangement of the watches might seem, and unimportant as I thought it at the time, whether I undertook the first or the second, yet was my choice, in this respect, the means under God's providence of my life being saved, and the cause of the loss of that of my overseer.

The night was cold, and the wind blowing hard from the south-west, whilst scud and nimbus were passing very rapidly by the moon. The horses fed tolerably well, but rambled a good deal, threading in and out among the many belts of scrub which intersected the grassy openings, until at last I hardly knew exactly where our camp was, the fires having apparently expired some time ago. It was now half past ten, and I headed the horses back in the direction in which I thought the camp lay, that I might be ready to call the overseer to relieve me at eleven. Whilst thus engaged, and looking steadfastly around among the scrub to see if I could anywhere detect the embers of our fires, I was startled by a sudden flash, followed by the report of a gun, not a quarter of a mile away from me.

Imagining that the overseer had mistaken the hour of the night and, not being able to find me or the horses, had taken that method to attract my attention, I immediately called out, but as no answer was returned I got alarmed and, leaving the horses, hurried up towards the camp as rapidly as I could. About a hundred yards from it, I met the King George's Sound native (Wylie), running towards me, and in great alarm crying out, 'Oh massa, oh massa, come here'—but could gain no information from him as to what had occurred. Upon reaching the encampment, which I did in about five minutes after the shot was fired, I was horror-struck to find my poor overseer lying on the ground, weltering in his blood and in the last agonies of death.

Glancing hastily around the camp I found it deserted by the two younger native boys, whilst the scattered fragments of our baggage, which I left carefully piled under the oilskin, lay thrown about in wild disorder, and at once revealed the cause of the harrowing scene before me.

Upon raising the body of my faithful but ill-fated follower, I found that he was beyond all human aid. He had been shot through the left breast with a ball, the last convulsions of death were upon him and he expired almost immediately after our arrival.

The frightful, the appalling truth now burst upon

me, that I was alone in the desert. He who had faithfully served me for many years, who had followed my fortunes in adversity and in prosperity, who had accompanied me in all my wanderings, and whose attachment to me had been his sole inducement to remain with me in this last, and to him, alas, fatal journey, was now no more.

For an instant, I was almost tempted to wish that it had been my own fate instead of his. The horrors of my situation glared upon me in such startling reality as for an instant almost to paralyse the mind. At the dead hour of night, in the wildest and most inhospitable wastes of Australia, with the fierce wind raging in unison with the scene of violence before me, I was left with a single native, whose fidelity I could not rely upon, and who for aught I knew might be in league with the other two, who perhaps were even now lurking about with the view of taking away my life as they had done that of the overseer. Three days had passed away since we left the last water, and it was very doubtful when we might find any more. Six hundred miles of country had to be traversed before I could hope to obtain the slightest aid or assistance of any kind, whilst I knew not that a single drop of water or an ounce of flour had been left by these murderers from a stock that had previously been so small.

With such thoughts rapidly passing through my mind, I turned to search for my double-barrelled gun which I had left covered with an oilskin at the head of my own break-wind. It was gone, as was also the double-barrelled

gun that had belonged to the overseer. These were the only
weapons at the time that were in serviceable condition, for
though there were a brace of pistols they had been packed
away, as there were no cartridges for them, and my rifle
was useless, from having a ball sticking fast in the breech,
and which we had in vain endeavoured to extract. A few
days previous to our leaving the last water, the overseer
had attempted to wash out the rifle not knowing it was
loaded, and the consequence was that the powder became
wetted and partly washed away, so that we could neither
fire it off nor get out the ball. I was, therefore, temporarily
defenceless, and quite at the mercy of the natives, had they
at this time come upon me.

Having hastily ripped open the bag in which the
pistols had been sewn up, I got them out, together with
my powder flask, and a bag containing a little shot and
some large balls. The rifle I found where it had been left,
but the ramrod had been taken out by the boys to load
my double-barrelled gun with, its own ramrod being
too short for that purpose; I found it, however, together
with several loose cartridges, lying about near the place
where the boys had slept, so that it was evident they had
deliberately loaded the firearms before they tried to move
away with the things they had stolen; one barrel only of
my gun had been previously loaded, and I believe neither
barrel in that of the overseer.

After obtaining possession of all the remaining
arms, useless as they were at the moment, with some

ammunition, I made no further examination then, but hurried away from the fearful scene, accompanied by the King George's Sound native, to search for the horses, knowing that if they got away now no chance whatever would remain of saving our lives.

Already the wretched animals had wandered to a considerable distance; and although the night was moonlight, yet the belts of scrub intersecting the plains were so numerous and dense that for a long time we could not find them; having succeeded in doing so at last, Wylie and I remained with them, watching them during the remainder of the night; but they were very restless, and gave us a great deal of trouble.

With an aching heart, and in most painful reflections, I passed this dreadful night. Every moment appeared to be protracted to an hour, and it seemed as if the daylight would never appear. About midnight the wind ceased, and the weather became bitterly cold and frosty. I had nothing on but a shirt and a pair of trousers, and suffered most acutely from the cold; to mental anguish was now added intense bodily pain. Suffering and distress had well nigh overwhelmed me, and life seemed hardly worth the effort necessary to prolong it. Ages can never efface the horrors of this single night, nor would the wealth of the world ever tempt me to go through similar ones again.

April 30—At last, by God's blessing, daylight dawned once more, but sad and heart-rending was the scene it presented to my view, upon driving the horses to what had been our last night's camp. The corpse of my poor companion lay extended on the ground, with the eyes open but cold and glazed in death. The same stern resolution and fearless open look which had characterised him when living stamped the expression of his countenance even now. He had fallen upon his breast four or five yards from where he had been sleeping, and was dressed only in his shirt. In all probability, the noise made by the natives in plundering the camp had awoke him; and upon his jumping up with a view of stopping them they had fired upon and killed him.

Around the camp lay scattered the harness of the horses, and the remains of the stores that had been the temptation to this fatal deed...

Among the principal things carried off by the natives were the whole of our baked bread, amounting to twenty pounds weight, some mutton, tea and sugar, the overseer's tobacco and pipes, a one-gallon keg full of water, some clothes, two double-barrelled guns, some ammunition and a few other small articles.

There were still left forty pounds of flour, a little tea and sugar, and four gallons of water, besides the arms and ammunition I had secured last night.

From the state of our horses, and the dreadful circumstances we were placed in, I was now obliged to abandon everything but the bare necessaries of life...A little bread was then baked, and I endeavoured once more to put the rifle in serviceable condition, as it was the only weapon we should have to depend upon in any dangers that might beset us.

Unable in any way to take out the breech, or to extract the ball, I determined to melt it out, and for that purpose took the barrel off the stock and put the breech in the fire, holding the muzzle in my hand. Whilst thus engaged, the rifle went off, the ball whizzing close past my head; the fire, it seems, had dried the powder, which had been wetted, not washed out; and when the barrel was sufficiently heated the piece had gone off, to the imminent danger of my life from the incautious way in which I held it. The gun, however, was again serviceable; and after carefully loading it I felt a degree of confidence and security I had before been a stranger to.

At eight o'clock we were ready to proceed; there remained but to perform the last sad offices of humanity towards him whose career had been cut short in so untimely a manner. This duty was rendered even more than ordinarily painful by the nature of the country where we happened to have been encamped. One vast unbroken surface of sheet rock extended for miles in every direction, and rendered it impossible to make a grave. We were some miles away from the seashore, and even had we been nearer could not have got down the cliffs to bury the corpse in the sand. I could only, therefore, wrap a blanket around the body of the overseer and, leaving it enshrouded where he fell, escape from the melancholy scene accompanied by Wylie, under the influence of feelings which neither time nor circumstances will ever obliterate.

Though years have now passed away since the enactment of this tragedy, the dreadful horrors of that time and scene are recalled before me with frightful vividness, and make me shudder even now when I think of them. A lifetime was crowded into those few short hours, and death alone may blot out the impressions they produced.

For some time we travelled slowly and silently onwards, Wylie preceding, leading one of the horses, myself following behind and driving the others after him, through a country consisting still of the same alternations of scrub and open intervals as before. The day became very warm, and at eleven, after travelling ten miles to the west, I determined to halt until the cool of the evening.

After baking some bread and getting our dinners, I questioned Wylie as to what he knew of the sad occurrence of yesterday. He positively denied all knowledge of it— said he had been asleep and was awoke by the report of the gun, and that upon seeing the overseer lying on the ground he ran off to meet me. He admitted, however, that after the unsuccessful attempt to leave us and proceed alone to King George's Sound the elder of the other two natives had proposed to him again to quit the party, and try to go back to Fowler's Bay to the provisions buried there. But he had heard or knew nothing, he said, of either robbery or murder being first contemplated.

My own impression was that Wylie had agreed with

the other two to rob the camp and leave us—that he had been cognisant of all their proceedings and preparations, but that when, upon the eve of their departure, the overseer had unexpectedly awoke and been murdered, he was shocked and frightened at the deed and, instead of accompanying them, had run down to meet me.

My opinion upon this point received additional confirmation from the subsequent events of this day; but I never could get Wylie to admit even the slightest knowledge of the fatal occurrence, or that he had even intended to have united with them in plundering the camp and deserting. He had now become truly alarmed; and independently of the fear of the consequences which would attach to the crime, should we ever reach a civilised community again, he had become very apprehensive that the other natives, who belonged to quite a different part of Australia to himself and who spoke a totally different language, would murder him as unhesitatingly as they had done the white man.

We remained in camp until four o'clock, and were again preparing to advance when my attention was called by Wylie to two white objects among the scrub at no great distance from us, and I at once recognised the native boys, covered with their blankets only, and advancing towards us. From Wylie's account of their proposal to go back towards Fowler's Bay I fully hoped that they had taken that direction, and left us to pursue our way to the Sound unmolested. I was therefore surprised and somewhat alarmed at finding them so near us.

With my rifle and pistols I felt myself sufficiently a match for them in an open country or by daylight. Yet I knew that as long as they followed like bloodhounds on our tracks our lives would be in their power at any moment that they chose to take them, whilst we were passing through a scrubby country or by night. Whatever their intention might be, I knew that if we travelled in the same direction with them our lives could only be safe by their destruction. Although they had taken fully one-third of the whole stock of our provisions, their appetites were so ravenous and their habits so improvident that this would soon be consumed, and then they must either starve or plunder us; for they had already tried to subsist themselves in the bush and had failed.

As these impressions rapidly passed through my mind, there appeared to me but one resource left to save my own life and that of the native with me: that was to shoot the elder of the two. Painful as this would be, I saw no other alternative if they still persisted in following us. After packing up our few things, and putting them upon the horses, I gave the bridles to Wylie to hold whilst I advanced alone with my rifle towards the two natives. They were now tolerably near, each carrying a double-barrelled gun, which was pointed towards me, elevated across the left arm and held by the right hand. As I attempted to approach nearer they gradually retreated.

Finding that I was not likely to gain ground upon them in this way, I threw down my weapons and advanced unarmed, hoping that if they let me near them I might suddenly close with the eldest and wrest his gun from him. After advancing about sixty or seventy yards towards them, I found that they again began to retreat, evidently determined not to let me approach any nearer, either armed or unarmed.

Upon this I halted and endeavoured to enter into parley with them, with a view to persuading them to return towards Fowler's Bay, and thus obviate the painful necessity I should have been under of endeavouring, for my own security, to take away the life of the eldest whenever I met with him, should they still persist in going the same road as myself. The distance we were apart was almost too great for parley, and I know not whether they heard me or not; though they halted and appeared to listen, they did not reply to what I said, and plainly wished to avoid all closer contact.

They now began to call incessantly to Wylie and, in answer to my repeated efforts to get them to speak to me, only would say, 'Oh massa, we don't want you, we want Wylie'—thus fully confirming me in the opinion I had formed that Wylie had agreed to go with them before the deed of violence was committed. It was now apparent to me that their only present object in following us had been to look for Wylie and get him to join them. In this they were unsuccessful; for he still remained quietly where

I left him holding the horses, and evidently afraid to go near them.

There was no use wasting further time, as I could not get them to listen to me. The sun, too, was fast sinking in the horizon, we had been four days without finding water, and the probability was we had very far still to go before we could hope to procure any; every moment, therefore, was precious.

Having returned to Wylie, I made him lead one of the horses in advance, and I followed behind, driving the rest after him, according to the system of march I had adopted in the morning. As soon as the two natives saw us moving on, and found Wylie did not join them, they set up a wild and plaintive cry, still following along the brush parallel to our line of route, and never ceasing in their importunities to Wylie, until the denseness of the scrub and the closing in of night concealed us from each other.

I was now resolved to make the most of the opportunity afforded me, and by travelling steadily onwards to gain so much distance in advance of the two natives as to preclude the possibility of their again overtaking us until we had reached the water, if indeed we were ever destined to reach water again. I knew that they would never travel more than a few miles before lying down, especially if carrying all the bread they had taken, the keg of water, guns, and other articles. We had, however, seen none of these things with them, except the firearms...

After pushing on for eighteen miles, I felt satisfied we

had left the natives far behind and, finding a patch of grass for the horses, halted for the remainder of the night...

Moving on again on the 1st of May, as the sun was above the horizon, we passed through a continuation of the same kind of country for sixteen miles, and then halted for a few hours during the heat of the day. We had passed many recent traces of natives both yesterday and today, who appeared to be travelling to the westward. After dividing a pot of tea between us, we again pushed on for twelve miles, completing a stage of twenty-eight miles, and halting, with a little dry grass for the horses. It was impossible they could endure this much longer; they had already been five days without water, and I did not expect to meet with any for two days more, a period which I did not think they could survive...

May 2—We again moved away at dawn, through a country which gradually became more scrubby, hilly and sandy. The natives whose tracks we had so frequently met with, taking the same course as ourselves to the westward, seemed now to be behind us; during the morning we had passed many freshly lit fires, but the people themselves remained concealed; we had now lost all traces of them and the country seemed untrodden and untenanted.

In the course of our journey this morning, we met with many holes in the sheets of limestone which occasionally coated the surface of the ground; in these holes the natives appeared to procure an abundance of water after rains, but it was so long since any had fallen that all were dry and empty now. In one deep hole only did we find the least trace of moisture; this had at the bottom of it perhaps a couple of wine glasses full of mud and water, and was most carefully blocked up from the birds with huge stones; it had evidently been visited by natives not an hour before we arrived at it, but I suspect they were as much disappointed as we were, upon rolling away all the stones, to find nothing in it...

We had now traversed 138 miles of country from the last water and, according to my estimate of the distance we had to go, ought to be within a few miles of the termination of the cliffs of the Great Bight.

May 3—The seventh day's dawn found us early commencing our journey. The poor horses still crawled on, though slowly. I was surprised that they were still alive, after the continued sufferings and privations they had been subject to. As for ourselves, we were both getting very weak and worn out, as well as lame, and it was with the greatest difficulty I could get Wylie to move, if he once sat down. I had myself the same kind of apathetic feeling, and would gladly have laid down and slept forever. Nothing but a strong sense of duty prevented me from giving way to this pleasing but fatal indulgence...

At ten miles from where we had slept, a native road led us down a very steep part of the cliffs, and we descended to the beach. The wretched horses could scarcely move. It was with the greatest difficulty we got them down the hill; and now, although within sight of our goal, I feared two of them would never reach it. By perseverance we still got them slowly along for two miles from the base of the cliffs and then, turning in among the sand-drifts, to our great joy and relief, found a place where the natives had dug for water. Thus at twelve o'clock on the seventh day since leaving the last depot we were again encamped at water, after having crossed 150 miles of a rocky, barren and scrubby tableland...

July 7—...Having turned our horses loose, and piled up our baggage, now again greatly reduced, I took my journals and charts, and with Wylie forded the river about breast high. We were soon on the other side, and rapidly advancing towards the termination of our journey. The rain was falling in torrents, and we had not a dry shred about us, whilst the whole country through which we passed had, from the long-continued and excessive rains, become almost an uninterrupted chain of puddles. For a great part of the way we walked up to our ankles in water. This made our progress slow, and rendered our last day's march a very cold and disagreeable one.

Before reaching the Sound, we met a native who at once recognised Wylie, and greeted him most cordially. From him we learnt that we had been expected at the Sound some months ago but had long been given up for lost, whilst Wylie had been mourned for and lamented as dead by his friends and his tribe. The rain still continued falling heavily as we ascended to the brow of the hill immediately overlooking the town of Albany—not a soul was to be seen—not an animal of any kind—the place looked deserted and uninhabited, so completely had the inclemency of the weather driven both man and beast to seek shelter from the storm.

For a moment I stood gazing at the town below me—that goal I had so long looked forward to, had so laboriously toiled to attain, was at last before me. A thousand confused images and reflections crowded through my mind, and the events of the past year were recalled in rapid succession. The contrast between the circumstances under which I had commenced and terminated my labours stood in strong relief before me. The gay and gallant cavalcade that accompanied me on my way at starting, the small but enterprising band that I then commanded, the goodly array of horses and drays, with all their well-ordered appointments and equipment, were conjured up in all their circumstances of pride and pleasure; and I could not restrain a tear as I called to mind the embarrassing difficulties and sad disasters that had broken up my party, and left myself and Wylie the two sole wanderers remaining at the close of an undertaking entered upon under such hopeful auspices.

Whilst standing thus upon the brow overlooking the town, and buried in reflection, I was startled by the loud shrill cry of the native we had met on the road and who still kept with us: clearly and powerfully that voice rang through the recesses of the settlement beneath, whilst the blended name of Wylie told me of the information it conveyed. For an instant there was a silence still almost as death—then a single repetition of that wild joyous cry, a confused hum of many voices, a hurrying to and fro of human feet, and the streets which had appeared so shortly before gloomy and untenanted were now alive with natives—men, women, and children, old and young, rushing rapidly up the hill to welcome the wanderer on his return and to receive their lost one almost from the grave.

It was an interesting and touching sight to witness the meeting between Wylie and his friends. Affection's strongest ties could not have produced a more affecting and melting scene—the wordless, weeping pleasure, too deep for utterance, with which he was embraced by his relatives, the cordial and hearty reception given him by his friends, and the joyous greeting bestowed upon him by all, might well have put to the blush those heartless calumniators who, branding the savage as the creature only of unbridled passions, deny to him any of those better feelings and affections which are implanted in the breast of all mankind, and which nature has not denied to any colour or to any race.

Ludwig Leichhardt

Commandant! Come Here, Very Good, 1844

 Ludwig Leichhardt, Prussian by birth and educated in Paris, arrived in Australia in 1840, and died somewhere in the vast outback sometime after 26 February 1848. Attempts to solve the mystery of Leichhardt's disappearance did much to spur further exploration.

His greatest work was the expedition from Brisbane to Port Essington, north-east of Darwin, in 1844–45. Here we join him in the vicinity of what is now Kakadu National Park, on the final leg home. He encounters not only Aborigines who speak English, but water buffaloes escaped from the abandoned settlement at Raffles Bay. Leichhardt's willingness to experiment with native foods doubtless contributed to his success as an explorer.

December 2—Whilst we were waiting for our bullock, which had returned to the running brook, a fine native stepped out of the forest with the ease and grace of an Apollo, with a smiling countenance, and with the confidence of a man to whom the white face was perfectly familiar. He was unarmed, but a great number of his companions were keeping back to watch the reception he should meet with. We received him, of course, most cordially; and upon being joined by another good-looking little man, we heard him utter distinctly the words, 'Commandant!', 'Come here!', 'Very good!', 'What's your name?'

If my readers have at all identified themselves with my feelings throughout this trying journey, if they have only imagined a tithe of the difficulties we have encountered, they will readily imagine the startling effect which these, as it were, magic words produced—we were electrified— our joy knew no limits, and I was ready to embrace the fellows who, seeing the happiness with which they inspired us, joined, with a most merry grin, in the loud expression of our feelings.

We gave them various presents, particularly leather belts, and received in return a great number of bunches of goose feathers, which the natives use to brush away the flies. They know the white people of Victoria, and called them Balanda, which is nothing more than 'Hollanders', a name used by the Malays from whom they received it.[†]

We had most fortunately a small collection of words, made by Mr Gilbert when at Port Essington, so that we were enabled to ask for water (*obert*); for the road (*allun*); for *limbo cardja*, which was the name of the harbour. I wished very much to induce them to become our guides; and the two principal men, Eooanberry and Minorelli,

---

[†] Victoria: the settlement at Port Essington

promised to accompany us, but they afterwards changed their minds.

My first object was to find good water, and our sable friends guided us with the greatest care, pointing out to us the most shady road to some wells surrounded with ferns which were situated in some tea-tree hollows at the confines of the plains and the forest. These wells, however, were so small that our horses could not approach to drink, so that we had to go to another set of wells, where I was obliged to stop, as one of our horses refused to go any farther. This place was about four miles ENE from our last camp. The wells were about six or eight feet deep, and dug through a sandy clay to a stiff bed of clay, on which the water collected...

It was evident, from the pains which the natives had taken in digging them, that the supply of fresh water was very precarious. In many instances, however, I observed that they had been induced to do so simply by the want of surface water in the immediate neighbourhood of places where they obtained their principal supply of food. This was particularly the case near the sea-coast, where no surface water is found...

The natives were remarkably kind and attentive and offered us the rind of the rose-coloured eugenia apple, the cabbage of the seaforthia palm, a fruit which I did not know, and the nut-like swelling of the rhizoma of either a grass or a sedge. The last had a sweet taste, was very mealy and nourishing, and the best article of the food of the natives we had yet tasted. They called it *allamurr* (the natives of Port Essington, *murnatt*) and were extremely fond of it. The plant grew in depressions of the plains, where the boys and young men were occupied the whole day in digging for it.

The women went in search of other food; either to the sea-coast to collect shellfish—and many were the broad paths which led across the plains from the forest land to the salt water—or to the brushes to gather the fruits of the season, and the cabbage of the palms.

The men, armed with a wommala, and with a bundle of goose spears, made of a strong reed or bamboo (?), gave up their time to hunting.[†] It seemed that they speared the geese only when flying, and would crouch down whenever they saw a flight of them approaching: the geese, however, knew their enemies so well that they immediately turned upon seeing a native rise to put his spear into the throwing stick. Some of my companions asserted that they had seen them hit their object at the almost incredible distance of 200 yards: but, making all due allowance for the guess, I could not help thinking how formidable they would have been had they been enemies instead of friends.

They remained with us the whole afternoon, all the tribe and many visitors, in all about seventy persons, squatting down with crossed legs in the narrow shades of the trunks of trees, and shifting their position as the sun advanced. Their wives were out in search of food

---

[†] Wommala: woomera

but many of their children were with them, which they duly introduced to us. They were fine, stout, well-made men, with pleasing and intelligent countenances. One or two attempts were made to rob us of some trifles; but I was careful; and we avoided the unpleasant necessity of showing any discontent on that head...

They went to the digging ground, about half a mile in the plain, where the boys were collecting *allamurr*, and brought us a good supply of it; in return for which various presents were made to them. We became very fond of this little tuber: and I dare say the feast of *allamurr* with Eooanberry's and Minorelli's tribe will long remain in the recollection of my companions.

They brought us also a thin grey snake, about four feet long, which they put on the coals and roasted. It was poisonous, and was called *yullo*. At nightfall, after filling their coolamons with water, there being none at their camp, they took their leave, and retired to their camping place on the opposite hill where a plentiful dinner awaited them. They were very urgent in inviting us to accompany them and, by way of inducement, most unequivocally offered us their sable partners.

We had to take great care of our bullock, as the beast invariably charged the natives whenever he obtained a sight of them, and he would alone have prevented their attacking us; for the whole tribe were so much afraid of him that, upon our calling out, 'The bullock,' they were immediately ready to bolt—with the exception of Eooanberry and Minorelli, who looked to us for protection.

I had not, however, the slightest fear and apprehension of any treachery on the part of the natives; for my frequent intercourse with the natives of Australia had taught me to distinguish easily between the smooth tongue of deceit, with which they try to ensnare their victim, and the open expression of kind and friendly feelings, or those of confidence and respect. I remember several instances of the most cold-blooded smooth-tongued treachery, and of the most extraordinary gullibility of the natives; but I am sure that a careful observer is more than a match for these simple children of nature, and that he can easily read the bad intention in their unsteady, greedy, glistening eyes.

Dec. 3—The natives visited us very early in the morning, with their wives and children, whom they introduced to us. There could not have been less than 200 of them present; they were all well made, active, generally well-looking, with an intelligent countenance: they had in fact all the characters of the coast blacks of a good country, but without their treacherous dispositions. I started in a north-east direction and, as we were accompanied by the natives, I led our bullock by the nose-rope behind my horse. After crossing a plain, we were stopped by a large sheet of salt water, about three or four miles broad, at the opposite side of which a low range was visible; when Eooanberry explained that we had to go far to the south-east and south, before we could cross the river, and that we had to follow it down again at the other side. He expressed his great attachment to his wife and child, and obtained leave of us to return to his tribe, which had already retired before him...

We now steered for a distant smoke to the south-east by east, and had travelled fully seventeen miles on or along extensive plains, when we perceived seven natives returning on a beaten footpath from the salt water to the forest.

We cooeed—they ran! But when we had passed, and Charley stopped behind alone, they came up to him and, having received some presents, they showed us some miserable wells between two tea-tree groves; after which they hastened home. Our cattle were tired and thirsty, but we could give them nothing to drink except about six quarts of brackish water which fell to the share of our bullock...

Dec. 4—The natives returned very early to our camp. I went up to them and made them some presents, in return for which they offered me bunches of goose feathers, and the roasted leg of a goose, which they were pleased to see me eat with a voracious appetite. I asked for *allamurr*, and they expressed themselves sorry in not having any left, and gave us to understand that they would supply us, if we would stay a day. Neither these natives nor the tribe of Eooanberry would touch our green hide or meat: they took it, but could not overcome their repugnance, and tried to drop it without being seen by us. Poor fellows!

They did not know how gladly we should have received it back! They were the stoutest and fattest men we had met...

Charley, Brown and John had gone into the brush to a camp of flying-foxes, and returned with twelve, which we prepared for luncheon, which allowed our bullock time to recover. They gave an almost incredible account of the enormous numbers of flying-foxes, all clustering round the branches of low trees, which drooped by the weight so near to the ground that the animals could easily be killed by cudgels...

After a delay of two hours, we again started, and travelled in a due south direction towards some thick smoke rising between two steep and apparently isolated rocky hills: they were about four miles distant and, when we arrived at their base, we enjoyed the pleasing sight of large lagoons surrounded with mangrove myrtles (*Stravadium*), with pandanus, and with a belt of reeds and nelumbiums. Man, horse and bullock rushed most eagerly into the fine water, determined to make up for the privation and suffering of the three last days. The lagoons were crowded with geese and, as the close vegetation allowed a near approach, Brown made good use of the few slugs that were still left, and shot ten of them, which allowed a goose to every man; a great treat to my hungry party...

Dec. 6—The natives visited us again this morning, and it was evident that they had not been with their gins. They invited us to come to their camp, but I wished to find a crossing place and, after having tried in vain to pass at the foot of the rocky hills, we found a passage between the lagoons, and entered into a most beautiful valley...The natives now became our guides, and pointed out to us a sound crossing place of the creek, which proved to be the head of the saltwater branch of the East Alligator River. We observed a great number of long conical fish and crab traps at the crossing place of the creek and in many of the tributary saltwater channels...

Here I took leave of our guides, the leader of whom appeared to be Apirk, a young and slender, but an intelligent and most active man. We now travelled again to the northward, following the outline of the rocky ridges at the right side of the creek and, having again entered upon the plains, we encamped at a very broad, shallow, sedgy, boggy lagoon...

Dec. 7—Apirk, with seven other natives, visited us again in the morning, and it seemed that they had examined the camp we had last left. They gave us to understand that we could travel safely to the northward without meeting any other creek. Apirk carried a little pointed stick, and a flat piece of wood with a small hole in it, for the purpose of obtaining fire. I directed my course to a distant mountain, due north from the camp, and travelled seven or eight miles over a large plain, which was composed of a rich dark soil, and clothed with a great variety of excellent grasses. We saw many columns of dust raised by whirlwinds and again mistook them for the smoke of so many fires of the natives...it seemed as if the giant spirits of the plain were holding a stately corroboree around us...

At this time we were all sadly distressed with boils and with a prickly heat; early lancing of the former saved much pain. The cuts and sores of the hands festered quickly, but this depended much more on the want of cleanliness than anything else. A most dangerous enemy grew up amongst us in the irresistible impatience to come to the end of our journey; and I cannot help considering it a great blessing that we did not meet with natives who knew the settlement of Port Essington at an earlier part of our journey, or I am afraid we should have been exposed to the greatest misery, if not destruction, by an inconsiderate, thoughtless desire of pushing onward.

Dec. 8—...We encamped at a fine lagoon...Immediately after our arrival, Brown went to shoot some geese, and met with two natives who were cooking some roots, but they withdrew in great haste as soon as they saw him. Soon afterwards, however, a great number of them came to the opposite side of the lagoon, and requested a parley.

I went down with some presents, and a young man came over in a canoe to meet me. I gave him a tin canister, and was agreeably surprised that the stock of English words increased considerably, that very few things we had were new to him, and that he himself had been at the settlement. His name was Bilge. He called me Commandant, and presented several old men to me under the same title. Several natives joined us, either using the canoe or swimming across the lagoon and, after having been duly introduced to me, I took four of them to the camp, where they examined everything with great intelligence, without expressing the least desire of possessing it.

They were the most confiding, intelligent, inquisitive natives I had ever met before. Bilge himself took me by the hand and went to the different horses, and to the bullock and asked their names and who rode them. The natives had always been very curious to know the names of our horses, and repeated 'Jim Crow', 'Flourbag', 'Caleb', 'Irongrey', as well as they could, with the greatest merriment. Bilge frequently mentioned 'Devil devil', in referring to the bullock, and I think he alluded to the wild buffaloes, the tracks of which we soon afterwards saw. We asked him for *allamurr*, and they expressed their readiness to bring it, as soon as the children and women, who both went under the denomination of piccaninnies, returned to the camp. The day being far advanced, and their camp a good way off, they left us, after inviting us to accompany them: but this I declined.

About ten o'clock at night, three lads came to us with *allamurr*; but they were very near suffering for their kindness and confidence, as the alarm of 'blackfellows' at night was a call to immediate and desperate defence. Suspecting, however, the true cause of this untimely visit,

I walked up to them and led them into the camp, where I divided their *allamurr* between us; allowing them a place of honour on a tarpaulin near me for the remainder of the night, with which attention they appeared highly pleased...

Dec. 9—The natives came to our camp at break of day, and Bilge introduced several old warriors of a different tribe, adding always the number of piccaninnies that each of them had; they appeared very particular about the latter, and one of the gentlemen corrected Bilge very seriously when he mentioned only two instead of three. Bilge had promised to go with us to Balanda but, having probably talked the matter over during the night with his wife, he changed his intentions; but invited us in the most urgent manner to stay a day at their camp.

Although no place could be found more favourable for feed and water, and a day's rest would have proved very beneficial to our cattle, yet our meat bags, on which we now solely depended, were so much reduced that every day of travelling was of the greatest importance; as the natives told us that four days would bring us to the peninsula, and two more to Balanda...

Dec. 10—...we saw a great number of natives occupied in burning the grass, and digging for roots...

I left my companions in the shady belt of drooping tea-trees, and rode with Charley towards the natives in order to obtain information. They were, however, only women and children, and they withdrew at my approach, although I had dismounted and left my horse far behind with Charley. They had, however, allowed me to come near enough to make them understand my incessant calls for *obcit*, water, adding occasionally, 'Balanda; very good; no good.' When they had disappeared in the forest, Charley came with the horse, and we reconnoitred along the boundaries of the plain to find water but, not succeeding, we returned; and, when opposite to the place where I had left my companions, I cooeed for them to come over with me.

My cooee was answered by natives within the forest, and shortly afterwards four men came running out of it, and approached us most familiarly. They spoke English tolerably, knew the pipe, tobacco, bread, rice, ponies, guns etc., and guided us to a fine lagoon which I named, after the leading man of their tribe, Nyuall's Lagoon. Two of them promised to pilot us to Balanda and to *rambal*, which meant houses. They were very confiding, and women and children entered for the first time freely into our camp.

They examined everything, but made not the slightest attempt to rob us even of a trifle. When the women returned at night, they did not bring *allamurr* or, as it was here called, *murnatt*, but plenty of *imberbi*, the root of convolvulus, which grow abundantly in the plain. They gave us a very seasonable supply of it, but would not taste our dried beef, which they turned, broke, smelled, and then with a feeling of pity and disgust returned to us.

Nyuall gave an amusing account of our state: 'You no bread, no flour, no rice, no backi—you no good! Balanda plenty bread, plenty flour, plenty rice, plenty backi! Balanda very good!'

He, Gnarrangan and Carbaret promised to go with us; and the first intended to take his wife with him. They imitated with surprising accuracy the noises of the various domesticated animals they had seen at the settlement; and it was amusing to hear the crowing of the cock, the cackling of the hens, the quacking of ducks, grunting of pigs, mewing of the cat etc., evident proofs that these natives had been in Victoria...

Dec. 11—...When we approached the forest, several tracks of buffaloes were seen...As the dung and tracks of the buffaloes were fresh, Charley went to track them, whilst Brown tried to shoot some ibises, which had been at the water and were now perched on a tree about 300 yards off. At the discharge of the gun a buffalo started out of a thicket, but did not seem inclined to go far. Brown returned, loaded his gun with ball, went after the buffalo and wounded him in the shoulder.

When Charley came back to the camp, he, Brown and Mr Roper pursued the buffalo on horseback and, after a long run, and some charges, succeeded in killing it. It was a young bull, about three years old, and in most excellent condition. This was a great, a most fortunate event for us; for our meat bags were almost empty and, as we did not wish to kill Redmond, our good companion, we had the prospect of some days of starvation before us.

We could now share freely with our black friends, and they had not the slightest objection to eat the fresh meat, after baking it in their usual manner. They called the buffalo *anaborro*, and stated that the country before us was full of them. These buffaloes are the offspring of the stock which had either strayed from the settlement at Raffles Bay, or had been left behind when the establishment was broken up. They were originally introduced from the Malay islands. I was struck with the remarkable thickness of their skin (almost an inch) and with the solidity of their bones, which contained little marrow; but that little was extremely savoury.

Dec. 12—Part of the meat was cut up and dried, and part of it was roasted to take with us; a great part of it was given to the natives who were baking and eating the whole day; and when they could eat no more meat, they went into the plains to collect *imberbi* and *murnatt* to add the necessary quantum of vegetable matter to their diet. The sultry weather, however, caused a great part of the meat to become tainted and maggoty. Our friend Nyuall became ill, and complained of a violent headache, which he tried to cure by tying a string tightly round his head.

Charles Sturt

At Noon I Took a Thermometer, 1845

 In 1844, aged forty-nine and partially blind from earlier expeditionary work, Charles Sturt left his beloved wife Charlotte and started on a third and final expedition—this time aimed straight at the heart of the continent. There, he believed he would find 'a large body of inland waters', so he equipped the expedition with a boat for sailing on this mythical sea. Instead, he discovered a sea of seemingly endless sand dunes—the Simpson Desert—and temperatures so extreme they shrivelled his supplies, overwhelmed his horses and burst his thermometer.

Sturt was possessed by an almost manic obsession. Scurvy was turning his men's skin black, and large pieces of spongy flesh hung from the roofs of their mouths. They were rotting where they stood, but still Sturt, now all but blind, pushed on. He wrote that he preferred death to defeat by this terrible land.

Sturt survived. At midnight on 19 January 1846, ten days in advance of the rest of the party, the skeletal explorer rode up to his isolated seaside house in Adelaide and knocked on the door. Charlotte, answering the unexpected call, had all but given him up for dead.

This account begins with Sturt's thoughts about the grand quest he was about to undertake. We then join him in November 1845 retracing his steps towards where Innamincka is today.

Let any man lay the map of Australia before him, and regard the blank upon its surface, and then let me ask him if it would not be an honourable achievement to be the first to place foot in its centre.

Men of undoubted perseverance and energy in vain had tried to work their way to that distant and shrouded spot. A veil hung over Central Australia that could neither be pierced or raised. Girt round about by deserts, it almost appeared as if nature had intentionally closed it upon civilised man, that she might have one domain on the earth's wide field over which the savage might roam in freedom.

I had traced down almost every inland river of the continent, and had followed their courses for hundreds of miles, but they had not led me to its central regions. I had run the Castlereagh, the Macquarie, the Lachlan, the Murrumbidgee, the Hume, the Darling and the Murray down to their respective terminations, but beyond them I had not passed—yet—I looked upon Central Australia as a legitimate field to explore which no man had a greater claim than myself, and the first wish of my heart was to close my services in the cause of Geography by dispelling the mists that hung over it...

The drought had now continued so long, and the heat been so severe, that I apprehended we might be obliged to remain another summer in these fearful solitudes. The weather was terrifically hot, and appeared to have set in unusually early.

Under such circumstances, and with so many causes to render my mind anxious, the reader will believe I did not sleep much. The men were as restless as myself, so that we commenced our journey before the sun had risen on the morning of the 10th of November, to give the horses time to take their journey leisurely. Slowly we retraced our steps, nor did I stop for a moment until we had got to within five miles of our destination, at which distance we saw a single native running after us and, taking it into my head that he might be a messenger from Mr Browne, I pulled up to wait for him; but curiosity alone had induced him to come forward.[†] When he got to within a hundred yards, he stopped and approached no nearer.

This little delay made it after sunset before we reached the upper pool (not the one Mr Browne and I had discovered), and were relieved from present anxiety by finding a thick puddle still remaining in it, so that I halted for the night. Slommy, Bawley and the colt had hard work to keep up with the other horses, and it really grieved me to see them so reduced. My own horse was even now beginning to give way, but I had carried a great load upon him.

---

† J. H. Browne was medical officer to the expedition. He had been left in charge of the depot when Sturt and his party advanced.

As we approached the water, three ducks flew up and went off down the creek southwards, so I was cheered all night by the hope that water still remained at the lower pool. On the 11th, therefore, early we pushed on, as I intended to stop and breakfast at that place before I started for the depot.

We had scarcely got there, however, when the wind, which had been blowing all the morning hot from the NE, increased to a heavy gale, and I shall never forget its withering effect. I sought shelter behind a large gum tree, but the blasts of heat were so terrific that I wondered the very grass did not take fire. This really was nothing ideal: everything, both animate and inanimate, gave way before it; the horses stood with their backs to the wind, and their noses to the ground, without the muscular strength to raise their heads; the birds were mute, and the leaves of the trees, under which we were sitting, fell like a snow shower around us.

At noon I took a thermometer, graduated to 127°, out of my box, and observed that the mercury was up to 125°. Thinking that it had been unduly influenced, I put it in the fork of a tree close to me, sheltered alike from the wind and the sun. In this position I went to examine it about an hour afterwards, when I found that the mercury had risen to the top of the instrument, and that its further expansion had burst the bulb, a circumstance that I believe no traveller has ever before had to record.

I cannot find language to convey to the reader's mind

an idea of the intense and oppressive nature of the heat that prevailed. We had reached our destination, however, before the worst of the hot wind set in; but all the water that now remained in the once broad and capacious pool to which I have had such frequent occasion to call the attention of the reader was a shining patch of mud nearly in the centre. We were obliged to dig a trench for the water to filter into during the night, and by this means obtained a scanty supply for our horses and ourselves.

Just as the morning was breaking, we left the creek and travelled for thirty-six miles. I then halted until the moon should rise, and was glad to see that the horses stood it well. At seven we resumed the journey, and got on tolerably well until midnight, when poor Bawley, my favourite horse, fell; but we got him up again and, abandoning his saddle, proceeded onwards. At a mile, however, he again fell, when I stopped, and the water revived him. I now hoped he would struggle on, but in about an hour he again fell. I was exceedingly fond of this poor animal, and intended to have purchased him at the sale of the remnants of the expedition, as a present to my wife. We sat down and lit a fire by him, but he seemed fairly worn out.

I then determined to ride on to the depot and, if Mr Browne should still be there, to send a dray with water to the relief of the men. I told them, therefore, to come slowly on, and with Mr Stuart pushed for the camp. We reached the plain just as the sun was descending, without having dismounted from our horses for more than fifteen hours and, as we rode down the embankment into it, looked around for the cattle, but none were to be seen. We looked towards the little sandy mound on which the tents had stood, but no white object there met our eye; we rode slowly up to the stockade, and found it silent and deserted.

I was quite sure that Mr Browne had had urgent reasons for retiring. I had indeed anticipated the measure: I hardly hoped to find him at the fort, and had given him instructions on the subject of his removal, yet a sickening feeling came over me when I saw that he was really gone; not on my own account for, with the bitter feelings of disappointment with which I was returning home, I could calmly have laid my head on that desert, never to raise it again. The feeling was natural, and had no mixture whatever of reproach towards my excellent companion.

We dismounted and led our horses down to water before I went to the tree under which I had directed Mr Browne to deposit a letter for me. A good deal of water still remained in the channel, but nevertheless a large pit had been dug in it as I had desired. I did not drink, nor did Mr Stuart—the surface of the water was quite green, and the water itself was of a red colour, but I believe we were both thinking of anything but ourselves at that moment.[†]

As soon as we had unsaddled the horses, we went

[†] Mr Stuart: the thirty-year-old John McDouall Stuart who accompanied Sturt on this expedition.

to the tree and dug up the bottle into which, as agreed upon, Mr Browne had put a letter; informing me that he had been most reluctantly obliged to retreat; the water at the depot having turned putrid, and seriously disagreed with the men; he said that he should fall back on the old depot along the same line on which we had advanced, and expressed his fears that the water in Strzelecki's Creek would have dried, on the permanence of which he knew our safety depended.

Under present circumstances the fate of poor Bawley, if not of more of our horses, was sealed. Mr Stuart and I sat down by the stockade, and as night closed in lit a fire to guide Morgan and Mack on their approach to the plain. They came up about 2 p.m., having left Bawley on a little stony plain, and the colt on the sand ridges nearer to us, and in the confusion and darkness had left all the provisions behind; it therefore became necessary to send for some, as we had not had anything for many hours.

The horses Morgan and Mack had ridden were too knocked up for further work, but I sent the latter on my own horse with a leather bottle that had been left behind by the party, full of water for poor Bawley, if he should still find him alive. Mack returned late in the afternoon, having passed the colt on his way to the depot, towards which he dragged himself with difficulty, but Bawley was beyond recovery; he gave the poor animal the water, however, for he was a humane man, and then left him to die.

We had remained during the day under a scorching

heat, but could hardly venture to drink the water of the creek without first purifying it by boiling, and as we had no vessel until Mack should come up we had to wait patiently for his arrival at 7 p.m. About nine we had a damper baked, and broke our fast for the first time for more than two days.

While sitting under a tree in the forenoon Mr Stuart had observed a crow pitch in the little garden we had made, but which never benefited us, since the sun burnt up every plant the moment it appeared above the ground. This bird scratched for a short time in one of the soft beds, and then flew away with something in his bill. On going to the spot Mr Stuart scraped up a piece of bacon and some suet, which the dogs of course had buried. These choice morsels were washed and cooked, and Mr Stuart brought me a small piece of bacon, certainly not larger than a dollar, which he assured me had been cut out of the centre and was perfectly clean. I had not tasted the bacon since February, nor did I now feel any desire to do so, but I ate it because I thought I really wanted it in the weak state in which I was.

Perhaps a physician would laugh at me for ascribing the pains I felt the next morning to so trifling a cause, but I was attacked with pains at the bottom of my heels and in my back. Although lying down I felt as if I was standing balanced on stones; these pains increased during the day, insomuch that I anticipated some more violent attack, and determined on getting to the old depot as soon as possible; but as the horses had not had sufficient rest I put off my journey to 5 p.m. on the following day, when I left Fort Grey with Mr Stuart, directing Mack and Morgan to follow at the same hour on the following day, and promising that I would send a dray with water to meet them.

I rode all that night until 3 p.m. of the 17th, when we reached the tents...we rode without stopping, and might truly be said to have been twenty hours on horseback.

Sincere I believe was the joy of Mr Browne, and indeed of all hands, at seeing us return, for they had taken it for granted that our retreat would have been cut off. I too was gratified to find that Mr Browne was better, and to learn that everything had gone on well...

Mr Browne informed me that the natives had frequently visited the camp during my absence. He had given them to understand that we were going over the hills again, on which they told him that if he did not make haste all the water would be gone. It now behoved us therefore to effect our retreat upon the Darling with all expedition...

On the 18th I sent Flood to a small creek, between us and the pine forest, but he returned on the following day with information that it had long been dry. Thus then were my fears verified, and our retreat to the Darling apparently cut off...The heat was greater than that of the previous summer; the thermometer ranging between 110° and 123° every day; the wind blowing heavily from NE to ESE filled the air with impalpable red dust, giving the sun the most foreboding and lurid appearance as we looked upon him. The ground was so heated that our matches, falling on it, ignited; and, having occasion to make a night signal, I found the whole of our rockets had been rendered useless, as on being lit they exploded at once without rising from the ground...

When we first arrived on the 27th of January, 1845, the cereal grasses had ripened their seed, and the larger shrubs were fast maturing their fruit; the trees were full of birds, and the plains were covered with pigeons—having nests under every bush. At the close of November of the same year—that is to say six weeks earlier—not an herb had sprung from the ground, not a bud had swelled, and, where the season before the feathered tribes had swarmed in hundreds on the creek, scarcely a bird was now to be seen. Our cattle wandered about in search for food, and the silence of the grave reigned around us day and night.

Was it instinct that warned the feathered races to shun a region in which the ordinary course of nature had been arrested, and over which the wrath of the Omnipotent appeared to hang? Or was it that a more genial season in the country to which they migrate rendered their desertion of it at the usual period unnecessary? Most sincerely do I hope that the latter was the case, and that a successful destiny will await the bold and ardent traveller who is now crossing those regions.[†]

On the 20th I sent Flood down the creek to ascertain if

[†] Sturt is referring to Leichhardt's expedition to Port Essington.

water remained in it or the farther holes mentioned by the natives, thinking that in such a case we might work our way to the eastward; but on the 23rd he returned without having seen a drop of water from the moment he left us. The deep and narrow channel I had so frequently visited, and which I had hoped might still contain water, had long been dry, and thus was our retreat cut off in that quarter also. There was apparently no hope for us—its last spark had been extinguished by this last disappointment; but the idea of a detention in that horrid desert was worse than death itself.

At this time Mr Stuart was taken ill with pains similar to my own, and Davenport had an attack of dysentery.

On the 23rd it blew a fierce gale and a hot wind from west by north, which rendered us still more uncomfortable: nothing indeed could be done without risk in such a temperature and such a climate. The fearful position in which we were placed caused me great uneasiness; the men began to sicken, and I felt assured that if we remained much longer the most serious consequences might be apprehended.

On the 24th, Mr Browne went with Flood to examine a stony creek about sixteen miles to the south, and on our way homewards. We had little hope that he would find any water in it but, if he did, a plan had suggested itself by which we trusted to effect our escape. It being impossible to stand the outer heat, the men were obliged to take whatever things wanted repair to our underground room, and I was happy to learn from Mr Stuart, who I sent up to superintend them, that the natives had not in the least disturbed Mr Poole's grave.[†]

On the 25th Mr Browne returned, and returned unsuccessful; he could find no water anywhere, and told me it was fearful to ride down the creeks and to witness their present state.

We were now aware that there could be no water nearer to us than 118 miles, i.e., at Flood's Creek, and even there it was doubtful if water any longer remained...I was myself laid up, a helpless being, for I had gradually sunk under the attack of scurvy which had so long hung upon me. The day after I arrived in camp I was unable to walk: in a day or two more, my muscles became rigid, my limbs contracted and I was unable to stir; gradually also my skin blackened, the least movement put me to torture, and I was reduced to a state of perfect prostration.

Thus stricken down, when my example and energies were so much required for the welfare and safety of others, I found the value of Mr Browne's services and counsel... and a plan at length occurred by which I hoped he might venture on the journey to Flood's Creek without risk.

This plan was to shoot one of the bullocks, and to fill his hide with water. We determined on sending this in a dray, a day in advance, to enable the bullock driver to get as far as possible on the road; we then arranged that Mr

---

[†] Some months earlier James Poole, Sturt's second-in-command, had died of scurvy, a disease caused by lack of vitamin C.

Browne should take the light cart, with thirty-six gallons of water, and one horse only; that on reaching the dray, he should give his horse as much water as he would drink from the skin, leaving that in the cart untouched until he should arrive at the termination of his second day's journey, when I proposed he should give his horse half the water and, leaving the rest until the period of his return, ride the remainder of the distance he had to go.

I saw little risk in this plan, and we accordingly acted upon it immediately: the hide was prepared and answered well, since it easily contained 150 gallons of water. Jones proceeded on the morning of the 27th, and on the 28th Mr Browne left me on this anxious and to us important journey accompanied by Flood. We calculated on his return on the eighth day, and the reader will judge how anxiously those days passed. On the day Mr Browne left me, Jones returned, after having deposited the skin at the distance of thirty-two miles.

On the eighth day from his departure, every eye but my own was turned to the point at which they had seen him disappear. About 3 p.m., one of the men came to inform me that Mr Browne was crossing the creek, the camp being on its left bank, and in a few minutes afterwards he entered my tent. 'Well, Browne,' said I, 'what news? Is it to be good or bad?'

'There is still water in the creek,' said he, 'but that is all I can say. What there is is as black as ink, and we must make haste, for in a week it will be gone.'

John Ainsworth Horrocks

Shot by Camel, 1846

 In July 1846 John Ainsworth Horrocks set out towards Lake Torrens in search of good pastoral land. Relations between the humans and the grazing species were strained from the very start. Indeed, open warfare seems to have broken out between them. At one point Horrocks 'killed a goat—the one that has given us so much trouble, and which Jimmy (an Aborigine) was delighted to see slaughtered, having in his hatred of the animal promised Garlick, the tentkeeper, a pint of ale if he would kill it next'.

But one member of Horrocks' expedition was trouble from the very start—Harry the cantankerous camel who bit Garlick severely on the head leaving 'two wounds of great length above his temples and another severe gash on his cheeks'. Earlier, Harry had attempted to eat an expedition goat.

The goats had their own strategy, for they became 'with the exception of one...very lame. They amused themselves last night by leaping on our tent, and tearing it in several places'. But worse was to come, for Harry bit through the flour bags, wasting the expedition supplies, and was eventually to have the ultimate revenge when he shot Horrocks.

Horrocks dictated this letter to the expedition secretary on 8 September 1846. How he managed to transmit it despite severe wounds to his right hand and mouth, and how he maintained such a calm, detached tone, remain mysterious. He died on 23 September. Harry, incidentally, was the first camel used in inland Australia. After Horrocks' death, it took two bullets to kill him, and he managed to bite a stockman on the head before succumbing.

It is with the greatest regret I have to inform the committee and my fellow-colonists who subscribed towards the expenses of the expedition of its untimely and unfortunate termination. Having made an excursion, accompanied by Mr Gill, to the tableland on the west of Lake Torrens, to ascertain if it were practicable to form a depot in that neighbourhood, and not succeeding in finding either water or grass, I returned to Depot Creek, determined to make an excursion with the camel, as it was impracticable to take horses sufficiently far, from what I saw of the desolate and barren country.[†]

With this view I started on the 28th of August, accompanied by Mr Gill and Bernard Kilroy, with provisions sufficient for three weeks and ten gallons of water, the camel being loaded with about 356 pounds...

[†] Mr Gill: this was S. T. Gill who was to earn fame for his drawings and lithographs of colonial Australia.

we reached a large saltwater lake about ten miles long and five miles broad. The land we were making for we distinctly saw I supposed about twenty-five miles distant. In rounding this lake, which I named Lake Gill, Bernard Kilroy, who was walking ahead of the party, stopped, saying he saw a beautiful bird which he recommended me to shoot to add to the collection.

My gun being loaded with slugs in one barrel and ball in the other, I stopped the camel to get at the shot belt, which I could not get without his laying down.

Whilst Mr Gill was unfastening it I was screwing the ramrod into the wad over the slugs, standing close alongside of the camel. At this moment the camel gave a lurch to one side, and caught his pack in the cock of my gun, which discharged the barrel I was unloading, the contents of which first took off the middle fingers of my right hand between the second and third joints, and entered my left cheek by my lower jaw, knocking out a row of teeth from my upper jaw.

In this dilemma I was fortunate in having two most excellent companions. We were now sixty-five miles from the depot or any water that we knew of, and all the water remaining was about five gallons. With very great reluctance I consented to Bernard Kilroy's entreaty for him to return back and fetch Mr Theatstone and two horses, as I knew part of the country was inhabited by a fierce lot of natives, as they had attacked Mr Gill and myself on my previous excursion. He said he was not afraid. Therefore he left and reached the depot the next morning by about nine o'clock. Having missed the tracks during the night, he could not have walked less than 100 miles from the morning of the accident to the time he reached the depot, having most bravely accomplished his task.

Mr Gill stopped to nurse me and his attention and kindness were not to be surpassed. Considering the distance we were away and the uncertainty of Kilroy's reaching the depot, Mr Gill showed himself to be a brave and steady companion by remaining with me. He has taken several sketches of this country, which will show to those interested how very improbable it is that any stations can be made to the west of Lake Torrens…I did not find a spot where there was any probability of finding a spring. Grass there is none except a little wild oaten grass, which grows in the sand here and there, and that not sufficient to feed a horse.

It is with extreme sorrow I am obliged to terminate the expedition, as the two that were with me, the camel and myself were in excellent working condition; and had it not been for this accident it was my intention to have followed down this low land running to the NNE, and returned by Lake Torrens, a distance of between 300 and 400 miles; and would then have been able to have given a more accurate account, although I am convinced we should not have found one acre of ground to make a station on, judging from the land I have gone over and what I could discern with my eye, there being a sterile sameness throughout.

Had it been earlier in the season and my wounds healed up I should have started again. On Sunday last I returned to the depot, horses, myself and party all completely knocked up.

I remain, yours truly,
J. HORROCKS.

Jackey Jackey

I Turned Round Myself and Cried, 1848

 Jackey Jackey's tale of the tragic end of John Kennedy's Cape York expedition forms one of the most moving narratives in Australian exploration history. It is beautifully and economically told—a riveting piece of literature.

Jackey Jackey, a native of the Hunter Valley, was a born leader who slowly assumed command as the crisis deepened. His account reveals an individual of exceptional resourcefulness and humanity, for he stayed with Kennedy to the very end.

After he was rescued, Jackey Jackey led a relief party to the spot where eight members of the original expedition had been left behind. He should be remembered among the first rank of Australian explorers.

I started with Mr Kennedy from Weymouth Bay for Cape York, on the 13th November, 1848, accompanied by Costigan, Dunn and Luff, leaving eight men at the camp at Weymouth Bay. We went on till we came to a river which empties itself into Weymouth Bay. A little further north we crossed the river; next morning a lot of natives camped on the other side of the river. Mr Kennedy and the rest of us went on a very high hill and came to a flat on the other side and camped there. I went on a good way next day; a horse fell down a creek; the flour we took with us lasted three days; we had much trouble in getting the horse out of the creek; we went on, and came out, and camped on the ridges; we had no water.

Next morning we went on and Luff was taken ill with a very bad knee. We left him behind, and Dunn went back again and brought him on; Luff was riding a horse named Fiddler; then we went on and camped at a little creek; the flour being out this day we commenced eating horse flesh, which Carron gave us when we left Weymouth Bay; as we went on we came on a small river, and saw no blacks there; as we proceeded we gathered nondas, and lived upon them and the meat. We stopped at a little creek and it came on raining, and Costigan shot himself; in putting his saddle under the tarpaulin, a string caught the trigger and the ball went in under the right arm and came out at his back under the shoulder.

We went on this morning all of us, and stopped at another creek in the evening, and the next morning we killed a horse named Browney, smoked him that night and went on next day, taking as much of the horse as we could with us, and went on about a mile and then turned back again to where we killed the horse, because Costigan was very bad and in much pain; we went back again because there was no water; then Mr Kennedy and

I had dinner there, and went on in the afternoon leaving Dunn, Costigan and Luff at the creek.

This was at Pudding-pan Hill, near Shelburne Bay. Mr Kennedy called it Pudding-pan Hill.

We left some horse meat with the three men at Pudding-pan Hill, and carried some with us on a pack horse. Mr Kennedy wanted to make great haste when he left this place, in order to get the doctor to go down to the men that were ill. This was about three weeks after leaving Weymouth Bay. One horse was left with the three men at Pudding-pan Hill, and we (Kennedy and myself) took with us three horses. The three men were to remain there until Mr Kennedy and myself had gone to and returned from Cape York for them. Mr Kennedy told Luff and Dunn when he left them if Costigan died they were to come along the beach till they saw the ship, and then to fire a gun; he told them he would not be long away, so it was not likely they would move from there for some time. They stopped to take care of the man that was shot; we (me and Mr Kennedy) killed a horse for them before we came away.

Having left these three men, we camped that night where there was no water; next morning Mr Kennedy and me went on with the four horses, two pack horses, and two saddle horses; one horse got bogged in a swamp. We tried to get him out all day, but could not; we left him there, and camped at another creek. The next day Mr Kennedy and I went on again, and passed up a ridge very scrubby, and had to turn back again, and went along gullies to get clear of the creek and scrub. Now it rained, and we camped; there were plenty of blacks here, but we did not see them, but plenty of fresh tracks, and camps and smoke.

Next morning we went on and camped at another creek, and on the following morning we continued going on, and camped in the evening close to a scrub; it rained in the night. Next day we went on in the scrub, but could not get through. I cut and cleared away, and it was near sundown before we got through the scrub—there we camped. It was heavy rain next morning, and we went on in the rain, then I changed horses and rode a black colt, to spell the other, and rode him all day, and in the afternoon we got on clear ground, and the horse fell down, me and all; the horse lay upon my right hip.

Here Mr Kennedy got off his horse and moved my horse from my thigh; we stopped there that night, and could not get the horse up; we looked to him in the morning and he was dead; we left him there; we had some horse meat left to eat and went on that day and crossed a little river and camped. The next day we went a good way; Mr Kennedy told me to go up a tree to see a sandy hill somewhere; I went up a tree, and saw a sandy hill a little way down from Port Albany. That day we camped near a swamp; it was a very rainy day.

The next morning we went on, and Mr Kennedy told me we should get round to Port Albany in a day;

we travelled on all day till twelve o'clock (noon), and then we saw Port Albany; then he said, 'There is Port Albany, Jackey—a ship is there—you see that island there,' pointing to Albany Island; this was when we were at the mouth of Escape River.

We stopped there a little while; all the meat was gone; I tried to get some fish but could not; we went on in the afternoon half a mile along the riverside, and met a good lot of blacks, and we camped. The blacks all cried out '*Powad, powad*,' and rubbed their bellies; and we thought they were friendly, and Mr Kennedy gave them fish hooks all round.

Everyone asked me if I had anything to give away, and I said, 'No?' And Mr Kennedy said, 'Give them your knife, Jackey.' This fellow on board was the man I gave the knife to, I am sure of it; I know him well; the black that was shot in the canoe was the most active in urging all the others on to spear Mr Kennedy; I gave the man on board my knife. We went on this day, and I looked behind, and they were getting up their spears, and ran all round the camp which we had left; I told Mr Kennedy that very likely those blackfellows would follow us, and he said, 'No, Jackey, those blacks are very friendly.'

I said to him, 'I know these blackfellows well; they too much speak.'

We went on some two or three miles and camped; I and Mr Kennedy watched them that night, taking it in turns every hour all night; by and by I saw the blackfellows; it was a moonlight night; and I walked up to Mr Kennedy, and said to him, 'There is plenty of blackfellows now.'

This was in the middle of the night; Mr Kennedy told me to get my gun ready; the blacks did not know where we slept, as we did not make a fire; we both sat up all night; after this, daylight came, and I fetched the horses and saddled them; then we went on a good way up the river, and then we sat down a little while, and we saw three blackfellows coming along our track, and they saw us, and one fellow ran back as hard as he could run, and fetched up plenty more, like a flock of sheep almost; I told Mr Kennedy to put the saddles on the two horses and go on, and the blacks came up, and they followed us all the day; all along it was raining, and I now told him to leave the horses and come on without them, that the horses made too much track.

Mr Kennedy was too weak, and would not leave the horses. We went on this day till towards evening, raining hard, and the blacks followed us all the day, some behind, some planted before; in fact, blacks all around following us. Now we went on into a little bit of a scrub, and I told Mr Kennedy to look behind always; sometimes he would do so, and sometimes he would not look behind to look out for the blacks. Then a good many blackfellows came behind in the scrub, and threw plenty of spears, and hit Mr Kennedy in the back first. Mr Kennedy said to me, 'Oh! Jackey, Jackey! shoot 'em, shoot 'em.'

Then I pulled out my gun and fired, and hit one fellow

all over the face with buckshot; he tumbled down, and got up again and again and wheeled right round, and two blackfellows picked him up and carried him away. They went away then a little way, and came back again, throwing spears all around, more than they did before: very large spears. I pulled out the spear at once from Mr Kennedy's back, and cut out the jag with Mr Kennedy's knife; then Mr Kennedy got his gun and snapped, but the gun would not go off.

The blacks sneaked all along by the trees, and speared Mr Kennedy again in the right leg, above the knee a little, and I got speared over the eye, and the blacks were now throwing their spears all ways, never giving over, and shortly again speared Mr Kennedy in the right side; there were large jags to the spears, and I cut them out and put them into my pocket. At the same time we got speared, the horses got speared too, and jumped and bucked all about, and got into the swamp.

I now told Mr Kennedy to sit down, while I looked after the saddle-bags, which I did; and when I came back again, I saw blacks along with Mr Kennedy; I then asked him if he saw the blacks with him, he was stupid with the spear wounds, and said, 'No.' Then I asked, where was his watch? I saw the blacks taking away watch and hat as I was returning to Mr Kennedy; then I carried Mr Kennedy into the scrub. He said, 'Don't carry me a good way,' then Mr Kennedy looked this way, very bad (Jackey rolling his eyes).

I said to him, 'Don't look far away,' as I thought he would be frightened; I asked him often, 'Are you well now?' and he said, 'I don't care for the spear wound in my leg, Jackey, but for the other two spear wounds in my side and back,' and said, 'I am bad inside, Jackey.'

I told him blackfellow always die when he got spear in there (the back); he said, 'I am out of wind, Jackey.' I asked him, 'Mr Kennedy, are you going to leave me?' and he said, 'Yes, my boy, I am going to leave you.' He said, 'I am very bad, Jackey; you take the books, Jackey, to the captain, but not the big ones—the governor will give anything for them.' I then tied up the papers. He then said, 'Jackey, give me paper and I will write.'

I gave him paper and pencil, and he tried to write, and then he fell back and died, and I caught him as he fell back and held him, and I then turned round myself and cried. I was crying a good while until I got well; that was about an hour, and then I buried him; I digged up the ground with a tomahawk, and covered him over with logs, then grass, and my shirt and trousers.

That night I left him near dark; I would go through the scrub, and the blacks threw spears at me, a good many, and I went back again into the scrub; then I went down the creek which runs into Escape River, and I walked along the water in the creek very easy, with my head only above water, to avoid the blacks, and get out of their way; in this way I went half a mile; then I got out of the creek, and got clear of them, and walked on all night nearly, and slept in the bush without a fire.

I went on next morning, and felt very bad, and I spelled for two days; I lived on nothing but salt water; next day I went on and camped one mile away from where I left, and ate one of the pandanus fruits; next morning I went on two miles, and sat down there, and I wanted to spell a little there, and go on; but when I tried to get up, I could not, but fell down again very tired and cramped, and I spelled here two days; then I went on again one mile, and got nothing to eat but one nonda; and I went on that day and camped, and on again next morning, about half a mile, and sat down where there was good water, and remained all day.

On the following morning, I went a good way, went round a great swamp and mangroves, and got a good way by sundown; the next morning I went and saw a very large track of blackfellows; I went clear of the track and of swamp or sandy ground; then I came to a very large river and a large lagoon; plenty of alligators in the lagoon, about ten miles from Port Albany.

I now got into the ridges by sundown, and went up a tree and saw Albany Island; then next morning at four o'clock, I went on as hard as I could go all the way down, over fine clear ground, fine ironbark timber, and plenty of good grass; I went on round the point (this was towards Cape York, north of Albany Island) and went on and followed a creek down, and went on top of the hill, and saw Cape York; I knew it was Cape York, because the sand did not go on further.

I sat down then a good while; I said to myself, this is Port Albany, I believe inside somewhere; Mr Kennedy also told me that the ship was inside, close up to the mainland; I went on a little way, and saw the ship and boat; I met close up here two black gins and a good many piccaninnies; one said to me, '*Powad, powad.*' Then I asked her for eggs, she gave me turtle's eggs, and I gave her a burning glass; she pointed to the ship which I had seen before; I was very frightened of seeing the black men all along here, and when I was on the rock cooeeing, and murry murry glad when the boat came for me.

John Macgillivray

Sir, I Am a Christian, 1848

 Just eight years after Eliza Fraser's experience, Barbara Thomson was shipwrecked and adopted by the Aborigines of Muralag Island, Torres Strait. There she lived as a wife of Boroto until she was 'rescued' four years later by the crew of the HMS *Rattlesnake,* commanded by Captain Owen Stanley. Speaking a mixture of English and the Kowrárega language she told of being well-treated by the Muralag men, if not the women. John MacGillivray, the naturalist on the *Rattlesnake* expedition, recorded her story of life beyond the frontier.

On the day after our arrival at Cape York the vessel from Sydney with our supplies anchored beside us and, besides provisions and stores, we had the additional pleasure of receiving five months' news from home.

On Oct. 16th, a startling incident occurred to break the monotony of our stay. In the afternoon some of our people on shore were surprised to see a young white woman come up to claim their protection from a party of natives from whom she had recently made her escape and who, she thought, would otherwise bring her back. Of course she received every attention, and was taken on board the ship by the first boat, when she told her story, which is briefly as follows.

Her name is Barbara Thomson: she was born at Aberdeen in Scotland and, along with her parents, emigrated to New South Wales. About four years and a half ago she left Moreton Bay with her husband in a small cutter (called the *America*), of which he was owner, for the purpose of picking up some of the oil from the wreck of a whaler, lost on the Bampton Shoal, to which place one of her late crew undertook to guide them...

The man who acted as pilot was unable to find the wreck and, after much quarrelling on board in consequence, and the loss of two men by drowning, and of another who was left upon a small uninhabited island, they made their way up to Torres Strait, where, during a gale of wind, their vessel struck upon a reef on the eastern Prince of Wales Island.

The two remaining men were lost in attempting to swim on shore through the surf, but the woman was afterwards rescued by a party of natives on a turtling excursion, who when the gale subsided swam on board, and supported her on shore between two of their number. One of these blacks, Boroto by name, took possession of the woman as his share of the plunder; she was compelled to live with him, but was well treated by all the men, although many of the women, jealous of the attention shown her, for a long time evinced anything but kindness.

A curious circumstance secured for her the protection of one of the principal men of the tribe, a party from which had been the fortunate means of rescuing her and which she afterwards found to be the Kowrárega, chiefly inhabiting Múralug, or the western Prince of Wales Island. This person, named Piaquai, acting upon the belief (universal throughout Australia and the islands of Torres Strait so far as hitherto known) that white people are the ghosts of the Aborigines, fancied that in the stranger he recognised a long-lost daughter of the name of Gi(a)om, and at once admitted her to the relationship which he thought had formerly subsisted between them; she was immediately acknowledged by the whole tribe as one of themselves, thus ensuring an extensive connection in relatives of all denominations.

From the headquarters of the tribe, with which Gi'om thus became associated, being upon an island which all vessels passing through Torres Strait from the eastward must approach within two or three miles, she had the mortification of seeing from twenty to thirty or more ships go through every summer without anchoring in the neighbourhood, so as to afford the slightest opportunity of making her escape. Last year she heard of our two vessels (described as two war canoes, a big and a little one) being at Cape York—only twenty miles distant—from some of the tribe who had communicated with us and been well treated, but they would not take her over, and even watched her more narrowly than before. On our second and present visit, however, which the Cape York people immediately announced by smoke signals to their friends in Múralug, she was successful in persuading some of her more immediate friends to bring her across to the mainland within a short distance of where the vessels lay.

The blacks were credulous enough to believe that 'as she had been so long with them, and had been so well treated, she did not intend to leave them—only she felt a strong desire to see the white people once more and shake hands with them'; adding that she would be certain to procure some axes, knives, tobacco, and other much prized articles. This appeal to their cupidity decided the question at once.

After landing at the sandy bay on the western side of Cape York, she hurried across to Evans Bay as quickly as her lameness would allow, fearful that the blacks might change their mind; and well it was that she did so, as a small party of men followed to detain her, but arrived too late. Three of these people were brought on board at her own request and, as they had been instrumental in saving her from the wreck, they were presented with an axe apiece, and other presents.

Upon being asked by Captain Stanley whether she really preferred remaining with us to accompanying the natives back to their island, as she would be allowed her free choice in the matter, she was so much agitated as to find difficulty in expressing her thankfulness, making use of scraps of English alternately with the Kowrárega language, and then, suddenly awaking to the recollection that she was not understood, the poor creature blushed all over, and with downcast eyes beat her forehead with her hand, as if to assist in collecting her scattered thoughts.

At length, after a pause, she found words to say, 'Sir, I am a Christian, and would rather go back to my own friends.'

At the same time, it was remarked by everyone that she had not lost the feelings of womanly modesty—even after having lived so long among naked blacks, she seemed acutely to feel the singularity of her position—dressed only in a couple of shirts, in the midst of a crowd of her own countrymen.

When first seen on shore our new shipmate presented so dirty and wretched an appearance that some people who were out shooting at first mistook her for a gin, and were passing by without taking further notice, when she called out to them in English, 'I am a white woman, why do you leave me?' With the exception of a narrow fringe of leaves in front, she wore no clothing, and her skin was tanned and blistered with the sun, and showed the marks of several large burns which had been received from sleeping too near the fire on cold nights; besides, she was suffering from ophthalmia, which had previously deprived her of the sight of one eye.[†] But good living,

---

[†] Although Patrick White based his novel *A Fringe of Leaves* on the story of Eliza Fraser, it is Barbara Thomson who gave him his title.

and every comfort (for Captain Stanley kindly provided her with a cabin and a seat at his table), combined with medical attention, very soon restored her health, and she was eventually handed over to her parents in Sydney in excellent condition.

Although perfectly illiterate, Mrs Thomson had made good use of her powers of observation, and evinced much shrewdness in her remarks upon various subjects connected with her residence among the blacks, joined to great willingness to communicate any information which she possessed...

Several hundred words of the Kowrárega language, and a portion of its grammar, were also obtained from time to time, and most of these were subsequently verified. And, although she did not understand the language spoken at Cape York, yet, as some of the Gúdang people there knew the Kowrárega, through its medium I was usually able to make myself tolerably well understood, and thus obtain an explanation of some matters which had formerly puzzled me, and correct various errors into which I had fallen. It was well, too, that I took an early opportunity of procuring these words, for my informant afterwards forgot much of her lately acquired language, and her value as an authority on that subject gradually diminished.

Gi'om was evidently a great favourite with the blacks, and hardly a day passed on which she was not obliged to hold a levee in her cabin for the reception of friends from the shore, while other visitors, less favoured, were content to talk to her through the port. They occasionally brought presents of fish and turtle, but always expected an equivalent of some kind.

Her friend Boroto, the nature of the intimacy with whom was not at first understood, after in vain attempting by smooth words and fair promises to induce her to go back to live with him, left the ship in a rage, and we were not sorry to get rid of so impudent and troublesome a visitor as he had become. Previous to leaving, he had threatened that, should he or any of his friends ever catch his faithless spouse on shore, they would take off her head to carry back with them to Múralug; and so likely to be fulfilled did she consider this threat, being in perfect accordance with their customs, that she never afterwards ventured on shore at Cape York.

John McDouall Stuart

What He Imagined I Was, 1858–60

 Stuart was an independent, even lonely man with a fierce pride. He had a reputation as a hard drinker but achieved great things. His lasting innovation was to avoid large overland expeditions in favour of exploration by small, mobile parties. Stuart's great ambition was to cross the continent from south to north.

We first meet him here at a rather comic moment in 1858 in the vicinity of Lake Torrens when he asks directions from a solitary Aboriginal hunter. Then we join him two years later at his celebrations upon reaching the geographic centre of Australia.

Thursday, 24th June, Sandhills—At 8.30 we left on a course of 340°, commencing with about two miles of rather heavy sandhills…At twelve miles changed our course to 79° to examine a gum creek (Yarraout), which we ran down for water, but did not obtain it before four miles, when we found a small hole of rainwater. This creek seems to be a hunting ground of the natives, as we saw a great many summer wurleys on its banks.[†]

[†] Wurley: Aboriginal shelter.

They had evidently been here today, for a little above where we first struck the creek we saw some smoke, but on following it up we found they had gone; mostly likely they had seen us and run away. The latter part of our journey today was over a stony plain, bounded on the west by the stony tableland with the sandhills on the top. All this country seems to have been under water, and is mostly likely the bed of Lake Torrens, or Captain Sturt's inland sea. In travelling over the plains, one is reminded of going over a rough, gravelly beach; the stones are all rounded and smooth. Distance today, thirty miles.

Friday, 25th June, Yarraout Gum Creek—...My doubt of the blackfellow's knowledge of the country is now confirmed; he seems to be quite lost and knows nothing of the country, except what he has heard other blacks relate; he is quite bewildered and points all round when I ask him the direction of Wingillpin. I have determined to push into the westward, keeping a little north of west. Bearing 292° for five miles, sandhills; thence 327° to a table-hill nine miles. Camped without water...

We came across some natives who kept a long distance off. I sent our black up to them to ask in which direction Wingillpin lay. They pointed to the course I was then steering, and said, 'Five sleeps.' They would not come near to us. About three-quarters of an hour afterwards I came suddenly upon another native who was hunting in the sandhills. My attention being engaged in keeping the bearing, I did not observe him until he moved, but I pulled up at once, lest he should run away, and called to him. What he imagined I was I do not know; but when he turned round and saw me I never beheld a finer picture of astonishment and fear. He was a fine muscular fellow, about six feet in height, and stood as if riveted to the spot, with his mouth wide open, and his eyes staring.

I sent our black forward to speak with him, but omitted to tell him to dismount. The terrified native remained motionless, allowing our black to ride within a few yards of him, when, in an instant, he threw down his waddies, and jumped up into a mulga bush as high as he could, one foot being about three feet from the ground, and the other about two feet higher, and kept waving us off with his hand as we advanced. I expected every moment to see the bush break with his weight. When close under the bush, I told our black to inquire if he were a Wingillpin native.

He was so frightened he could not utter a word, and trembled from head to foot. We then asked him where Wingillpin was. He mustered courage to let go one hand and, emphatically snapping his fingers in a north-west direction, again waved us off. I take this emphatic snapping of his fingers to mean a long distance. Probably this Wingillpin may be Cooper's Creek. We then left him, and proceeded on our way through the sandhills...Distance today, twenty-four miles.

Sunday, 22nd April [1860], Small Gum Creek, under

John McDouall Stuart

Mount Stuart, Centre of Australia—Today I find from my observations of the sun, 111° 00' 30", that I am now camped in the centre of Australia.

William Wills

My Pulse Is at Forty-Eight, 1861

 William Wills' father was heartbroken by the failure of his son to return from the tragically incompetent expedition in which he and Robert O'Hara Burke, together with John King and Charles Gray, became the first men to cross the continent from south to north.

Two years after their deaths, Wills senior published a book stubbornly titled *A Successful Exploration through the Interior of Australia.* In it he lovingly describes the future explorer as his friend and equal. I wonder how this very un-Victorian father felt as he read these entries from his son's diary? The young Wills reserved the last of his strength to write a farewell letter to his father.

Stranded at Cooper Creek after the depot party left for Menindie on the very day the explorers struggled back into camp, Wills describes dying of starvation on a full stomach. But was it the nardoo or the greens he was eating that decided his fate? Gray was already dead; Burke and King had gone along the creek to find the Aborigines who were their only hope of survival. Back in Melbourne, Wills senior was desperately trying to raise the alarm to organise a rescue.

Monday, 3rd June 1861—Started at seven o'clock, and keeping on the south bank of the creek was rather encouraged at about three miles by the sound of numerous crows ahead; presently fancied I could see smoke, and was shortly afterwards set at my ease by hearing a cooee from Pitchery, who stood on the opposite bank, and directed me round the lower end of the waterhole, continually repeating his assurance of abundance of fish and bread.

Having with some considerable difficulty managed to ascend the sandy path that led to the camp, I was conducted by the chief to a fire where a large pile of fish were just being cooked in the most approved style. These I imagined to be for the general consumption of the half-dozen natives gathered around, but it turned out that they had already had their breakfast. I was expected to dispose of this lot—a task which, to my own astonishment, I soon accomplished, keeping two or three blacks pretty steadily at work extracting the bones for me.

The fish being disposed of, next came a supply of nardoo cake and water until I was so full as to be unable to eat any more; when Pitchery, allowing me a short time to recover myself, fetched a large bowl of the raw nardoo flour mixed to a thin paste, a most insinuating article, and one that they appear to esteem a great delicacy.[†] I was then invited to stop the night there, but this I declined, and

---

[†] Nardoo is the spore bundle of an aquatic fern which resembles a four-leafed clover.

proceeded on my way home.

Tuesday, 4th June 1861—Started for the blacks' camp intending to test the practicability of living with them, and to see what I could learn as to their ways and manners...

Thursday, 6th June 1861—Returned to our own camp: found that Mr Burke and King had been well supplied with fish by the blacks. Made preparation for shifting our camp nearer theirs on the morrow...

Friday, 7th June 1861—Started in the afternoon for the blacks' camp with such things as we could take; found ourselves all very weak in spite of the abundant supply of fish that we have lately had. I, myself, could scarcely get along, although carrying the lightest swag, only about thirty pounds. Found that the blacks had decamped, so determined on proceeding tomorrow up to the next camp, near the nardoo field.

Saturday, 8th June 1861—With the greatest fatigue and difficulty we reached the nardoo camp. No blacks, greatly to our disappointment; took possession of their best mia-mia and rested for the remainder of the day.

Sunday, 9th June 1861—King and I proceeded to collect nardoo, leaving Mr Burke at home.

Monday, 10th June 1861—Mr Burke and King collecting nardoo; self at home too weak to go out; was fortunate enough to shoot a crow...

Tuesday, 11th June 1861—King out for nardoo; Mr Burke up the creek to look for the blacks.

Wednesday, 12th June 1861—King out collecting

nardoo; Mr Burke and I at home pounding and cleaning. I still feel myself, if anything, weaker in the legs, although the nardoo appears to be more thoroughly digested.

Saturday, 15th June 1861—King out for nardoo; brought in a fine supply. Mr Burke and I pounding and cleaning; he finds himself getting very weak, and I am not a bit stronger.

I have determined on beginning to chew tobacco and eat less nardoo, in hopes that it may induce some change in the system. I have never yet recovered from the constipation, the effect of which continues to be exceedingly painful.

Sunday, 16th June 1861—...We finished up the remains of the camel Rajah yesterday, for dinner; King was fortunate enough to shoot a crow this morning...

Thursday, 20th June 1861—...I am completely reduced by the effects of the cold and starvation. King gone out for nardoo; Mr Burke at home pounding seed; he finds himself getting very weak in the legs. King holds out by far the best; the food seems to agree with him pretty well.

Finding the sun come out pretty warm towards noon, I took a sponging all over; but it seemed to do little good beyond the cleaning effects, for my weakness is so great that I could not do it with proper expedition.

I cannot understand this nardoo at all—it certainly will not agree with me in any form; we are now reduced to it alone, and we manage to consume from four to five pounds per day between us; it appears to be quite indigestible, and cannot possibly be sufficiently nutritious to sustain life by itself.

Friday, 21st June 1861—…I feel much weaker than ever and can scarcely crawl out of the mia-mia. Unless relief comes in some form or other, I cannot possibly last more than a fortnight.

It is a great consolation, at least, in this position of ours, to know that we have done all we could, and that our deaths will rather be the result of the mismanagement of others than of any rash acts of our own. Had we come to grief elsewhere, we could only have blamed ourselves; but here we are returned to Cooper's Creek, where we had every reason to look for provisions and clothing; and yet we have to die of starvation, in spite of the explicit instructions given by Mr Burke: 'That the depot party should await our return'; and the strong recommendation to the committee 'that we should be followed up by a party from Menindie'…

Saturday, 22nd June 1861—…Mr Burke and King out for nardoo; the former returned much fatigued. I am so weak today as to be unable to get on my feet…

Monday, 24th June 1861—A fearful night. At about an hour before sunset, a southerly gale sprung up and continued throughout the greater portion of the night; the cold was intense, and it seemed as if one would be shrivelled up…

King went out for nardoo in spite of the wind, and came in with a good load; but he himself terribly cut up.

He says that he can no longer keep up the work and, as he and Mr Burke are both getting rapidly weaker, we have but a slight chance of anything but starvation, unless we can get hold of some blacks...

26th—Mr Burke and King remain at home cleaning and pounding seed; they are both getting weaker every day; the cold plays the deuce with us, from the small amount of clothing we have: my wardrobe consists of a wide-awake, a merino shirt, a regatta shirt without sleeves, the remains of a pair of flannel trousers, two pairs of socks in rags, and a waistcoat, of which I have managed to keep the pockets together.[†] The others are no better off. Besides these, we have between us, for bedding, two small camel pads, some horse-hair, two or three little bits of rag, and pieces of oilcloth saved from the fire.

Wednesday, 27th June 1861—...Mr Burke and King are preparing to go up the creek in search of the blacks. They will leave me some nardoo, wood and water, with which I must do the best I can until they return. *I think this is almost our only chance.* I feel myself, if anything, rather better, but I cannot say stronger: the nardoo is beginning to agree better with me; but without some change I see little chance for any of us. They have both shown great hesitation and reluctance with regard to leaving me, and have repeatedly desired my candid opinion in the matter. I could only repeat, however, that

---

[†] Wide-awake: a felt hat.

I considered it our only chance, for I could not last long on the nardoo, even if a supply could be kept up…

Friday, 29th June 1861—…Burke suffers greatly from the cold and is getting extremely weak; he and King start tomorrow up the creek to look for the blacks; it is the only chance we have of being saved from starvation. I am weaker than ever, although I have a good appetite and relish the nardoo much; but it seems to give us no nutriment, and the birds here are so shy as not to be got at. Even if we got a good supply of fish, I doubt whether we could do much work on them and the nardoo alone.

Nothing now but the greatest good luck can save any of us; and as for myself I may live four or five days if the weather continues warm. My pulse is at forty-eight, and very weak, and my legs and arms are nearly skin and bone. I can only look out, like Mr Micawber, 'for something to turn up'.[†] Starvation on nardoo is by no means very unpleasant, but for the weakness one feels, and the utter inability to move one's self; for as far as appetite is concerned it gives the greatest satisfaction. Certainly fat and sugar would be more to one's taste; in fact those seem to me to be the great stand-by for one in this extraordinary continent: not that I mean to depreciate the farinaceous food, but the want of sugar and fat in all

---

[†] Mr Micawber: the incurable optimist from Dickens' *David Copperfield* who, after many failed schemes, migrated to Australia and made his fortune at last.

substances obtainable here is so great that they become almost valueless to us as articles of food, without the addition of something else.[†]

W. J. WILLS

[†] Farinaceons: containing starch, a natural carbohydrate substance.

John King

 The Burke and Wills expedition had set out to discover ' if there really existed within their great continent a Sahara...great lakes... or watered plains which might tempt men to build new cities'. The expedition foundered, near the centre of the continent, in good if dry country, on the ignorance and prejudice of its leader Burke. He feared the Aborigines, and the constant use of his revolver in turn inspired fear in them.

John King was a young Irishman, an ex-soldier who had served in India and came to Australia specifically to join the expedition. As the sole survivor, cared for by the Aborigines, King is a fascinating figure. He was barely twenty when the relief party found him 'half-demented by starvation and loneliness'. Here King tells us what happened after he and Burke left Wills to search for the Aborigines. This account is taken from the evidence he presented to the subsequent royal commission into the disaster.

John King

Mr Wills having returned, it was decided to go up the creek and live with the natives if possible, as Mr Wills thought we should have but little difficulty in obtaining provisions from them if we camped on the opposite side of the creek to them. He said he knew where they were gone, so we packed up and started. Coming to the gunyahs where we expected to have found them, we were disappointed, and seeing a nardoo field close by halted, intending to make it our camp.

For some time we were employed gathering nardoo, and laying up a supply. Mr Wills and I used to collect and carry home a bag each day, and Mr Burke generally pounded sufficient for our dinner during our absence; but Mr Wills found himself getting very weak, and was shortly unable to go out to gather nardoo as before, or even strong enough to pound it, so that in a few days he became almost helpless...

Mr Burke now proposed that I should gather as much as possible in three days, and that with this supply we should go in search of the natives—a plan which had been urged upon us by Mr Wills as the only chance of saving him and ourselves as well, as he clearly saw that I was no longer able to collect sufficient for our wants.

Having collected the seed as proposed, and having pounded sufficient to last Mr Wills for eight days, and two days for ourselves, we placed water and firewood within his reach and started; before leaving him, however,

Mr Burke asked him whether he still wished it, as under no other circumstance would he leave him, and Mr Wills again said that he looked on it as our only chance. He then gave Mr Burke a letter and his watch for his father, and we buried the remainder of the field-books near the gunyah. Mr Wills said that, in case of my surviving Mr Burke, he hoped that I would carry out his last wishes, in giving the watch and letter to his father.

In travelling the first day, Mr Burke seemed very weak, and complained of great pain in his legs and back. On the second day he seemed to be better, and said that he thought he was getting stronger, but on starting did not go two miles before he said he could go no further. I persisted in his trying to go on, and managed to get him along several times, until I saw that he was almost knocked up, when he said he could not carry his swag, and threw all he had away. I also reduced mine, taking nothing but a gun and some powder and shot, and a small pouch and some matches.

In starting again, we did not go far before Mr Burke said we should halt for the night; but as the place was close to a large sheet of water and exposed to the wind, I prevailed on him to go a little further, to the next reach of water, where we camped.

We searched about and found a few small patches of nardoo, which I collected and pounded, and with a crow, which I shot, made a good evening's meal. From the time we halted Mr Burke seemed to be getting worse, although he ate his supper; he said he felt convinced he could not last many hours, and gave me his watch, which he said belonged to the committee, and a pocketbook to give to Sir William Stawell, and in which he wrote some notes.[†] He then said to me, 'I hope you will remain with me here till I am quite dead—it is a comfort to know that someone is by; but, when I am dying, it is my wish that you should place the pistol in my right hand, and that you leave me unburied as I lie.'

That night he spoke very little, and the following morning I found him speechless, or nearly so, and about eight o'clock he expired. I remained a few hours there, but as I saw there was no use in remaining longer I went up the creek in search of the natives. I felt very lonely, and at night usually slept in deserted wurleys belonging to the natives.

Two days after leaving the spot where Mr Burke died, I found some gunyahs where the natives had deposited a bag of nardoo, sufficient to last me a fortnight, and three bundles containing various articles. I also shot a crow that evening; but was in great dread that the natives would come and deprive me of the nardoo.

I remained there two days to recover my strength, and then returned to Mr Wills. I took back three crows; but found him lying dead in his gunyah, and the natives had been there and had taken away some of his clothes. I buried the corpse with sand and remained there some days

---

[†] Sir William Stawell: chairman of the Exploration Fund Committee.

but, finding that my stock of nardoo was running short, and as I was unable to gather it, I tracked the natives who had been to the camp by their footprints in the sand, and went some distance down the creek shooting crows and hawks on the road.

The natives, hearing the report of the gun, came to meet me, and took me with them to their camp, giving me nardoo and fish; they took the birds I had shot and cooked them for me, and afterwards showed me a gunyah where I was to sleep with three of the single men. The following morning they commenced talking to me, and putting one finger on the ground and covering it with sand, at the same time pointing up the creek saying 'whitefellow', which I understood to mean that one white man was dead.

From this I knew that they were the tribe who had taken Mr Wills's clothes. They then asked me where the third white man was, and I also made the sign of putting two fingers on the ground and covering them with sand, at the same time pointing up the creek. They appeared to feel great compassion for me when they understood that I was alone on the creek, and gave me plenty to eat.

After being four days with them, I saw that they were becoming tired of me, and they made signs that they were going up the creek and that I had better go downwards; but I pretended not to understand them. The same day they shifted camp and I followed them, and on reaching their camp I shot some crows, which pleased them so much that they made me a break-wind in the centre of their camp, and came and sat round me until such time as the crows were cooked, when they assisted me to eat them.

The same day one of the women, to whom I had given part of a crow, came and gave me a ball of nardoo, saying that she would give me more only she had such a sore arm that she was unable to pound. She showed me a sore on her arm, and the thought struck me that I would boil some water in the billy and wash her arm with a sponge. During the operation, the whole tribe sat round and were muttering one to another. Her husband sat down by her side, and she was crying all the time. After I had washed it, I touched it with some nitrate of silver, when she began to yell, and ran off, crying out, '*Mokow! Mokow!*' (Fire! Fire!)

From this time, she and her husband used to give me a small quantity of nardoo both night and morning, and whenever the tribe was about going on a fishing excursion he used to give me notice to go with them. They also used to assist me in making a wurley or break-wind whenever they shifted camp. I generally shot a crow or a hawk, and gave it to them in return for these little services.

Every four or five days the tribe would surround me and ask whether I intended going up or down the creek; at last I made them understand that if they went up I should go up the creek, and if they went down I should also go down; and from this time they seemed to look upon me as one of themselves, and supplied me with fish and nardoo regularly. They were very anxious, however, to know where Mr Burke lay, and one day, when we were fishing in the waterholes close by, I took them to the spot. On seeing his remains, the whole party wept bitterly, and covered them with bushes.

After this, they were much kinder to me than before, and I always told them that the white men would be here before two moons; and in the evening when they came with nardoo and fish they used to talk about the 'whitefellows' coming, at the same time pointing to the moon. I also told them they would receive many presents, and they constantly asked me for tomahawks, called by them *bomay ko*. From this time to when the relief party arrived, a period of about a month, they treated me with uniform kindness, and looked upon me as one of themselves.

Alfred Howitt

Our Black Friends, 1861

 It was a search party led by Alfred Howitt, explorer, magistrate, geologist and ethnographer, which finally located John King. Howitt enjoyed the company of Aborigines and was intrigued by their culture. They in turn esteemed and trusted him. If Howitt had led the great expedition in place of the bellicose Burke, how different would have been the outcome.

September 15th—...I crossed at a neck of sand, and at a little distance again came on the track of a camel going up the creek; at the same time I found a native, who began to gesticulate in a very excited manner, and to point down the creek, bawling out, '*Gow, gow!*' as loud as he could. When I went towards him he ran away, and finding it impossible to get him to come to me I turned back to follow a camel track, and to look after my party. The track was visible in sandy places, and was evidently the same I had seen for the last two days. I also found horse traces in places, but very old.

Crossing the creek, I cut our track and rode after the party. In doing so I came upon three pounds of tobacco, which had lain where I saw it for some time. This, together with a knife-handle, fresh horse tracks and the camel track going eastward, puzzled me extremely, and led me into a hundred conjectures. At the lower end of the large reach of water before mentioned, I met Sandy and Frank looking for me, with the intelligence that King, the only survivor of Mr Burke's party, had been found.

A little further on I found the party halted, and immediately went across to the blacks' wurleys, where I found King sitting in a hut which the natives had made for him. He presented a melancholy appearance—wasted to a shadow, and hardly to be distinguished as a civilised being but by the remnants of clothes upon him. He seemed exceedingly weak, and I found it occasionally difficult to follow what he said. The natives were all gathered round, seated on the ground, looking with a most gratified and delighted expression...

September 18th—Left camp this morning with Messrs Brahe, Welsh, Wheeler and King to perform a melancholy duty, which has weighed on my mind ever since we have encamped here, and which I have only put off until King should be well enough to accompany us. We proceeded down the creek for seven miles, crossing a branch running to the southward, and followed a native track leading to that part of the creek where Mr Burke, Mr Wills and King encamped after their unsuccessful attempt to reach Mount Hopeless and the northern settlements of South Australia, and where poor Wills died.

We found the two gunyahs situated on a sandbank between two waterholes and about a mile from the flat where they procured nardoo seed, on which they managed to exist so long. Poor Wills's remains we found lying in the wurley in which he died, and where King, after his return from seeking for the natives, had buried him with sand and rushes. We carefully collected the remains and interred them where they lay; and, not having a prayer-book, I read chap. xv of 1 Cor., that we might at least feel a melancholy satisfaction in having shown the last respect to his remains. We heaped sand over the grave, and laid branches upon it, that the natives might understand by their own tokens not to disturb the last repose of a fellow being. I cut the following inscription on a tree close by, to mark the spot:

```
W. J. WILLS,
    V. Yds.
W.N.W.
A. H.
```

The fieldbooks, a notebook belonging to Mr Burke, various small articles lying about, of no value in themselves but now invested with a deep interest from the circumstances connected with them, and some of the nardoo seed on which they had subsisted, with the small wooden trough in which it had been cleaned, I have now in my possession...

September 21st—Finding that it would not be prudent for King to go out for two or three days, I could no longer defer making a search for the spot where Mr Burke died, and with such directions as King could give I went up to the creek this morning with Messrs Brahe, Welsh, Wheeler and Aitkin. We searched the creek upwards for eight miles, and at length, strange to say, found the remains of Mr Burke lying among tall plants under a clump of box-trees, within two hundred yards of our last camp, and not thirty paces from our track. It was still more extraordinary that three or four of the party and the two black boys had been close to the spot without noticing it.

The bones were entire, with the exception of the hands and feet; and the body had been removed from the spot where it first lay, and where the natives had placed branches over it, to about five paces' distance. I found the revolver which Mr Burke held in his hand when he expired partly covered with leaves and earth, and corroded with rust. It was loaded and capped. We dug a grave close to the spot, and interred the remains wrapped in the Union Jack—the most fitting covering in which the bones of a brave but unfortunate man could take their last rest. On a box-tree, at the head of the grave, the following inscription is cut in a similar manner to the above:

```
R. O'H. B.
21 | 9 | 61
A. H.
```

Alfred Howitt

September 23rd—Went down the creek today in search of the natives...I could not think of leaving without showing them that we could appreciate and reward the kindness they had shown to Burke's party and particularly to King...Passed the first feeder of Strzelecki's Creek, going to the southward, and at a large reach of water below found the natives camped.

They made a great commotion when we rode up, but seemed very friendly. I unpacked my blanket, and took out specimens of the things I intended giving them—a tomahawk, a knife, beads, a looking-glass, comb and flour and sugar. The tomahawk was the great object of attraction, after that the knife, but I think the looking-glass surprised them most. On seeing their faces reflected, some seemed dazzled, others opened their eyes like saucers and made a rattling noise with their tongues expressive of wonder. We had quite a friendly palaver, and my watch amused them immensely. I made them understand that they were to bring the whole tribe up next morning to our camp to receive their presents, and we parted the best of friends.

September 24th—This morning, about ten o'clock, our black friends appeared in a long procession, men, women and children or, as they here also call them, piccaninnies; and at a mile distance they commenced bawling at the top of their voices as usual. When collected all together on a little flat, just below our camp, they must have numbered between thirty and forty, and the uproar was deafening.

With the aid of King, I at last got them all seated

before me and distributed the presents—tomahawks, knives, necklaces, looking-glasses, combs—amongst them. I think no people were ever so happy before, and it was very interesting to see how they pointed out one or another whom they thought might be overlooked. The piccaninnies were brought forward by their parents to have red ribbon tied round their dirty little heads. An old woman, Carrawaw, who had been particularly kind to King, was loaded with things.

I then divided fifty pounds of sugar between them, each one taking his share in a Union-Jack pocket-handkerchief, which they were very proud of. The sugar soon found its way into their mouths; the flour, fifty pounds of which I gave them, they at once called 'whitefellow nardoo', and explained that they understood that these things were given to them for having fed King. Some old clothes were then put on some of the men and women, and the affair ended in several of our party and several of the blackfellows having an impromptu 'corroboree', to the intense delight of the natives, and I must say, very much to our amusement.

They left, making signs expressive of friendship, carrying their presents with them. The men all wore a net girdle; and of the women some wore one of leaves, others of feathers. I feel confident that we have left the best impression behind us, and that the 'whitefellows', as they have already learned to call us, will be looked on henceforth as friends, and that, in case of emergency, anyone will receive the kindest treatment at their hands.

Georg Neumayer

Storm on Kosciusko, 1862

 The exploration of the Australian Alps seems inextricably linked with Germans and Poles: Lhotsky, Strzelecki, Neumayer and von Guérard. Georg Balthasar von Neumayer was a German-born scientist with a passion for terrestrial magnetism, hydrography and meteorology. He came to Australia in the 1850s, established an observatory in Melbourne and set about conducting a magnetic survey of Victoria. His account of his visit to the summit of Mt Kosciusko in the late spring of 1862, in the company of the artist Eugène von Guérard, provides a terrifying example of Australia's fickle alpine weather. Von Guérard went on to paint one of his most memorable works from the view he obtained on that dramatic November day.

It was a day which Edward Brinkmann, assistant to Neumayer, would certainly never have forgotten. In the storm that blew across the mountain he became separated from the party and was given up for dead. Neumayer continued on with his magnetic survey and three weeks later the expedition, having travelled hundreds of kilometres, was near Albury.

Thick fog in the valley on the morning of the 18th but sky clear. Preparing everything for the ascent of Mt Kosciusko. Left three horses at Groggan's and took only Tommy with me packed with all the blankets and rations...Descended a steep incline towards the valley of the Leather Jacket Creek (3184) where we arrived at 10.30 a.m.; temp. of the creek 56.7°; that of the air 84.5°.[†] Left the place and ascended the steep banks of the creek under much difficulty although the horse behaved admirably. Continued ascending till we arrived at the region of dead timber (4663). The weather was quite calm, but the sky very threatening.

About this time all of our party except myself felt very ill so that we were obliged to stop here for some time and take some brandy and water, which enabled them better to resist the effects of heat and fatigue. Crossed an extensive flat at 1.46 p.m., then after a continual ascent came to the upper limit of dwarf timber (6254) (*Eucalyptus*), and resolved to pitch our tents...

We arrived at this spot at 5 p.m.; it must be mentioned, however, that the ascent would not have taken all this time had we been able to keep up a proper pace, for with the exception of the crossing of the Leather Jacket the ascent of Mt Kosciusko from the Victorian side is an easy one when compared with that of some of the equally high mountains in other parts of the world; but, throughout, our progress was retarded partly by the necessity of

---

[†] Numbers in parentheses indicate feet above sea level.

clearing a path, and the illness of the men. The vegetation near the camping place reminds one very much of that of the Alps except that the strange look of the dwarf gum trees introduces rather a new feature...

The temp. of the boiling point 200.27°; 9 p.m., few drops of rain but calm and overcast. An immense number of Bogong moths about the camp. By 10 p.m. a strong breeze rose from the north, which continued in puffs nearly throughout the night. The flapping of the tent although very annoying did not seriously interfere with our sound rest.

November 19th at 5 a.m. ...Packed some of the magnetic instruments on Tommy and left our camp at 7 a.m. and after crossing some extensive snowfields arrived at what I named the Pinnacle Hill (7038) at 8 a.m. Resolved to make some observations on terrestrial magnetism and placed the theodolite on a hill, composed of granite boulders; the weather, however, becoming unsettled and the wind being still strong from the north, I deferred these observations until my return.

The instruments were consequently packed up again and as it evidently would be extremely difficult to take the horse any farther on, I ordered Edward to secure him properly and provide him with food for the time of our absence, and then started for what we supposed, and subsequently found to be, the highest point of Mt Kosciusko...A few hundred feet higher up and we reached the watershed between the Murray and Snowy Rivers, the

one flowing towards the Indian, the other into the Pacific
Ocean. Passing over some snowfields of considerable
extent, we arrived at the summit (7176) at 11 a.m.; temp.
54.5°.

As the wind blew very strong from the north and rain
fell occasionally in showers, I gave Edward my maps to
put under shelter during the observations, and I hurried
them as much as possible in order that we might yet
have time to ascend the Snowy Peak, another point of
Mt Kosciusko, which from its being thickly covered
with snow has frequently been believed to be its highest
point. Descended into a flat and made a short halt for the
purpose of taking dinner, during which I learned that my
friend M. de Guérard celebrated his fiftieth birthday on
this very day and we accordingly drank his health.

All at once Edward recollected that he had forgotten to
bring my maps with him on leaving the last hill; not much
importance was attached to this at the time, as I thought
it an easy matter to go and fetch them on our return. At
1 p.m. we reached the Snowy Peak (7140), but the wind
was so very strong and the granite boulders, of which
the summit is composed, were so piled up that I did not
think it prudent to take the barometers to the top and
accordingly mounted them some forty feet lower down.
Temp. of boiling point 198.62°.

M. de Guérard, meanwhile, had seated himself
on the summit, which affords a beautiful view of the
mountainous country of New South Wales and Victoria,

as well as the plains of the Murray River, and was taking a sketch of the scenery when, just as I was completing my observations, he called out that it appeared to him a heavy storm was approaching from the New South Wales side. It was apparent from the barometrical readings that the pressure of air was rapidly decreasing, and on ascending to the top I became convinced there was no time to be lost and that we must hasten our return to camp as much as possible…

Left the Snowy Peak at 2.25 p.m. When we reached the snowfields at the foot of the summit, I told Edward to run up and fetch the maps he had forgotten and advised him to take our dog Hector with him. He had scarcely quitted our party five minutes when a terrific gale set in from west and the whole top of the mount was enveloped in dense clouds, the rain falling in torrents. Seeing the danger he was exposed to from the state of the weather, of becoming separated from our party, I cried out to him in order to recall him, but unfortunately this had the effect only of recalling the dog and thus leaving Edward to his own resources.

It was a very difficult task indeed to find our way against wind and weather but, the watershed once crossed, we could scarcely fail to strike the camp, provided only we maintained ordinary presence of mind. I entertained the hope that perhaps Edward would succeed in making his way to the little lake above mentioned, but as the fog was so dense that we could hardly see each other and had to steer by the compass and the terrain, we ourselves could not make this lake and it was not till about half an hour later, on the weather clearing up for a moment, that we perceived we had passed it.

The roaring of the wind was at this time so loud that it was by no means an easy matter to communicate with each other, and thus it happened that another of our party, Weston, dropped off and could not be found.

Another difficulty now was to find Pinnacle Hill that we might relieve the poor horse and fetch the instruments, and at times the attempt appeared almost hopeless, the more so from the chilly state of the atmosphere. Mr Twynham, now perfectly exhausted, became quite stiff and unable to move. By great good fortune, however, M. de Guérard and myself, dragging him between us through fog and mist, hit upon the very spot where horse and instruments had been left in the morning.

I had now to pack the horse—by no means an easy task as neither of my companions was able to assist me, and the animal, terrified by the storm, had become entangled in the rope by which he was tethered...After immense difficulties, it being now nearly dark, M. de Guérard and I—Mr Twynham had been lost a short time before—reached the camp by eight o'clock. We found it in a terrible state, everything wet through and torn. After fastening the horse and putting things a little in order we went back for Mr Twynham, who could hardly be more than half a mile from us, and were fortunate enough to recover him. Had to carry him as he was in a perfectly helpless state.

We were now most anxious to light a fire but, as Edward had the matchbox with him and we had but few left, it was no easy thing; but after an hour and a half we succeeded in kindling a fire, which was soon blown into a good blaze by the terrific galenow raging, the roaring of the wind interrupted occasionally only by the thunder...

My delight can scarcely be imagined when the barking of the dog announced the return of one of our missing men. It was Weston, who said that, attracted by the light of our fire, he had made his last effort to reach the camp.

At 4 a.m. on the 20th, clear morning, so that I was able to have a good view of the whole country, climbed up a rock in order to fix a piece of canvas to serve as a flag, hoping this might perhaps direct Edward to the camp. Resolved to proceed at once in search of him, M. de Guérard volunteering to accompany me, neither of the other two men being in a fit state to do so, and even he, after walking with me for an hour, declared himself unable to proceed any farther.

The search was now left to me alone and my first care was to ascertain whether Edward had reached the summit and taken the maps with him; therefore, when crossing the snowfield, I looked carefully for his footprints, but though I could plainly make out those of the dog I could discover none of his. On reaching the top, I found my maps untouched and concluded that he had not succeeded in crossing the snowfield or in ascending the summit, and that, in his bewilderment, he had travelled down into the valley of the Snowy River...

At 7 p.m., just as we had taken supper and it was already dark, our horse, who had been nibbling at some scanty herbage near the spot, made off and could not be found any more. It seems that the poor animal cared to stop no longer where he hardly could get anything to eat and had to suffer severely from a temperature of 37.5°.

Morning of the 21st cold and foggy. Got up at 4 a.m. and started with the intention of tracking the horse but without success. Weston, who went in another direction, returned at 7.45 a.m. without having seen a trace of him and it was now quite clear that he had tried to find his way to Groggan's station—no very pleasant prospect for us, being thus left without any means of transport and our stores fast running out. Sent Weston again with strict injunctions to descend towards the station till he found the horse...

I therefore resolved to return to Groggan's station as soon as Weston should appear with the horse, which we had the satisfaction of seeing at 10 a.m. He had found him near the lower limit of the belt of dead timber; there is no doubt that, had it not been for the hobbles, he would have succeeded in reaching the station. In the course of the forenoon I made some few magnetic observations near the camp...

Leaving all the provisions yet in our possession and

exact instructions to Edward, should he ever return to the camp, how to follow our track, we packed the horse and started, after having given three cheers for the missing man. While descending I made it a point to blaze all the trees in such a manner that even a man in a reduced state of body would be able to follow the track...

Arrived at the Leather Jacket again by 4 p.m. Had great difficulty in getting the horse, in its exhausted state, up the Groggan's side of the banks of the creek. The brave animal tried it three times, and on each occasion succeeded in reaching a height of eighty feet, but rolled back again and there remained. There was no other course left but to unpack and carry the things ourselves to the top of the hill. Got to Groggan's station at last by 7.15 p.m., but heard nothing of our friend...

I regretted very much that in consequence of the absence of Edward, who carried the only suitable barometer for such occasions, it was impossible to record the oscillations in the pressure of the air during this NW gale, the comparison of which with observations made at the sea-level or in other localities of the mountainous part of the country would have proved of considerable interest...

The unfortunate affair with Edward interfered greatly with the scientific objects during my stay on the mount, my time being entirely taken up in looking for him, and the idea continually preying on my mind that he would not be able to make for the settled districts and thus extricate himself from his very perilous position. I was therefore now determined to hurry to Omeo and secure the assistance of the police, for the purpose of instituting another search after the poor fellow...

[3 December 1862]—The day very hot, and a haze, caused by bushfires, over the whole sky, so that nothing of the fine mountain scenery was visible. Returned to the Devil's Creek and arrived at Porepankah, on the crossing place of the Ovens River at 5 p.m. At Sleeve's place got some information about the road to Yackandandah, twenty-five miles from here. After leaving Sleeve's place on the 4th, we went up a steep gap (1688); found it very fatiguing, the weather being fearfully hot, and then descended into the Happy Valley (918). The creek here spread out into a swamp of considerable width and the crossing of it was very difficult. Had to construct a sort of bridge of brushwood over which our horses, when unpacked, might venture.

Mr Twynham, notwithstanding, fell into the mud together with his horse and we found it hard work to extricate him. Had to carry all our instruments and other things on our backs. Missed Edward very much, for it was very hard for me to attend to such things as I have just described, and conduct my observations as well...Fixed upon a station and made some magnetical and astronomical observations.

A calm, dull morning with sky overcast on the 5th... Started early and, travelling on a very fair track, through a slightly undulating country, we reached Yackandandah at noon. Went on to Adam's Flat gold diggings, about four to five miles from Yackandandah. M. de Guérard remained here for the night, in order to have an opportunity of speaking to Mr Lane, the police magistrate, about Edward and asking his advice as to the best mode of instituting an inquiry after him. He overtook us on the road and we arrived together at Belvoir at 11 a.m. on the 6th.

Our anxiety on approaching this place may be imagined, for we still entertained the hope that Edward might have made for it, knowing that we had left our waggon there and would be sure to direct our course thither as soon as we could. Went to the police court, but could hear nothing of him, so that the last hope of his safety was now quite destroyed.

Sat down to dinner, and had hardly done so when the lost man made his appearance in a most deplorable condition, having been without food and clothes for some time. My conjectures as to the route he had taken proved to be correct. Soon after leaving us on Mt Kosciusko, he endeavoured to return but missed the track to the camp and descended into the valley of the Thredbo River. For two days he wandered on, with scarcely anything to eat, until he fell in with some diggers in a lonely valley, who behaved most kindly to him and assisted him in making his way to Kiandra. From this place he worked his way to Albury, where he arrived on the same morning on which we reached Belvoir—a strange coincidence when we consider that we both had travelled upwards of 300 miles, in quite different directions, since parting on Mt Kosciusko.

I cannot quit this most annoying affair without expressing my appreciation of Edward's courageous behaviour, after separating from our party, and of the skill and care he bestowed upon the instruments entrusted to his charge; for the fine mountain barometer Fortin II did not receive the least injury during the whole of this rough and perilous journey.

Ernest Giles

Living, Raw, Dying, 1874

 Ernest Giles was retrenched from the Victorian Post Office in 1854. The post office's loss was our gain, for Giles went on to become one of the most daring and eloquent explorers in the history of the continent. For Giles, exploration was a huge and irresistible game of brinkmanship. It was a game in which he gambled his life, the lives of his horses, and even his men.

Here in the waterless wasteland later known as the Gibson Desert, we see Giles face his darkest moment. Yet even when things are at their most desperate, when the explorers are a hundred miles from nowhere, with just a few pints of water and one exhausted horse between them, all Giles can think of is the quest. 'Oh, how ardently I longed for a camel,' he writes, as he sees the distant and untouchable ranges on the horizon.

And then, when Giles is alone, without water and horse, he hangs grimly on in conditions that would have killed a lesser man. The tiny wallaby he eats alive, and which perhaps tips the balance from death to life, is a meal that few could have written about so enthusiastically.

20th April 1874—Gibson and I, having got all the gear we required, took a week's supply of smoked horse, and four excellent horses, two to ride and two to carry water, all in fine condition. I rode the Fair Maid of Perth, an excellent walker; I gave Gibson the big ambling horse, Badger, and we packed the big cob, a splendid bay horse and fine weight-carrier, with a pair of waterbags that contained twenty gallons at starting. The other horse was Darkie, a fine, strong, nuggetty-black horse, who carried two five-gallon kegs of water and our stock of smoked horse, rugs etc. We reached the Circus, at twenty miles, early, and the horses had time to feed and fill themselves after being watered, though the grass was very poor.[†]

21st—While I went for the horses Gibson topped up the water-bags and kegs, and poured a quantity of water out of the hole on to a shallow place, so that if we turned any horses back, they could drink without precipitating themselves into the deep and slippery hole when they returned here. As we rode away, I remarked to Gibson that the day was the anniversary of Burke and Wills's return to their depot at Cooper's Creek, and then recited to him, as he did not appear to know anything whatever about it, the hardships they endured, their desperate struggles for existence, and death there, and I casually remarked that Wills had a brother who also lost his life in the field of discovery. He had gone out with Sir

---

[†] The Circus: a waterhole.

John Franklin in 1845.[†]

Gibson then said, 'Oh! I had a brother who died with Franklin at the North Pole, and my father had a deal of trouble to get his pay from government.' He seemed in a very jocular vein this morning, which was not often the case, for he was usually rather sulky, sometimes for days together, and he said, 'How is it, that in all these exploring expeditions a lot of people go and die?'

I said, 'I don't know, Gibson, how it is, but there are many dangers in exploring, besides accidents and attacks from the natives, that may at any time cause the death of some of the people engaged in it; but I believe want of judgment or knowledge or courage in individuals often brought about their deaths. Death, however, is a thing that must occur to everyone sooner or later.'

To this he replied, 'Well, I shouldn't like to die in this part of the country, anyhow.'

In this sentiment I quite agreed with him, and the subject dropped. At eleven miles we were not only clear of the range, but had crossed to the western side of Lake Christopher, and were fairly enclosed in the sandhills, which were of course covered with triodia.[‡] Numerous fine casuarinas grew in the hollows between them, and some stunted bloodwood trees (red gum) ornamented the tops of some of the sandhills. At twenty-two miles, on a west

---

[†] Exploration must have run in the family. Wills' brother had joined Franklin's expedition to the Arctic, which vanished without trace until the grisly remains were found in 1857.

[‡] Triodia: spinifex.

course, we turned the horses out for an hour. It was very warm, there was no grass. The horses rested in the shade of a desert-oak tree, while we remained under another. These trees are very handsome, with round umbrageous tops; the leaves are round and fringe-like.

We had a meal of smoked horse; and here I discovered that the bag with our supply of horseflesh in it held but a most inadequate supply for two of us for a week, there being scarcely sufficient for one. Gibson had packed it at starting, and I had not previously seen it. The afternoon was oppressively hot—at least it always seems so when one is away from water. We got over an additional eighteen miles, making a day's stage of forty.

The country was all sandhills. The Rawlinson Range completely disappeared from view, even from the tops of the highest sandhills, at thirty-five miles...

The triodia here reigns supreme, growing in enormous bunches and plots, and standing three and four feet high, while many of the long dry tops are as high as a man. This gives the country the appearance of dry grassy downs; and as it is dotted here and there with casuarina and bloodwood trees, and small patches of desert shrubs, its general appearance is by no means displeasing to the eye, though frightful to the touch. No sign of the recent presence of natives was anywhere visible, nor had the triodia been burnt for probably many years...

22nd—The ants were so troublesome last night, I had to shift my bed several times. Gibson was not at all affected by them and slept well. We were in our saddles immediately after daylight. I was in hopes that a few miles might bring about a change of country, and so it did, but not an advantageous one to us. At ten miles from camp the horizon became flatter, the sandhills fell off, and the undulations became covered with brown gravel, at first very fine. At fifty-five miles it became coarser, and at sixty miles it was evident the country was becoming firmer, if not actually stony. Here we turned the horses out, having come twenty miles.

I found one of our large water-bags leaked more than I expected, and our supply of water was diminishing with distance. Here Gibson preferred to keep the big cob to ride, against my advice, instead of Badger, so, after giving Badger and Darkie a few pints of water each, Gibson drove them back on the tracks about a mile and let them go, to take their own time and find their own way back to the Circus. They both looked terribly hollow and fatigued, and went away very slowly. Sixty miles through such a country as this tells fearfully upon a horse. The poor brutes were very unwilling to leave us, as they knew we had some water, and they also knew what a fearful region they had before them to reach the Circus again.

We gave the two remaining horses all the water contained in the two large water-bags, except a quart or two for ourselves. This allowed them a pretty fair drink, though not a circumstance to what they would have swallowed. They fed a little while we remained here. The day was warm enough. The two five-gallon kegs with water we hung in the branches of a tree, with the pack-saddles, empty water-bags etc. of the other two horses.

Leaving the Kegs—I always called this place by that name— we travelled another twenty miles by night, the country being still covered with small stones and thickly clothed with the tall triodia...

It was late by the time we encamped, and the horses were much in want of water, especially the big cob, who kept coming up to the camp all night, and tried to get at our water-bags, pannikins etc. The instinct of a horse, when in the first stage of thirst in getting hold of any utensil that ever had water in it, is surprising and most annoying, but teaching us by most persuasive reasons how akin they are to human beings. We had one small water-bag hung in a tree. I did not think of this just at the moment when my mare came straight up to it and took it in her teeth, forcing out the cork and sending the water up, which we were both dying to drink, in a beautiful jet which, descending to earth, was irrevocably lost.

We now had only a pint or two left. Gibson was now very sorry he had exchanged Badger for the cob, as he found the cob very dull and heavy to get on; this was not usual, for he was generally a most willing animal, but he would only go at a jog while my mare was a fine walker.

The following morning there was a most strange dampness in the air, and I had a vague feeling, such as must have been felt by augurs, and seers of old, who trembled as they told events to come; for this was the last day on which I ever saw Gibson. It was a lamentable day in the history of this expedition. We left the camp even before daylight, and as we had camped on the top of a rim we knew we had seven or eight miles to go before another view could be obtained. The next rim was at least ten miles from the camp, and there was some slight indications of a change.

We were now ninety miles from the Circus water, and 110 from Fort McKellar...The ridges were five miles away, and there were others still farther preventing a view. When we reached them we had come ninety-eight miles from the Circus. Here Gibson, who was always behind, called out and said his horse was going to die, or knock up, which are synonymous terms in this region.

Now we had reached a point where at last a different view was presented to us, and I believed a change of country was at hand...for the first time in all the distance we had come we had reached a spot where water might run during rain, though we had not seen any place where it could lodge...

Oh, how ardently I longed for a camel! How ardently I gazed upon this scene! At this moment I would even my jewel eternal have sold for power to span the gulf that lay between! But it could not be, situated as I was; compelled to retreat—of course with the intention of coming again with a larger supply of water—now the sooner I retreated the better.

These far-off hills were named the Alfred and Marie Range, in honour of their Royal Highnesses the Duke and Duchess of Edinburgh. Gibson's horse having got so bad had placed us both in a great dilemma; indeed, ours was a most critical position. We turned back upon our tracks, when the cob refused to carry his rider any farther, and tried to lie down. We drove him another mile on foot, and down he fell to die. My mare, the Fair Maid of Perth, was only too willing to return; she had now to carry Gibson's saddle and things, and we went away walking and riding by turns of half an hour. The cob, no doubt, died where he fell; not a second thought could be bestowed upon him.

When we got back to about thirty miles from the Kegs I was walking and, having concluded in my mind what course to pursue, I called to Gibson to halt till I walked up to him. We were both excessively thirsty, for walking had made us so, and we had scarcely a pint of water left between us.

However, of what we had we each took a mouthful, which finished the supply, and I then said—for I couldn't speak before—'Look here, Gibson, you see we are in a most terrible fix with only one horse, therefore only one can ride, and one must remain behind. I shall remain: and now listen to me. If the mare does not get water soon she will die; therefore ride right on; get to the Kegs if possible tonight, and give her water. Now the cob is dead there'll be all the more for her; let her rest for an hour or two, then get over a few more miles by morning, so that early tomorrow you will sight the Rawlinson, at twenty-five miles from the Kegs. Stick to the tracks, and never leave them. Leave as much water in one keg for me as you can afford after watering the mare and filling up your own bags, and, remember, I depend upon you to bring me relief. Rouse Mr Tietkens, get fresh horses and more water-bags, and return as soon as you possibly can. I shall of course endeavour to get down the tracks also.'

He then said if he had a compass he thought he could go better at night. I knew he didn't understand anything about compasses, as I had often tried to explain them to him. The one I had was a Gregory's Patent, of a totally different construction from ordinary instruments of the kind, and I was very loath to part with it, as it was the only one I had. However, he was so anxious for it that I gave it him, and he departed. I sent one final shout after him to stick to the tracks, to which he replied, 'All right,' and the mare carried him out of sight almost immediately. That was the last ever seen of Gibson.

I walked slowly on, and the further I walked the more thirsty I became. I had thirty miles to go to reach the Kegs, which I could not reach until late tomorrow at the rate I was travelling, and I did not feel sure that I could keep on at that. The afternoon was very hot. I continued following the tracks until the moon went down, and then had to stop. The night was reasonably cool, but I was parched and choking for water. How I longed again for morning! I hoped Gibson had reached the Kegs, and that he and the mare were all right. I could not sleep for thirst, although towards morning it became almost cold. How I wished this planet would for once accelerate its movements and turn upon its axis in twelve instead of twenty-four hours, or rather that it would complete its revolution in six hours.

24th April to 1st May—So soon as it was light I was again upon the horse tracks, and reached the Kegs about the middle of the day. Gibson had been here, and watered the mare, and gone on. He had left me a little over two gallons of water in one keg, and it may be imagined how glad I was to get a drink. I could have drunk my whole supply in half an hour, but was compelled to economy, for I could not tell how many days would elapse before assistance could come: it could not be less than five, it might be many more.

After quenching my thirst a little I felt ravenously hungry and, on searching among the bags, all the food I could find was eleven sticks of dirty, sandy, smoked horse, averaging about an ounce and a half each, at the bottom of a pack-bag. I was rather staggered to find that I had a little more than a pound weight of meat to last me until assistance came. However, I was compelled to eat some at once, and devoured two sticks raw, as I had no water to spare to boil them in.

After this I sat in what shade the trees afforded, and reflected on the precariousness of my position. I was sixty miles from water, and eighty from food, my messenger could hardly return before six days, and I began to think it highly probable that I should be dead of hunger and thirst long before anybody could possibly arrive.

I looked at the keg; it was an awkward thing to carry empty. There was nothing else to carry water in, as Gibson had taken all the smaller water-bags, and the large ones would require several gallons of water to soak the canvas before they began to tighten enough to hold water. The keg when empty, with its rings and straps, weighed fifteen pounds, and now it had twenty pounds of water in it. I could not carry it without a blanket for a pad for my shoulder, so that with my revolver and cartridge-pouch, knife, and one or two other small things on my belt, I staggered under a weight of about fifty pounds when I put the keg on my back. I only had fourteen matches.

After I had thoroughly digested all points of my situation, I concluded that if I did not help myself providence wouldn't help me. I started, bent double by the keg, and could only travel so slowly that I thought it scarcely worth while to travel at all. I became so thirsty at each step I took that I longed to drink up every drop of water I had in the keg, but it was the elixir of death I was burdened with, and to drink it was to die, so I restrained myself.

By next morning I had only got about three miles away from the Kegs, and to do that I travelled mostly in the moonlight. The next few days I can only pass over as they seemed to pass with me, for I was quite unconscious half the time, and I only got over about five miles a day.

To people who cannot comprehend such a region it may seem absurd that a man could not travel faster than that. All I can say is, there may be men who could do so, but most men in the position I was in would simply have died of hunger and thirst, for by the third or fourth day—I couldn't tell which—my horse meat was all gone. I had to remain in what scanty shade I could find during the day, and I could only travel by night.

When I lay down in the shade in the morning I lost all consciousness, and when I recovered my senses I could not tell whether one day or two or three had passed. At one place I am sure I must have remained over forty-eight hours. At a certain place on the road—that is to say, on the horse tracks—at about fifteen miles from the Kegs—at twenty-five miles the Rawlinson could again be sighted—I saw that the tracks of the two loose horses we had turned back from there had left the main line of tracks, which ran east and west, and had turned about east south-east, and the tracks of the Fair Maid of Perth, I was grieved to see, had gone on them also.

I felt sure Gibson would soon find his error, and return to the main line. I was unable to investigate this any farther in my present position. I followed them about a mile, and then returned to the proper line, anxiously looking at every step to see if Gibson's horse tracks returned into them.

They never did, nor did the loose horse tracks either. Generally speaking, whenever I saw a shady desert-oak tree there was an enormous bulldog ants' nest under it, and I was prevented from sitting in its shade. On what I thought was the 27th I almost gave up the thought of walking any farther, for the exertion in this dreadful region, where the triodia was almost as high as myself, and as thick as it could grow, was quite overpowering and, being starved, I felt quite light-headed. After sitting down, on every occasion when I tried to get up again, my head would swim round, and I would fall down oblivious for some time.

Being in a chronic state of burning thirst, my general plight was dreadful in the extreme. A bare and level sandy waste would have been paradise to walk over compared to this. My arms, legs, thighs, both before and behind, were so punctured with spines, it was agony only to exist; the slightest movement and in went more spines, where they broke off in the clothes and flesh, causing the whole of the body that was punctured to gather into minute pustules, which were continually growing and bursting. My clothes, especially inside my trousers, were a perfect mass of prickly points.

My great hope and consolation now was that I might soon meet the relief party. But where was the relief party? Echo could only answer—where? About the 29th I had emptied the keg, and was still over twenty miles from the Circus. Ah! who can imagine what twenty miles means in such a case? But in this April's ivory moonlight I plodded on, desolate indeed, but all undaunted, on this lone, unhallowed shore.

At last I reached the Circus, just at the dawn of the day. Oh, how I drank! How I reeled! How hungry I was! How thankful I was that I had so far at least escaped from the jaws of that howling wilderness, for I was once more upon the range, though still twenty miles from home.

There was no sign of the tracks, of anyone having been here since I left it. The water was all but gone. The solitary eagle still was there. I wondered what could have become of Gibson; he certainly had never come here, and how could he reach the fort without doing so?

I was in such a miserable state of mind and body that I refrained from more vexatious speculations as to what had delayed him: I stayed here, drinking and drinking, until about 10 a.m., when I crawled away over the stones down from the water. I was very footsore, and could only go at a snail's pace.

Just as I got clear of the bank of the creek, I heard a faint squeak, and looking about I saw, and immediately caught, a small dying wallaby, whose marsupial mother had evidently thrown it from her pouch. It only weighed about two ounces, and was scarcely furnished yet with fur. The instant I saw it, like an eagle I pounced upon it and ate it, living, raw, dying—fur, skin, bones, skull and all. The delicious taste of that creature I shall never forget. I only wished I had its mother and father to serve in the same way.

I had become so weak that by late at night I had only accomplished eleven miles, and I lay down about five miles from the Gorge of Tarns, again choking for water. While lying down here, I thought I heard the sound of the footfalls of a galloping horse going campwards, and vague ideas of Gibson on the Fair Maid—or she without him—entered my head. I stood up, and listened, but the sound had died away upon the midnight air. On the 1st of May, as I afterwards found, at one o'clock in the morning, I was walking again, and reached the Gorge of Tarns long before daylight, and could again indulge in as much water as I desired; but it was exhaustion I suffered from, and I could hardly move.

My reader may imagine with what intense feelings of relief I stepped over the little bridge across the water, staggered into the camp at daylight, and woke Mr Tietkens, who stared at me as though I had been one new risen from the dead. I asked him had he seen Gibson, and to give me some food. I was of course prepared to hear that Gibson had never reached the camp; indeed I could see but two people in their blankets the moment I entered the fort, and by that I knew he could not be there.

None of the horses had come back, and it appeared that I was the only one of six living creatures—two men and four horses— that had returned, or were now ever likely to return, from that desert, for it was now, as I found, nine days since I last saw Gibson.

John Forrest

Fight for Water, 1874

 Such arrogance! To turn up at a waterhole in a remote part of the driest continent, to name it as if it was a new discovery, then camp by it and be surprised when you are told, in no uncertain terms, to clear off by those who have owned it for 50,000 years. John Forrest, who made his discovery near the Carnarvon Range in central Western Australia, was quick to see evidence of cannibalism among the Aborigines in a burned skull. Perhaps this made it a little easier to pull the trigger.

Forrest was a frontiersman, born and bred in the bush. The first city he ever saw was Melbourne, yet even its great sights failed to stir his imagination, for it seems that the only thing he rushed to see was the monument to Burke and Wills. Exploration, perhaps, was all to him.

June 1st—Barometer 28.38; thermometer 45° at 8 a.m. In collecting the horses we came on an old native camp and found the skull of a native, much charred, evidently the remains of one who had been eaten… Myself and Windich were in advance, and after reaching the range we followed down a flat about north for six miles, when it joined another large watercourse, both trending NNW and NW. We followed down this river for about seven miles, in hopes of finding water, without success...

2nd—Early this morning went with Pierre to look for water, while my brother and Windich went on the same errand. We followed up the brook about south for seven miles, when we left it and followed another branch about SSE, ascending which, Pierre drew my attention to swarms of birds, parakeets etc., about half a mile ahead.

We hastened on, and to our delight found one of the best springs in the colony...Overjoyed at our good fortune, we hastened back and, finding that my brother and Windich had not returned, packed up and shifted over to the springs, leaving a note telling them the good news. After reaching the springs we were soon joined by them. They had only found sufficient water to give their own horses a drink; they also rejoiced to find so fine a spot.

Named the springs the Weld Springs, after His Excellency Governor Weld, who has always taken such great interest in exploration, and without whose influence and assistance this expedition would not have been organised.† There is splendid feed all around. I intend giving the horses a week's rest here, as they are much in want of it, and are getting very poor and tired...

7th (Sunday)—Pierre shot an emu, and the others

† Sir Frederick Weld was governor of Western Australia between 1869 and 1875.

shot several pigeons. This is a splendid spot; emus and kangaroos numerous, pigeons and birds innumerable, literally covering the entire surface all round the place in the evenings. We have been living on game ever since we have been here. Intend taking a flying trip tomorrow; party to follow on our tracks on Tuesday. Read Divine Service. Barometer 28.38; thermometer 55° at 7 p.m...

10th—We travelled on to the springs, which were only about three miles from where we slept last night, and camped. I intend staying here for some time, until I find water ahead or we get some rain. We are very fortunate in having such a good depot, as the feed is very good. We found that about a dozen natives had been to the springs while we were away. They had collected some of the emu feathers, which were all lying about. Natives appear to be very numerous, and I have no doubt that there are springs in the spinifex or valleys close to it. Barometer 28.08; thermometer 62° at 5.30 p.m....

13th—About one o'clock Pierre saw a flock of emus coming to water, and went off to get a shot. Kennedy followed with the rifle. I climbed up on a small tree to watch them. I was surprised to hear natives' voices, and looking towards the hill I saw from forty to sixty natives running towards the camp, all plumed up and armed with spears and shields. I was cool, and told Sweeney to bring out the revolvers; descended from the tree and got my gun and cooeed to Pierre and Kennedy, who came running. By this time they were within sixty yards, and halted.

One advanced to meet me and stood twenty yards off; I made friendly signs; he did not appear very hostile. All at once one from behind (probably a chief) came rushing forward, and made many feints to throw spears. He went through many manoeuvres, and gave a signal, when the whole number made a rush towards us, yelling and shouting, with their spears shipped. When within thirty yards I gave the word to fire: we all fired as one man, only one report being heard. I think the natives got a few shots, but they all ran up the hill and there stood, talking and haranguing and appearing very angry.

We reloaded our guns, and got everything ready for a second attack, which I was sure they would make. We were not long left in suspense. They all descended from the hill and came on slowly towards us. When they were about 150 yards off I fired my rifle, and we saw one of them fall, but he got up again and was assisted away. On examining the spot we found the ball had cut in two the two spears he was carrying; he also dropped his woomera which was covered with blood. We could follow the blood-drops for a long way over the stones. I am afraid he got a severe wound.

My brother and Windich being away we were short-handed. The natives seem determined to take our lives, and therefore I shall not hesitate to fire on them should they attack us again. I thus decide and write in all humility, considering it a necessity, as the only way of saving our lives. I write this at 4 p.m., just after the occurrence, so that, should anything happen to us, my brother will know how and when it occurred.

5 p.m. The natives appear to have made off. We intend sleeping in the thicket close to camp, and keeping a strict watch, so as to be ready for them should they return to the attack this evening. At 7.30 my brother and Windich returned, and were surprised to hear of our adventure. They had been over fifty miles from camp ESE, and had passed over some good feeding country, but had not found a drop of water. They and their horses had been over thirty hours without water.

14th (Sunday)—The natives did not return to the attack last night. In looking round camp we found the traces of blood where one of the natives had been lying down. This must have been the foremost man, who was in the act of throwing his spear, and who urged the others on. Two therefore, at least, are wounded, and will have cause to remember the time they made their murderous attack upon us.

We worked all day putting up a stone hut, ten by nine feet, and seven feet high, thatched with boughs. We finished it; it will make us safe at night. Being a very fair hut, it will be a great source of defence. Barometer 28.09; thermometer 68° at 5 p.m. Hope to have rain, as without it we cannot proceed.

Emily Caroline Creaghe

The Little Explorer's Diary, 1883

 'E. Carrie Creaghe. The Little Explorer's Diary'. Thus did Emily Caroline Creaghe sign the title page of her extraordinary, unpublished diary of frontier adventure. Accompanying her husband Harry, Creaghe was the only female member of Ernest Favenc's exploring expedition, which pushed deep into the Gulf country in 1882–83. Her account is of especial interest because of her perspective on Australia's barbarous northern frontier—well illustrated when she enters a settler's hut to see forty pairs of Aboriginal ears nailed to the walls. We drop in on her just as an expedition member dies of sunstroke, and later at first contact with some Aborigines.

18 January 1883—Found today that Mrs Favenc is not strong enough to go out to the exploring expedition so, much to our disgust, we have to give up all idea of going. She is going back to Sydney with Mr Favenc and I am going to Mr Shadforth's station 220 miles inland with Harry. When Mr Favenc returns in March the two will go out with one man and get the work done in three months instead of four and a half as they

would have done if we had gone...

20 January—Left Normanton at half past three p.m. for 'Magowrah', Mr Trimble's station, a distance of sixteen miles. Arrived there at seven, about a dozen men camped all night and eight of us belonging to the party going inland. Mr Shadforth, Mr Murray, McNaught, Power, two men and ourselves. Being the only female except one in the kitchen I felt decidedly queer amongst such a number of men.

21 January—Left Magowrah, at nine a.m. passed the Bynoe River, Flinders River and had dinner at Armstrong Creek. The men left almost immediately after dinner for L Creek, a distance of thirty-two miles, called after Leichhardt the explorer whose initials are on a tree on the bank of the creek. I felt nearly done up when we got to Armstrong Creek, having come sixteen miles (and not yet being accustomed to long riding and poor food). Managed to get to the end of the second stage but was nearly knocked up. Got into camp at half past seven p.m. Rather hot, scarcely anything but bare plains all the way.

22 January—Made a start at half past six a.m. Arrived at camp a mile and a half this side of M Lagoon, twenty-two miles from L Creek, called after Morrel—Leichhardt's companion—at about noon. We, Harry and I, did intend remaining in camp at L Creek all today as I am nearly 'finished' but there is every appearance of rain, so we must push on to cross the River Leichhardt before it is flooded. The hottest weather I have ever felt today; the flies are something dreadful. Mr McNaught and his man left the camp in the afternoon. Still the country is level and bare.

23 January—Left M Lagoon at half past five a.m. Passed Diary Creek and camped on Packsaddle Creek where the mosquitoes were something terrible...Diary Creek gets its name from an old diary being found there, and Packsaddle Creek from an old saddle being found there, both articles supposed to have belonged to Leichhardt's party. Nicely timbered country.

24 January—Left Packsaddle at half past eight a.m., the horses having got away and the men were from half past five looking for them. Travelled all the morning, passed Margaret Lagoon and are now camped on the banks of the River Leichhardt. There is an old tumbled-down public house close to the river crossing. The country is again plains and not much timber. The heat is intense, no rain yet but every appearance of it. Yesterday we did about twenty miles and today eighteen. There are plenty of crocodiles in the rivers but I have not seen many. Mr Warner had a fearful headache when we got to camp and we hope he has not had a touch of the sun.

25 January—Left the Leichhardt camp at 7 a.m. and arrived at 'The Rocky' at half past ten, a distance of fourteen or fifteen miles. Warner (Mr Murray's man) who had not been well last night got some terrible fits and has evidently had a sunstroke. He managed to drive the packhorses into camp but got ill immediately on arrival. Mr Watson and two men from his station twelve miles distant came up and he, being a friend of Harry's, stopped all day and night with us. He gave us an account of his being speared by the blacks some little time ago. He was of great assistance in trying to hold Warner during his fits. We are afraid Warner won't get over it, as he is still unconscious.

26 January—A plague of beetles last night. Warner is slightly better and has not had a return of the fits, but our going any further this morning is quite out of the question. We did not put up the tents last night for the first time as it looked so very unlike rain and it was too hot to sleep in it, so when a thunderstorm broke in the middle of the night, we all had to turn out and put them up as fast as we could and only just put the finishing touches when down it came. Mr Watson went off before we were up. It is fine and very hot today (evening). Warner is much worse this evening. He is quite unconscious and has been so since 10 a.m. It is most painful to hear his groans. A terrific thunderstorm this evening at eight, got a little wet.

27 January—Warner died at three this morning. He never became conscious but his groans were something terrible at night. Poor Mr Murray sat with him. A death in a camping party is an awful thing. Mr Murray went away at 7 a.m. to Augustus Downs and brought back Mr Watson and two men with pick and shovel to dig a grave. Harry and I spent a miserable day until half past three by ourselves in camp guarding the body from native dogs. They have just sewn up his body in his blanket in the midst of a heavy thunderstorm, while some of the others are digging the grave. The poor fellow was quite young, strong, tall and healthy three days ago. 'In the midst of life we are in death.' Mr Watson and men will camp all night with us, and we shall leave early tomorrow morning.

Mr Watson brought us some milk, bread, plain cake and a watermelon which were great treats; at least the milk was. I have got into that state from not eating that I could not manage even cake. Our food in camp consists of nasty dirty hairy dried salt beef, dark brown sugar (half dust) and hard dry damper. There are some tinned meats, but the jolting has made them uneatable. There is some jam, but who can eat it with hard dry damper and no butter.

28 January—They finished the grave at 2 a.m. and so poor Warner was buried in the dead of night. The horses were troublesome so we did not start till twenty to nine this morning. Only went seven miles as the heat became so intense it was dangerous to travel, and camped till five o'clock at the side of a waterhole. Travelled till half past eight and them camped at the Ridgepoll on Fiery Creek about nineteen miles from the Rocky. The food we are living upon is something horrible, and I have scarcely touched a thing since we left Normanton; just two or three mouthfuls at each meal, but make up for the want of food by drinking any amount of tea (without milk) which is detestable...

20 February—The rainy season seems to have set in properly. Mr Shadforth and Ernest came home...They brought a new black gin with them who can't speak a word of English. The usual method here of bringing in a new wild gin is to put a rope around her neck and drag her along from horseback, the gin on foot.

21 February—The new gin whom they call Bella is chained up to a tree a few yards from the house, and is not to be loosed until they think she is tamed.

23 February—Still raining heavily. The new gin Bella made Topsy (an old one) jealous and the latter threw a firestick at her and said she would kill her. The stick flew past Mrs Shadforth's face, so Madame Topsy got a thrashing.

24 February—Bella, the new gin, decamped in the night, whether it was because of Topsy's threat to kill her, or discontent at this life we don't know. They tracked her as far as the O'Shanassy but that river is a 'banker' so they could not afford to go after her any further. There is no mail expected for two months owing to the floods...

2 May—Mr Favenc and Mr Crawford took the horses back to the waterhole we were at yesterday to get a drink as they could not go on, as it was so probable we might be some time in finding more water. They left at half past six and returned at three and we packed up immediately after they had had a hurried lunch and left at four. Harry and I remained about the camp doing odd jobs all the morning. We are reduced to damper and honey as we have finished our cooked meat and have no water with which to boil the one piece that remains. We have some anchovy paste, but are afraid to eat it owing to its tendency to create thirst. We came on until about eight tonight, Mr Favenc carrying the lantern as on the previous night. We have not come upon water, but the horses can do without it for some hours tomorrow and we trust we shall come upon it soon.

I had a tiny scrap of water spared me this morning to rinse my hands and face, but I feel extremely 'grubby'. We came over very rough country this afternoon, and at times we all had narrow escapes from being thrown off our horses, for the holes were so numerous and deep that it was only by holding on tightly and being on our guard that we managed to stay in our saddles when the horses stumbled into the holes.

3 May—It has been a very eventful day. We left camp soon after 8 a.m., anxious to hurry on as much as possible to reach water early. We continued our right course (west) for an hour and seeing no signs of water (viz. emus and native dog tracks or flocks of birds), we changed our course north. We went on till 2 p.m. and were despairing of getting water, when we saw not three miles straight ahead of us a blacks' fire (or smoke rather) and we made for it in desperation, knowing there would be water where niggers were.

We reached the fire and were going round it, when Favenc made a gallop and Crawford followed from behind with us, and we knew they must have seen blacks. Presently we got up to them and saw Favenc holding a man with one hand and in the other pointing his revolver at him, and Crawford holding a gin. They were a peculiar sight. The blacks had never seen a white man before, we soon found out by their showing no fear when Favenc pulled out his revolver.

When Mr Favenc came upon them, they climbed a small tree, and when he made signs for them to come down the nigger threw his gin down, thinking that might satisfy him, and it was some time before the black was induced to come down himself. Favenc tied him with a strap to prevent his running away before he had led us to water.

We were not going to do them any harm, so they remained captives till we had shown them, by giving them some drops of water to drink (which we had kept specially for the purpose) and signing to them what we wanted them to do. They then went on with a great many gesticulations which we suppose meant fright, and after taking us about three miles we came upon the main blacks' camp and a waterhole. There were seven men and nine gins and some piccaninnies. The gins bolted at our appearance and we saw nothing of them. One poor little baby was left by the mother in her fright and it was toddling about crying.

The blacks wear no clothing of any sort, and one of them had a carpet snake which he had killed tied round his waist ready to cook for his supper. The poor things were quiet and frightened, but not having been molested by white men they did not attempt to do us any harm. When we went down to the waterhole they all took up their boomerangs, so Harry remained on the bank with his revolver ready to fire at the first throw. They soon put them down however and came and stood about twenty yards away while we had dinner. We gave them some damper and they seemed pleased.

We left their camp at 4 p.m. and came on till eight through a dreadful scrub. How we got through in the dark without accident I don't know. We soon had the fire lit and the billy boiling for our meagre supper. We saw spears and things lying on the ground in the blacks' camp, but we took nothing away as harm has been done so often by white men stealing the blacks' only means of gaining their food. The man we caught first had a white plaited string made of bark round his head, and he threw it down when Favenc let him loose, as a sign of submission and peace. All the men amongst these blacks are circumcised.

David Carnegie

Sorry As I Was to Be Rude to a Lady, 1896

 David Carnegie began his career as an explorer by necessity. He was a miner, but his searches took him so far from the beaten track that getting home again became a matter of life and death. Later, his urge to explore seems to have got the better of his wish to become rich from gold, and carried him on a truly remarkable exploration through the centre of Western Australia.

We meet him here in the Gibson Desert, desperately tracking Aborigines so that he can force them to reveal the whereabouts of their waterholes. In this episode Carnegie treats an elderly Aboriginal woman abominably. Did he ever consider how he would react if someone had treated his own mother so?

Sorry as I was to be rude to a lady, I had to make her prisoner, but not without a deal of trouble. 'Dah, dah, dah!' she shouted, scratching, biting, spitting, and tearing me with her horrid long nails, and using, I feel sure, the worst language that her tongue could command. I had to carry this unsavoury object back to her camp, she clutching at every bush we passed, when her hands were not engaged in clawing and scratching me. After her anger had somewhat abated she pointed out a rock-hole from which they had got their water. Securing the woman with a light rope, I put her in Warri's charge, who kept watch above, lest the natives should return and surprise us, whilst I descended the rock-hole to see what supply was there. A little water was visible, which I quickly baled into the canvas bags we had brought for the purpose.

The bottom of the hole was filled in with dead sticks, leaves, the rotting bodies of birds and lizards, bones of rats and dingoes. Into this ghastly mass of filth I sunk up to my middle, and never shall I forget the awful odour that arose as my feet stirred up the mess. Nevertheless water was there, and thankful I was to find it, even to drink it as it was. After half an hour's work in this stinking pit, sick from the combination of smells—distinguishable above every other being the all-pervading perfume of aboriginals—I was rewarded by some twelve gallons of water, or, more properly speaking, liquid.

I decided to take the gin back with us, as it had been clear to me for some time past that without the aid of natives we could not hope to find water. With our small caravan it was impossible to push on and trust to chance, or hope to reach the settled country still nearly 500 miles ahead in a bee-line. Even supposing the camels could do this enormous stage, it was beyond our power to carry sufficient water for ourselves. The country might improve or might get worse; in such weather as we now experienced no camel could go for more than a few days without water.

I felt myself justified, therefore, in unceremoniously making captives from what wandering tribes we might fall in with. And in light of after events I say unhesitatingly that, without having done so, and without having to a small extent used rough treatment to some natives so caught, we could not by any possibility have succeeded in crossing the desert, and should not only have lost our own lives, but possibly those of others who would have made search for us after.

'A man arms himself where his armour is weakest', so I have read; that, however, is not my case. I am not justifying myself to myself, or defending a line of action not yet assailed. I write this in answer to some who have unfavourably criticised my methods, and to those I would say, 'Put yourselves in our position, and when sitting in a comfortable armchair at home, in the centre of civilisation, do not, you who have never known want or suffered hardship, be so ready to judge others who, hundreds of miles from their fellow-men, threatened every day with possible death from thirst, were doing their best to lay bare the hidden secrets of an unknown region, as arid and desolate as any the world can show.'

On starting back for camp the gin refused to walk or move in any way, so we had to pack her on Czar, making her as comfortable as possible on Warri's blankets, with disastrous results thereto. Arrived at camp, I found that the rock-hole was bottomed, and now quite dry. Straining the putrid water brought by me through a flannel shirt, boiling it, adding ashes and Epsom salts, we concocted a serviceable beverage. This, blended with the few gallons of muddy water from the well, formed our supply, which we looked to augment under the guidance of the gin.

After completing our work the well presented the appearance of a large rock-hole, thirty feet, deep, conical in shape, of which one half of the contents had been dug out. This confirmed my opinion that the native wells of these regions are nothing more than holes in the bed-rock, which have been covered over and in by the general deposit of sand...

From September 8th, 9 a.m. until September 12th, 12.30 a.m. we had worked almost continuously, only taking in turn what sleep we could snatch when one could be spared; and the result, 140 gallons as sum total, inclusive of mud and other matter.

We left Patience Well on the 12th, at 10 a.m., taking the woman with us. Breaden was the only one in whose charge she would consent to be at all calm; to him therefore was allotted the duty of looking after her. At eleven we reached the dry well to which Warri and I had tracked the natives. The water we were forced to use was so uninviting that I decided to make another effort to find a supply in this locality. The gin was of no use whatever, and would only repeat whatever we said to her—*gabbi*, which King Billy had understood, was wasted on her. '*Gabbi, gabbi*,' she repeated, waving her arm all round the horizon.[†]

Leaving the rest to bottom the dry well, which might have water lower down, Warri and I again started off on the tracks of a buck, and these we followed due north on foot for four and a half hours, hoping every moment to come on a well. Soon after starting, an apparently old track joined the other, and together they marched still north. Presently the old tracks changed into fresh ones, and close by I found two rough sandals made of strips of bark. One I kept, the other was nearly worn out. There was no change in the dreary appearance of the country; through scrubs, over stones and sand we held our way, until Warri, who was now a little way behind, called, 'No good, no more walk!' I could see the poor boy was knocked up, and felt little better myself; to go on did not guarantee water, and might end in disaster, so after a short rest we retraced our steps.

The night was now dark and oppressive, so hatless and shirtless we floundered through the spinifex, nearly exhausted from our walk, following so close on the last few days' work. I believe that but for Warri I should have been 'bushed'; my head was muddled and the stars not too clear. What a joyful sight met our eyes as we crested a rise of sand—a sight almost as reviving as the food and water we so anxiously looked forward to. Tongues of flame shot up in the air, a fire lit by our mates, but showing that, in spite of Warri's instinct, we had not been walking in quite

[†] King Billy: an Aborigine captured by Carnegie earlier in the expedition.

the right direction.

No welcome news greeted our arrival—the well was dry, and the native obdurate. We all agreed she was useless, and since she refused all forms of nutriment I feared she would die on our hands, so she regained her liberty, and fled away with a rapidity not expected in one of her years.

Hedley Herbert Finlayson

Oolacunta, 1931

 In December 1931 Hedley Herbert Finlayson made an extraordinary discovery. A chemist with a passion for the mammals of his native South Australia, Finlayson had heard rumours that a kind of rat-kangaroo or bettong, known to the Aborigines as oolacunta, existed in the far north of the state. He undertook an 1100-kilometre trek from Adelaide to investigate. Upon arriving at Appamunna station, among the stony plains and sand ridges, he found that the oolacunta was no other than the Desert rat kangaroo, a species described by John Gould in 1843 but never recorded again until Finlayson's rediscovery.

Remarkably, although Finlayson found the species to be common in northern South Australia and south-western Queensland between 1931 and 1935, this mysterious animal has never been heard of since.

We 'pulled off ' finally on a little stony plain with scattered saltbush, and made our depot camp under some corkwoods. We were five miles from water, but the boys seemed so assured that the country was 'right', that we decided to endure the discomforts of a waterless camp for the benefit of being near the coveted *Caloprymnus*. But I had grave misgivings. All the five bettongs that are the nearest allies of the oolacunta, I have seen in the country of their choice, and anything less promising than this stony, shelterless plain in the blaze of midsummer would be difficult to imagine. But the blacks were right.

The plan of campaign had been anxiously debated all the way in from Appamunna. The great open sweep of the country is so immense that all methods of procedure partook somewhat of hunting for a needle in a haystack. Snaring and trapping were out of the question, shooting was too damaging to skeletons, and the most practicable method (while the horses lasted) seemed to be for the whole party to beat up the country mounted, and gallop anything which was put up.

At this juncture Butcher created a sensation by announcing that he could catch oolacuntas by hand. When questioned, he explained that many years ago when 'big mob jump up alonga Barcoo', the blacks used to locate the grass nests and then, determining the direction in which the opening lay, would, if the wind were right, sneak up behind and, silently slipping a coolamon or their hands over the top, bag the occupant! Some jealousy existed between Butcher and Jimmy, and Reese and I were inclined to attribute this account to a desire to shine. Moreover, there was a certain Alice-in-Wonderlandish touch about this method of capture by the 'laying on of hands'. So much so that Reese, on reflection, was constrained to administer a grave rebuke to Butcher, suggesting indeed that he was a sanguinary liar. But in this we wronged him.

Seldom do the things one keenly desires come easily. But on our very first cast we got a prize. The six of us rode east in the early morning, and on a sandhill picked up fresh oolacunta tracks crossing to a flat on the far side...We had ridden less than half an hour when there came a shrill excited 'Yuchai' from the horseboy farthest out, and the chase was on. The pre-arranged plan was for each of us to take up the galloping in turn, the rat being headed whenever possible and turned in towards the rest of the party who remained in a group. When the first horse showed signs of losing heart, the next man took the first opportunity of replacing him, and so on.

Following the yell, Tommy came heading back down the line towards the sandhill, but it was only after much straining of eyes that the oolacunta could be distinguished—a mere speck, thirty or forty yards ahead. At that distance it seemed scarcely to touch the ground; it almost floated ahead in an eerie, effortless way that made the thundering horse behind seem, by comparison, like a coal hulk wallowing in a heavy sea.

They were great moments as it came nearer; moments filledwith curiosity and excitement, but with a steady undercurrent of relief and satisfaction. It was here!

Caloprymnus bears a strong external resemblance

to five or six other related species and from a distance there was little to distinguish that which was approaching from either of two other marsupials known to occur in adjoining tracts. But as it came down the flat towards me, a little pale ghost from the 1840s, all doubt fled. The thing was holding itself very differently from the bettongs. As I watched it through the shimmering heat haze, some sense of the incongruous brought back a vivid memory of a very different scene, two years before, when I had sought the nearest living relative of *Caloprymnus*, above the snowline on a Tasmanian range.

Imagine a little animal about the bulk of a rabbit, but built like a kangaroo, with long spindly hind legs, tiny forelegs folded tight on its chest, and a tail half as long again as the body but not much thicker than a lead pencil, and you have it in the rough. But its head, short and blunt and wide, is very different from that of any kangaroo or wallaby, and its coat is uniformly coloured a clear pale yellowish ochre—exactly like the great clay-pans and floodplains.

As it came up to us I galloped alongside to keep it under observation as long as possible. Its speed, for such an atom, was wonderful, and its endurance amazing. We had considerable difficulty in heading it with fresh horses. When we finally got it, it had taken the starch out of three mounts and run us twelve miles; all under such adverse conditions of heat and rough going, as to make it almost incredible that so small a frame should be capable of such an immense output of energy. All examples obtained subsequently by this method behaved similarly; they persisted to the very limit of their strength, and quite literally, they paused only to die.

Back at the camp all was jubilation. The afternoon and most of the next day were spent in examining, sketching, photographing, measuring, dissecting, and preserving—for luck is not to be trusted. And I wanted to make the very most of the first specimen lest it be also the last. We rode out each day, sometimes to success, sometimes not. In the afternoons we worked on the rats which the 'rat boss' had dug, while the heat under the corkwoods grew ever worse and worse.

Even the old hands, reared under the grim old tradition of 'salt beef, damper, and constipation', who love to hark back to the summers when it really was hot, admitted subsequently that it had been bad. I had thought the still days bad, but when the hot winds came I thought again. When the flies and ants and heat and sand could be endured no longer, we left the skinning and spelled. And while we gazed out over the white-hot flats and sandhills, we sipped boiling tea, and had torturing visions of iced Quellthaler in an old-time shady garden.[†]

On the day before we broke camp to start on the long ride to Cordilla and the Innamincka track, Butcher quashed for ever the soft impeachment which Reese had made on his veracity and covered himself with glory.

[†] Quellthaler: the name of a wine.

It was usual for two of the boys to take the horses to water each evening near sundown, and fill the canteens at the hole five miles away. On this afternoon they had been gone no more than half an hour when Butcher rode back into camp alone. With impassive face and in dignified silence, he handed over a bag tied at the mouth. Very cautious investigation showed it to contain a beautiful fully adult oolacunta and a half-grown joey— both alive and undamaged. Those we had run down were too exhausted to make good life-studies for a camera, but here were fitting subjects at last.

In riding over the country, we had had ample confirmation of Butcher's statement about the nest-building habit of *Caloprymnus*. In a fiery land, where a burrowing habit is the chief factor in the survival of most species, the oolacunta clings pathetically to a flimsy shelter of grass and leaves, which it makes in a shallow depression scratched out of the loam. And now, here was a splendid proof of his second claim. The Yalliyanda boy had, while riding with the others, spotted a nest and noted the head of the occupant in the opening, watching the party. He rode on without pause for a quarter of a mile, then, leaving his horse, made a rapid stalk up the wind and grabbed both mother and babe from behind.

The laying on of hands was no myth!

Olive Pink

Stabbed in Back by Fates, 1933

 Miss Olive Pink was a formidable individual who, in the early 1930s, left depression-struck Sydney for life as a field anthropologist among the Walbiri of central Australia. Her letters to her doctoral supervisor, Professor A. P. Elkin of Sydney University, are numerous and lengthy, her mounting frustration at delays in receiving funding indicated first by capitals, then red underlining, and finally by entirely vermilion missives. She is the only explorer in this anthology who sends a telegram. Ill with severe dysentery, she wired Elkin: 'STABBED IN BACK BY FATES'. On 30 October 1933 she headed a letter: 'Oonmundjee, Central Australia, about 280 miles W of Alice Springs (perhaps 230 only, am not sure until I return).'

A lost explorer maybe, but one who returned with fascinating insights. She scribbled into her notebook this list of items carried by an Aboriginal woman. It is a detailed inventory of a kind never made by male explorers.

Olive Pink

A Woman's Possessions & Requirements

Domestic Utensils
four types of wooden vessels (sometimes more than one
of a kind)
two grinding stones, one large and flat, one small old
digging sticks for pokers and loosening earth fine grass
or fine vine used to prevent water slopping over...

Personal Use
yam stick (digging-stick) used like spade
fire stick (i.e., a short piece of wood with smouldering
embers still attached)
ligatures and bandages of vine
a waddi (have not seen it in use)
flints for cutting food (now European knives)
native tobacco (chewed now, but whether prior to
whites' introduction to their tobacco I don't know)
improvised handkerchiefs (of grass or leaves)
? pubic apron only used at certain periods (if at all?)
(This is quite uncertain. I have never seen one worn.
Whether adults wear this is uncertain. A bride does on
her wedding night apparently.)
fur string upper chest protector
rabbit-bandicoot tails (for head)
neck bands of fur string
head bands of fur string

nose bone, whether of wood or bone (uncertain for
women). Men use both.

Cosmetics etc
larvae of termites
grease from animals and lizards
red ochre
yellow ochre
white lime
(charcoal—for women—uncertain. I think not used.)

For Babies
wooden scraps used as cradle and perambulator
dusting powder (the sandy soil) and perhaps powdered
charcoal
handkerchiefs (leaves and grass)
paperbark in place of baby's blanket

Robyn Davidson

Panic and Shake, 1977

 Robyn Davidson undertook one of the most remarkable journeys ever made in contemporary Australia—from Alice Springs to Shark Bay, alone and on camel back. Her account is bone-chillingly honest. The terror of isolation, of not knowing where water can be found, is something every explorer must have felt but would never admit to. Davidson's confrontations with wild bull camels also add a postscript to camel exploration in Australia. It will be even more difficult now that feral camels have become so widespread.

We join Davidson and her three camels, Diggity, Dookie and Bubby, as they set out from Docker River, several hundred kilometres west of Uluru.

As I left the settlement, alone, I was aware only of a flatness, a lack of substance in everything. My steps felt achingly slow, small and leaden. They led me nowhere. Step after step after step, the interminable walking dragged out, pulling my thoughts downwards into spirals. The country seemed alien, faded, muted, the silence hostile, overwhelming.

I was twenty miles out, tired and thirsty. I drank some beer. I was about to turn off and make camp when through the beer-hazed afternoon heat came striding three large strong male camels in full season.[†]

Panic and shake. Panic and shake. They attack and kill, remember. Remember now, one—tie up Bub securely, two— whoosh him down, three—take rifle from scabbard, four—load rifle, five—cock, aim and fire rifle. They were just thirty yards away and one was spurting a cylindrical arch of red blood. He didn't seem to notice it. They all came forward again.

I was scared deep in my bones. First, I could not believe it was happening, then I believed it was never going to stop. My ears thumped, cold sweat stuck to the hollow of my back. My vision was distorted by fear. Then I was past it, not thinking any more, just doing it.

Zzzzt. This time just behind his head and he turned and ambled away. Zzzt. Near the heart again, he slumped down but just sat there. Zzzt. In the head, dead. The other two trundled off into the scrub. Shake and sweat, shake and sweat. You've won for now.

I unsaddled the camels and hobbled them close, glancing around constantly. It was getting dark. They came back. Braver now, I shot one, but only wounded it. Night came too quickly.

The fire flickered on white moonstruck sand, the sky was black onyx. The rumbling sound of bulls circled the

---

[†] Her camel had been gelded and attracted the wild bull camels.

camp very close until I fell asleep. In the moonlight, I woke up and maybe twenty yards away was a beast standing in full profile. I didn't want to harm it. It was beautiful, proud. Not interested in me at all. I slept again. drifting off to the sound of bells on camels, peacefully chewing their cud.

Came dawn, I was already stalking, gun loaded and ready. They were both still there. I had to kill the wounded one. I tried to. Another cylinder of blood and he ran away nipping at his wound. I could not follow, I had my own survival to think of. There he was, the last young bull, a beautiful thing, a moonlight camel. I made a decision. This one of the three would be allowed to live until he did something directly to jeopardise my safety. Happy decision. 'Yes, maybe he'll tag along right to Carnarvon. And I'll call him Aldebaran and isn't he magnificent, Diggity, what a match for Dookie. I don't have to kill him at all.'

I snuck around to catch the camels. He watched me. Now, last camel to catch, Bub. Off he galloped in his hobbles, the new bull pacing lazily beside him. I couldn't catch him with the other bull so close. I tried for an hour, I was exhausted, I wanted to kill Bubby, to dismember him, rip his balls out, but they'd already gone. I took the rifle and walked to within thirty feet of the now excited and burbling young bull. I put a slug right where I knew it would kill him. It did not, and he bit and roared at his wound. He didn't understand this pain, I was crying.

I fired again into his head and he sat down, gurgling through his own blood. I walked up to his head, we stared at one another— he knew then. He looked at me, I shot him in the brain, point blank.

Bubby was puzzled. He walked up to the carcass and drank some blood. It was all over his nose, like clown's lipstick, and he threw his lips around. He allowed himself to be caught, I didn't hit him. I walked on.

I entered a new time, space, dimension. A thousand years fitted into a day and aeons into each step. The desert oaks sighed and bent down to me, as if trying to grab at me. Sandhills came and sandhills went. Hills rose up and hills slipped away. Clouds rolled in and clouds rolled out and always the road, always the road, always the road.

So tired, I slept in the creek and thought of nothing but failure. I could not even light a fire. I wanted to hide in the dark. I thought it was surely longer than two days, I had walked so far. But time was different here, it was stretched by step after step and in each step a century of circular thought. I didn't want to think like this, was ashamed of my thoughts but I could not stop them. The moon, cold marble and cruel, pushed down on me, sucked at me, I could not hide from it, even in dream.

And the next day and the next day too, the road and the sandhills and the cold wind sucked at my thoughts and nothing happened but walking.

The country was dry. How could the camels be so thirsty and thin. At night, they came into camp and tried to knock over the water drums. I hadn't enough to spare, I rationed them. The map said 'rockhole'. Thank god. I turned off the track somewhere in that haze of elastic time and walked in. More sandhills, then a stretch of gibberflat, wide and dry and desolate with one dead bird, and two empty holes. Some string somewhere inside me was starting to unravel. An important string, the one that held down panic. I walked on, That night I camped in those sandhills.

The sky was leaden and thick. All day it had been grey, smooth, translucent, like the belly of a frog. Spots of rain pattered on me but not enough to lay the dust. The sky was washing me out, emptying me. I was cold as I hunched over my meagre fire. And somewhere, between frozen sandhills, in a haunted and forgotten desert, where time is always measured by the interminable roll of constellations, or the chill call of a crow waking, I lay down on my dirty bundle of blankets. The frost clung like brittle cobwebs to the black bushes around me, while the sky turned thick with glitter. It was very still. I slept. The hour before the sun spills thin colour on the sand, I woke suddenly and tried to gather myself from a dream I could not remember. I was split. I woke into limbo and could not find myself. There were no reference points, nothing to keep the world controlled and bound together. There was nothing but chaos and the voices.

The strong one, the hating one, the powerful one was mocking me, laughing at me.

'You've gone too far this time. I've got you now and I hate you. You're disgusting, aren't you? You're nothing. And I have you now, I knew it would come, sooner or later. There's no use fighting me you know, there's no one to help you. I've got you, I've got you.'

Another voice was calm and warm. She commanded me to lie down and be calm. She instructed me to not let go, not give in. She reassured me that I would find myself again if I could just hold on, be quiet and lie down.

The third voice was screaming.

Diggity woke me at dawn. I was some distance from camp, cramped, and cold to my bones. The sky was cold, pale blue and pitiless, like an Austrian psychopath's eyes. I walked out into the time warp again. I was only half there, like an automaton. I knew what I had to do. 'You must do this, it will keep you alive. Remember.' I walked out into that evil whispering sea. Like an animal, I sensed a menace, everything was quite still, but threatening, icy, beneath the sun's heat. I felt it watching me, following me, waiting for me.

I tried to conquer the presence with my own voice. It croaked out into the silence and was swallowed by it. 'All we have to do,' it said, 'is reach Mount Fanny, and there is certain to be water there. Just one step and another, that's all I have to do, I must not panic.' I could see what had to be Mount Fanny in the hot blue distance, and I wanted to be there, protected by those rocks, more than anything I'd ever wanted. I knew I was being unreasonable. There was more than enough water to get by on to Wingelinna. But the camels, I'd been so sure they'd do a week comfortably. I hadn't planned on the sudden dryness— the lack of green feed. 'But there'll be water there, of course there will. Haven't they told me so? What if there's not? What if the mill's run dry? What if I miss it? What if this thin little piece of string that keeps me tied to my camels breaks? What then? Walk walk walk, sandhills for ever, they all looked the same. I walked as if on a treadmill—no progress, no change. The hill came closer so slowly. 'How long is it now? A day? This is the longest day. Careful. Remember, it's just a day. Hold on, mustn't let go. Maybe a car will come. No cars. What if there's no water, what will I do? Must stop this. Must stop. Just keep walking. Just one step at a time, that's all it takes.' And on and on and on went that dialogue in my head. Over and over and round and round.

Late in the afternoon—long creeping shadows. The hill was close. 'Please please let me be there before night. Please don't let me be here in the dark. It will engulf me.'

It must be over the next sandhill surely. No, then the next one. OK, all right, the next, no the next, no the next. Please god, am I mad. The hill is there, I can almost touch it. I started to yell. I started to shout stupidly at the dunes. Diggity licked my hand and whined but I could not stop. I had being doing this for ever. I walked in slow motion. Everything was slowing down.

[1977]

And then, over the last sandhill, I was out of the dunes. I crouched on the rocks, weeping, feeling their substance with my hands. I climbed steadily, up the rocky escarpment, away from that terrible ocean of sand. The rocks were heavy and dark and strong. They rose up like an island. I crawled over this giant spine, where it emerged from the waves in a fuzz of green. I looked back to the immensity of where I had been. Already the memory was receding—the time, the aching time of it. Already, I had forgotten most of the days. They had sunk away from memory, leaving only a few peaks that I could recall. I was safe.

Resources for Teachers and Students

The following activities are relevant to the study of the text as part of a unit on Australian history or as part of a unit on historical or Australian literature.

These activities will help students to develop skills and knowledge including:

Analysis of changes over time.

Analysis of links between historical and contemporary issues.

Understanding of the contribution of events to the cultural, political and social development of a nation.

Comprehension and synthesis of written evidence to support arguments and conclusions.

Recognition of multiple perspectives on events.

Evaluation of evidence which supports interpretations of events.

PART ONE

A closer reading

Students can respond to any of the journal entries by analysing the following:

What features of the landscape did the explorer observe and comment on? What was the importance of these features of the landscape to the explorer?

What difficulties and obstacles did the explorer confront and how were these dealt with?

What aspects of the landscape or journey did the explorer comment on positively or with surprise?

What conclusions did the explorer reach about the land and on what observations or assumptions were these conclusions based?

What comments did the explorer make about the people (Indigenous Australians) inhabiting the land?

How might the explorer's observations and comments have contributed to the developing understanding of the land mass we have come to know as Australia?

What does the explorer leave out of his or her entry?

What questions would you ask the explorer?

Students could present their responses as:

A labelled illustration depicting the scene described by the explorer and annotated to include answers to the questions above.

Writing on the reading—an enlarged version of the text is presented on a poster and students circle, highlight and annotate the relevant words, phrases or sections of the text.

A letter to the explorer commenting on the points above in a modern context and commenting on the changes to the landscape that have taken place.

A PowerPoint presentation which incorporates quotes from the journal entry to support the judgments made.

PART TWO

Specific entries

JOSEPH BANKS, 1770

Between 8 June and 12 June, 1770, Banks's boat experienced difficulties. What does his record of events tell us about:

The way his boat was constructed?

The lifestyle of sailors?

The tools and resources used by explorers of this era?

The risks involved in sea exploration during this era?

Write about the incident one of the crew, or from the perspective of an Indigenous Australian watching the events unfold.

EDWARD EYRE, 1841

Explorers had much to fear: thirst, betrayal and ultimately death. Consider these questions with respect to the fears Eyre was forced to confront.

What was Eyre afraid of? Find passages from the writing that indicate his fears.

In what ways did Eyre's relationship with Wylie differ from his relationship with the other two indigenous boys? What are some of the reasons for these differences?

Read page 174 and discuss what this tells us about the interactions between Indigenous Australians and explorers during this era.

Eyre writes, 'The gun, however, was again serviceable; and after carefully loading it I felt a degree of confidence and security I had before been a stranger to.' (page 172) Why do you think Eyre needed his gun to feel secure? What does this tell us about the fears faced by explorers during this era?

ROBYN DAVIDSON, 1977

Davidson confronts some unexpected challenges. She describes her reactions vividly. Answer the questions below:

What was Davidson most afraid of and why?

How did Davidson feel about shooting the camels? Find the phrases in her writing which explain her feelings.

Davidson experienced a 'dialogue in her head'. What was it telling her and how did she respond?

Are you surprised that Davidson's exploration took place in 1977? Give reasons for your answer.

PART THREE

Thematic explorations

INDIGENOUS AUSTRALIANS

Most explorers comment on the presence and characteristics of the Indigenous Australians they meet. The comments, however, are varied—some positive, some negative. Explore this theme by completing the following:

Make a list of the phrases and adjectives used to describe Indigenous Australians in the journal entries (make sure you record the page number, the explorer and the year of exploration).

Read at least ten entries and make note of how the explorers and their teams reacted to and treated the Indigenous Australians. Categorise their responses and present a summary in oral or written form.

Analyse how views, reactions and treatment changed over time. What reasons were there for these changes?

FLORA AND FAUNA

Observations of the surrounding vegetation and animals preoccupy many of the explorers—particularly the early ones. Consider the following:

What aspects of the plants did the explorers make note of, and why?

Are the same characteristics important to people who live on the land today? Why? Why not?

Look at the description of quokkas on page 14 and the animal on page 7. Try to write your own description of some native Australian animals for people who have never seen the animals. Read your descriptions aloud to other classmates and see if they can guess what animal you have described.

Find some examples of plants being used for the survival of the explorers. Make sure you provide complete page references.

The changes in the landscape between 1623 and today are immense. Find some passages from the text that describe the landscape and try describing the same area as you imagine it may look today.

CONFLICT

Regrettably many of the explorations were tarnished by fights, distrust and even death. The conflicts were often between

Indigenous Australian and the explorers, but not always.

What sorts of incidents or conditions created tensions between the members of the exploration teams?

Were the explorers more often challenged by the land or by its inhabitants?

What sorts of situations gave rise to distrust and conflict?

What sorts of actions or conditions enabled explorers to avoid conflict?

In what circumstances did the explorers demonstrate respect and appreciation for the Indigenous Australians they encountered?

PART FOUR

Written responses

Respond to the following writing prompts. Make sure you clearly reference the sections in the text which provide evidence for your response.

ANALYSIS

In what ways did the relationships between explorers and Indigenous Australians change over time?

In what different ways did the explorers react to the challenges they faced?

How did the availability of different tools or equipment change the ways in which the explorers operated?

COMPARISON

Select two explorers from different eras and comment on the changes over time which affected the manner and results of their explorations.

What experiences are common to explorers? Select a few entries and comment on the aspects of their experiences which are similar.

Did different explorers have different goals or motivations? How did the goals of the explorers change over time?

ARGUMENT

'Explorers only achieved success by conquering the lands and people they confronted.' Do you agree?

'Teamwork was the key to a successful exploration.' Do you agree?

'Exploration was a personal journey.' Discuss.

CREATIVE

JOB DESCRIPTION. Write an advertisement for a newspaper in which an explorer is sought. What personal and physical qualities are required?

READ ALL ABOUT IT. Write an article for a newspaper of the time explaining the results of an exploration. It could be a feature article or a factual report. It could be written by the wife of an explorer.

GUIDE and MAP. Provide an aspiring explorer with a map and guide for a journey to a particular region which has only once been visited—by one of the explorers in this book. What equipment would be recommended and why? What should one be wary of, and what should one make sure to observe?

PART FIVE

Further Research

Select one of the explorers and research secondary evidence describing and explaining their journey. Analyse the differences between the primary source of information and the secondary source. Which source tells you more about the explorer and their discoveries and why?

What was the role of women in the lives of these explorers? Research the involvement of women in the preparations and conduct of the explorations.

Map the areas and timelines of the explorations. Which were the last parts of Australia to be explored and why? Add explorations not included in this book.